PREACHER BOY IN THE HEARTLAND

PREACHER BOY IN THE HEARTLAND

Arthur B. McCaffry

iUniverse, Inc.
New York Lincoln Shanghai

PREACHER BOY IN THE HEARTLAND

Copyright © 2007 by Arthur B. McCaffry

All rights reserved. No part of this book may be used or reproduced by any means, graphic, electronic, or mechanical, including photocopying, recording, taping or by any information storage retrieval system without the written permission of the publisher except in the case of brief quotations embodied in critical articles and reviews.

iUniverse books may be ordered through booksellers or by contacting:

iUniverse
2021 Pine Lake Road, Suite 100
Lincoln, NE 68512
www.iuniverse.com
1-800-Authors (1-800-288-4677)

Because of the dynamic nature of the Internet, any Web addresses or links contained in this book may have changed since publication and may no longer be valid.

The views expressed in this work are solely those of the author and do not necessarily reflect the views of the publisher, and the publisher hereby disclaims any responsibility for them.

ISBN: 978-0-595-41479-6 (pbk)
ISBN: 978-0-595-85827-9 (ebk)

Printed in the United States of America

Contents

ACKNOWLEDGEMENT..................................... vii
PREFACE.. ix

Chapter 1	TIME OF DESPAIR........................... 1
Chapter 2	EDUCATION AND HOME LIFE............. 6
Chapter 3	THE CHURCH................................ 25
Chapter 4	THE HANGING OF MR. ROOSTER......... 34
Chapter 5	THE PREACHER COMES CALLING........ 39
Chapter 6	BEGINNING THE EVANGELISM........... 51
Chapter 7	MEETING ELMO............................. 65
Chapter 8	REVIVAL TIME IN KENTUCKY............. 76
Chapter 9	RETURNING HOME......................... 92
Chapter 10	UNCLE JOE AT PENDLETON.............. 99
Chapter 11	FISHIN' AT HART LINES................... 104
Chapter 12	CROSSING THE OHIO..................... 116
Chapter 13	MOUNT VERNON PENTECOST MEETING................................... 122
Chapter 14	WORLD'S FAIR............................. 140
Chapter 15	VISITING KENTUCKY RELATIVES........ 151
Chapter 16	THE INHERITANCE......................... 166
Chapter 17	ELECTION DAY............................. 179

Chapter 18	NEVER POOR AGAIN	186
Chapter 19	JAIL TIME FOR SPARE	196
Chapter 20	THE BARBERSHOP	207
Chapter 21	MAW'S DEATH	217

ACKNOWLEDGEMENT

I wish to express my sincere gratitude to my grandmother and her many children and grandchildren who helped me make it through The Great Depression. The guidance she gave to all of us during her years was something one cannot put a price upon. Many people living today have benefited from her life and character without knowing her, but their parents did.

I would like to express my gratitude to all the wonderful people who gave me encouragement during this period of my life. I would not want to be a part of any other generation. The values we learned during this period will always be remembered.

I also wish to express my sincere thanks to Mr. Eric Vonfuhrmann, Associate Professor of English at the University of Southern Indiana. He encouraged me to write my story and his friendship is valued.

A. B. McCaffry

PREFACE

ALL INCIDENTS AND LOCATIONS DESCRIBED IN THIS BOOK ARE TRUE. MANY OF THE PERSONS' NAMES REFERRED TO IN THE BOOK HAVE BEEN CHANGED AND MANY ARE DECEASED. THE TIME AND ERA OF THIS MEMOIR MAY BE BEST UNDERSTOOD BY ASSUMING THE ROLE OF THE AUTHOR DURING THIS PERIOD OF THE AMERICAN HEARTLAND AND ITS BELIEFS AND TRADITIONS. STRONG RELIGIOUS TIES TO THE PROTESTANT AND CATHOLIC FAITHS EXISTED ALONG WITH PATRIOTISM AND DEVOTION TO CHURCH AND COUNTRY.

1

TIME OF DESPAIR

I'm four, five, and six years old, and I can read, write, spell and ride a horse. I have a great memory of the Bible, which is part of my daily life. I've got wonderful aunts, uncles, cousins, a great grandmother and a loving but unreliable preacher father. I live in a four room house on the westside of Evansville, Indiana. This is the best part of my life.

The other side of my life is not so rosy. My mother died when I was two years of age; my father likes to preach the gospel, but he has a hard time resisting the temptations of the world. My Aunt Dorie and Grandmother tell me, he's gotta get some will-power, or he's goin' straight to hell for sure. The Great Depression is goin' on, but everything seems normal to me. My biggest problem in life is I cain't swim.

There's always a lot goin' on at our house with the family and friends coming and goin' all day long. The Virginia Insurance man comes once a week, takes his money from an envelope on the wall, marks his book, sits down, has his coffee, and talks to me and Maw. Sam Gander, the ice man, drives by our house every morning in the summer. He sees our sign in the window and brings us ice, sits down, has his coffee and leaves. Happy Jack, the black junk man, comes five days a week down the alley with his mule and wagon yelling, Rags, copper, brass, old iron. Every kid in the neighborhood hears him and runs to meet the rag man. We sell him our rags and junk, and he gives us pennies and nickels. We wait for the ice cream man while peddlers run up and down the street yelling, Cantaloupe, watermelons, corn and tomatoes while kids run and chase June bugs; tie a string of thread on their legs and let 'em fly. At night we pick fireflies out of the air, put 'em in jars, and watch their lights go off and on.

When the ice cream man comes, every kid in the neighborhood runs for his covered truck with a nickel in hand to get the best ice cream cone ever made. We hand him his nickel and he piles the ice cream on high. Sometimes kids who don't have the nickel ask for licks before we even start. A boy named Lindel lives across the street in a shed with his mother. We call him Snotty Nose Lindel 'cause his nose runs all year long, summer, spring, winter and fall. Snotty Nose never has a nickel, but he's always there wantin' his lick before anyone. We finish our licks and hand it to Snotty Nose. He walks away lickin' the cone and never talks, unless it's something he wants to know really bad.

BOY SHOT IN LEFT LUNG.

Member of Charivari Party Falls When Bridegroom Fires.

Evansville, Ind., June 23.—While in a charivari party at Howell, Vanderburg county, Arthur McCaffry, age eight, was shot in the left lung by Posey Beckham, who used a twenty-two calibre rifle. The lad is in a critical condition and may die. Beckham is under arrest, charged with assault and battery with intent to kill.

Beckham and wife were recently divorced, but became reconciled, and on Saturday were remarried. In the evening a party of their friends gathered at their home to charivari them and insisted that Beckham come out and treat them. Beckham refused, grabbed a rifle and, according to the story told the police, fired into the crowd from an open window in the hope of frightening them. Beckham's wife is prostrated over the affair and had to have the care of a physician.

My mother died of childbirth when I was two years old and my grandmother assumed the part of mother to me. Everyone refers to her as Maw and she loves me with all her heart. I have some very loving relatives and they understand the situation I'm in at the very beginning of my life. Maw made her mind up she's gonna teach me the difference between right and wrong, but she knows her biggest problem is Dad. She's in her fifties, physically strong, and stronger still in her faith.

I go to every church service Maw attends, and that's a lot. Sunday, I attend services from morning till night and go to prayer meetings on Wednesday evenings. I sit on the long wooden bench that runs across the front of the church interior and listen to Reverend Johnson read and preach from the Bible. At age four, some of what I'm hearing begins sifting through my brain, and I begin learning the Bible. I accept it as a long running story and believe it with heart and soul. I'm accepted in the family as an adult very early and I'm expected to perform my responsibilities. I'm always part of conversations concerning the Bible. Maw is planting the seed in my mind 'bout all the wonders and predictions of the Bible. She tells me 'bout goin' to heaven and how every knee will bow down before Jesus while he sits on his Great White Throne on Judgment Day. I ask her how she knows all this, and she says, it's in the Bible, Son, it's in the Bible and that's the law.

America is fascinated with air travel, and dirigibles are the talk of the year in 1931. The newspaper tells 'bout the dirigible *Akron* flying over Evansville on Friday evening, and Maw says I'm 'bout to see history in the making. I stand at the back door of Maw's house and look up as the *Akron* glides in the sky directly over our house. I see it and grab her arm while I gaze up to the sky. My imagination runs wild! The huge airship glides over my head, and I hear the humming of its motors as it passes so very low. I can see people sitting in the airship's dining room eating evening meals.

As it passes over, I'm thinkin' what Maw teaches me and 'bout prophesies in the Bible, the same as Reverend Johnson speaks 'bout while I lie on the bench at church half asleep. I hear him say, When, the last days come before the return of Christ, we'll see signs coming from heaven. I don't understand it, but I remember his words and can hardly believe what I'm seeing. I ask, Maw, Does this mean Jesus is coming back soon? She says, Son, nobody knows when He's coming, but He will come, and you be sure you're ready for Him. We walk inside the house after the dirigible passes over, and I'm still asking her the same question. She gives me the same answers, and no longer do I worry. Little did anyone then dream that two years later the *Akron* would be destroyed during an electrical storm over the Atlantic Ocean and that all passengers aboard would be killed. It's my first remembrance of Maw and I together. Those memories of her will never fade away.

2

<u>EDUCATION AND HOME LIFE</u>

I'm five years old, and the learning is coming fast. I sit in the living room, and Uncle Joe says, What's four times four? I say, Sixteen. Then we go through the set of multiplication tables till we're both tired. Maw comes into the room and reads the Holy Bible to me, explaining how everyone needs to get saved, baptized, and sanctified by the Holy Spirit. It's hard for me to understand, but somehow, I like it.

I ask Uncle Joe how far he went in school.
He says, I went clean through the second grade.
How far did Dad go?
He tells everybody he graduated, but he went clean through the fifth grade.
Maw says, Your Uncle Orie graduated from grade school, but he doesn't have time to teach you, 'cause he's married and got his own family to raise.
I ask, What 'bout Dad, can he teach me stuff like you and Uncle Joe?
Your dad is good at history, Son; he can tell you every battle they had in the Civil War and how General Sherman marched through Georgia, but I think he might exaggerate some. He's good at readin' and writin', but don't let him try to teach you manners.
Why not Maw?
When it comes to eatin' time, Son, your dad doesn't have manners.

I'm in grade school, and it's, Christmas time. Dad comes to me, hands me a pound box of Schrafft's finest chocolates all tied up with a fancy ribbon and says, Son, give this to the prettiest teacher you have in school. I tell him, Dad, nobody in my class gives chocolates to teachers; besides, why can't we eat 'em? He tells me he's trying to look out for me and doing the best he can to see that I know how to get along in life. I don't understand what giving the prettiest teacher in Rheinlander Grade School has to do with me gettin' along in life. Dad says if I give her the chocolates when my grade time comes she'll think of the chocolates and maybe add on a little something extra. I know Maw don't agree with this, but I'm gonna give Miss Strupp the big box of chocolates anyhow. I tell him, Dad, you don't know her. She's the prettiest, but she's pretty tough, and besides I already get the best grades in class. He says, Do as I say, Son, and don't you ever give any to a hairy legged man.

I stay after school the next day and hand Miss Strupp the chocolates. I like the way she smells, clean and fresh, with her nice fancy perfume. It smells better than the lilac powder Aunt Dorie puts on Cousin Kathryn's bottom after her bath. She says, why, thank you Arthur, but you shouldn't give these to me, but she takes my chocolates anyway. I tell her you're the prettiest, Miss Strupp, so they're for you. I sure won't give any to any hairy legged man like Mr. Cottrell even though he's the principal. She thanks me again, and I wanta get outta here before someone sees me giving her chocolates. I walk away thinking how well the chocolates must taste, and somehow, it doesn't seem just right. I've got holes in my shoes covered with cardboard and she's dressed like a queen; I'm beginning to wonder if what Dad thinks is exactly right 'bout giving the chocolates to the prettiest teacher.

Dad begins attending church more often and he decides to be a preacher. Reading the Bible and attending church with Maw is something he enjoys, and people are beginning to notice him. His memory of Bible scriptures and names of places in the Old and New Testaments is great, and he knows how to use it. He has charisma and charm. He stands 'bout

5 feet 9 inches, is slender, has dark hair and a pair of wandering blue eyes and his story-telling ability adds to his charm as a preacher. I hear him preaching to himself on hot Sunday afternoons for long hours, but he needs something more and that something is me. He feels I have enough knowledge of the Bible to begin preachin' and that's what he's counting on to gain a following.

I'm learning how to preach from Dad and he has me in the house on Sunday afternoons goin' over how to stand and face the audience. I know hundreds and hundreds of facts 'bout the, Bible, and he says this is goin' to be the big draw; me answering Bible questions. I stand before him many Sunday afternoons answering questions such as who was the oldest man who ever lived, how old was this or that prophet or disciple when he died, what's the shortest verse in the Bible, what's the longest verse in the Bible, what are the Ten Commandments and their meanings, where did all the disciples preach and how they died, and various questions 'bout Jesus' crucifixion and his promise to return. He says I should explain why drinking beer and wine is a sin, but don't dwell on it. Dad says, above all, talk 'bout heaven and how the streets are paved with gold, and if they worship idols they're goin' to hell for sure. Make sure they understand the altar is the only way to get there. This is Dad's message to me, and I learn it well.

It's time for me to deliver a sermon and Dad is good 'bout teaching me all the finer points. Dad says, I'm gonna show you the most important thing in your young life, even though you probably won't be using it while I'm with you. Hold out your hand, Son. I hold out my hand, he grabs it, shakes it good and says; Now that's what I call a real handshake. Whatever you do, don't be like a wimp; squeeze the other guy's hand firmly, and he'll know you're a man. I grab his hand again, squeeze it with all my might and Dad says, That's a good one; just keep up the good work, you're gettin' better.

Now he's gonna give me some more pointers on preaching. He says, Son, when you're on the podium the floor is yours, give it to 'em good.

Point your finger at them sinners, and they're all sinners; make 'em feel ashamed of all the things they're doing. I ask Dad if he ever sins, and he says, Don't, talk that way, Son, but there's times I have. He says, Walk around, never stand still, and keep waving the Bible in the air. I ask, Dad, if he ever feels guilty when the preacher points at him, and he says, Sure, Son, that's why you see me at the altar now and then, and maybe just a little more than some of the others in our church. Just remember one thing, Son, if you need help, your old dad will be looking out for you. I tell him, I know you will Dad, and if you're not, Maw will. Maw knows of Dad's teaching and doesn't disagree, but she knows his way of life is a bad example. She has problems at home, but we develop a strong bond that can't ever be broken. I accept her as Maw, and she's now my mother.

Uncle Joe runs a bootleg joint called 'The Greasy' in a small shed behind my aunt's house next door. I help him wash beer bottles, run to the store to get him malt and yeast and when Maw's not around, I cap the bottles. He puts me on a box and hands me some nickels, and says, Play the slot machines and win us a jackpot. I love it, but I worry Maw is gonna find out, 'cause she says gambling is sinful; Uncle Joe says it's part of life. His way I love, but I know she's right. I just don't wanta get caught.

It's springtime, and that means it's time to pick greens. Maw says, Son, today we're goin' to the nearest field, and you're gonna get a lesson 'bout eatin' and pickin' greens; they're good for you, especially in the spring. I don't wanta hear 'bout greens 'cause I ate 'em once and didn't like what I ate, but I'm not arguing with Maw. We take off for the nearest open field, and the greens are sprouting up all around.

Now it's time for her to begin teaching me the facts of life. Maw says the facts of life are the difference between right and wrong and what's goin' on in the world. They're also lessons in manners and being respectful to elders. She says time after time, It's all in the Bible, Son; it's all in the Bible. I like what she teaches me and wanta hear more. I especially like it when she tells me 'bout being an American and living in the Heartland of America where everyone is equal, only we don't have any money.

I ask Maw, Are we rich or poor?
She says, Not only poor, we're dirt poor.
Did you ever see anyone rich?
Probably, Son, but you can be rich inside, and that's what really counts.
I don't understand her remark, but someday I'll find out.

I love to hear her tell 'bout my momma and how pretty she was. I don't like it when she tells me 'bout when she died and how Dad wasn't always around. She tells me how Dad got out of the army and came home unexpectedly. She tells me how she met my grandfather and how they came down the Ohio River to Evansville. She tells how their only belongings were in the four suitcases they took with them. She tells me 'bout riding the wooden flatboat and a very bad storm occurred. She describes how my grandfather was rubbing his beads and making the sign of the cross while she was reading the 23rd Psalm. We both laugh, and she says, Honey, it sure wasn't funny the day of the storm, but it sure is now. I ask, Maw, When you're in trouble, do you read the 23rd Psalm? She says, Son, I've got something better than that to tell you someday and I'll tell you when you are a little older; it's all 'bout angels. I tell her, Don't ever forget to tell me, Maw, please don't? She smiles, and we both are satisfied. I'm being educated and can't wait to hear 'bout those angels and someday she'll tell me.

Maw says, Listen, Son, I know your Uncle Joe is letting you spend time in that sin place of his, and I don't think you need to go there any longer.
I know it's wrong, but Uncle Joe sure gives me a lot of nickels to play the slot machines, and I don't mind helping him cap beer bottles.
Son, you wouldn't wanta be in such a place if Jesus happens to come back, would you?
That kinda scares me, and I don't know what to say.

She says, It's O.K. this time, Son, but don't go again no matter what he says; he's just weak and hasn't learned his lesson yet.

Do, you believe Joe or Dad will ever learn?

I'm not sure, it takes a while longer for some people, and they're probably that kinda people.

Maw looks kinda worried and says, I'm gonna tell you something that I really have a hard time doing. She says, Should anyone come to the house and ask 'bout Uncle Joe, say nothing 'bout him making beer. I tell her, I won't, I won't, Maw, I'll never tell. She knows I'll never tell, they could kill me first, and I won't tell 'bout Uncle Joe making beer. She says, Fine, Son, fine, we just don't want Joe gettin' in trouble, do we? I tell her, No, Maw, we sure don't, and I'll never tell anyone he makes beer. We finish picking greens and head home.

I join my friends in a nearby field and play with my new dog, Bull. We romp and play, and then I go back to the house and there stands two large, well dressed men talkin' to Maw. I move inside the door and listen and it's not good; it's 'bout Uncle Joe and Maw warned me 'bout these guys, so they must be bad. I hear 'em talkin' and Maw says, No, Joe's not here at this time and I'm not sure when he's coming back. The men still ask and I still listen. I've gotta help her. I grab hold of her dress and pull forward towards the men. She shoves me back, and I grab again trying to reach the door. I don't understand why she won't let me help. Finally I make it and stand in front of the two big guys and blurt out, My Uncle Joe ain't here, and he's not makin' beer. They look at each other and burst out laughin' as they walk away. Maw shuffles me back in the kitchen and I know she's not happy; I've seen that look on her face before. She says, Son, please, just for once let me take care of these kinds of things. I only wanted to help, but she just doesn't understand. She throws her arms in the air muttering, My, oh, my, what's gonna happen next? I still don't understand, but I better leave well enough alone for now. It's only a day or two till Uncle Joe's joint is closed for good, but it's not long before another place opens and he's goin' strong again.

It's Saturday morning and Maw and me are alone in the kitchen. It's time for us to clean. I'm having problems understanding something I've been thinking about, so I ask her for answers. She always knows everything, and she asks, What's bothering you, Son? I tell her I just don't understand how come all my friends and kinfolks have names that really aren't their names. She says, like what, Son? I tell her, Maw, I know 'bout myself being called, Bid, and my real name is, Arthur, but only school teachers and prayer group women call me that. The rest of my friends call me, Bid, and I like it better. I ask, Why, did I get called Bid at the beginning? Maw says, Well, when your momma first saw you, she said, Look, at him, he's so itty-bitty, and your aunt Dorie said, We'll call him Biddy. Uncle Orie said, No, it sounds sissy, so we gotta call him, Bid. I'm glad Uncle Orie had his way and now I wanta find out 'bout all my other cousins, aunts and uncles and their names. I know Donald, my cousin next door is called, Cotton, and there's a lot more, but I don't know their real names. Maw says, It's like this, Son, a lot of names were given to them by friends, 'cause maybe they have something physical or something that looks or sounds like something else. For instance, Donald is called Cotton because of his white cotton-like hair. It's not supposed to be something that is disrespectful, but it's probably a little friendly type name. Do you understand? I answer, Yes, I do now, and I made a list out yesterday and I'd like to know if I'm right. She says, Fine Son, read it to me. Now, I'm gonna find some answers. She says, I'm always glad to help, read me your list.

Well first of all, Maw, I wrote down, Cotton, my older cousin, and now I know why. Then there's Leroy his brother, called Slim, 'cause no matter how much he eats, he's still slim. Then there's Jerald, his other brother, we call him Sky 'cause when you talk to him he always looks up at the sky. Then there's Forest, called Pete, 'cause Pete Fox is his favorite baseball player. Then there's Uncle Fred, we call Shave 'cause he started shavin' by the time he was twelve. Next, Uncle Orie and his brothers and sisters call him Big-shot, 'cause he always wears a hat and tie no matter what time of the day. Uncle Joe says Orie thinks he may be smarter than the rest of us 'cause he finished the eighth grade.

Maw says, Hold on a minute and who's tellin' you all this stuff? I tell her Uncle Joe, of course, he tells me everything. He did say that sometimes cousin Jason might get mad if you call him Titties in front of anybody, especially girls. Maw, he does have big tits for a boy. He got mad at Uncle Joe one time at the ballpark for just calling him Titties, and wouldn't play on the ball team. We got beat, and now Uncle Joe is mad at Titties for causing us to lose. She says, Son, these things really aren't important in life, it's the way you treat people that's important, do you understand? I tell her, Sure I do, Maw, Uncle Joe says the same thing, and that I should be nice to people, and any time you aren't around I can come to him. I can tell she doesn't like that idea either, and tells me it's best to wait on her. She tells me she knows he loves me, but sometimes his thinkin' isn't the same as hers. I ask, How 'bout me goin' to Dad? She says, that's even worse, just wait for me. I know she's always right, so I'll just have to wait.

It's wash day. This happens three times a week in the back yard. We start early in the morning, and I have my usual chore to perform preparing wash water in a huge iron kettle that sits close to the house. I build the fire, fill the rinse tubs, and get ready. Maw comes and begins scrubbing clothes on a small washboard all morning long till it's time to cook the meals over a Warm Morning stove that sits in the kitchen.

The summers seem hot as a person can stand, especially next to a hot blazing fire. We're busy and sweatin' but we find time to talk. This is a time for me to get things off my mind, and I tell Maw, Today's the day Mrs. White will be at our house and every time she comes, I break out with a fever after she leaves. Cousin Cotton tells me he knows how to help me. He said, Bid, I know all 'bout that old hag, she's just pissed-off 'cause you're on the side of Jesus, and she's on the side of the devil. She's puttin' a hex on you for sure, and that's why you get sick. Maw, I believe Cousin Cotton is right, and Uncle Joe and me been talkin'. He knows a way she won't bother me any longer and I'd like to try it this afternoon, 'cause he's gonna be here. Maw says, Well, what you got in mind? I tell her, I don't know, but Uncle Joe does, and he said to let him know when she leaves, and I told him I would. Maw acts like she doesn't know what I'm talkin' 'bout, but everyone else does. She finally says, Son, I don't care as long as you don't hurt her feelings or physically hurt her. Maw's still listening, but acts like she doesn't hear me, so I tell her again how the old witch wants to borrow a wash rag or something and that's the hex. Cousin Cotton told me 'bout it and he really knows. Finally Maw gives in to my wants and says, Go ahead and do it, Son, go ahead and do it. I'm gettin' tired of listening to her babbling crazy things anyhow. I'm glad Maw feels this way 'cause now I know Cotton is right.

Mrs. White is a small scrawny woman who lives three blocks from our house and comes to visit 'bout once a week. She's considered to be the witch of the neighborhood by everyone, and nobody but Maw talks to her and even Maw never goes to visit. Mrs. White knows 'bout my training and Bible studies due to newspaper coverage. As usual, she comes in the afternoon, down the alley from the east end hobbling with a cane, wearing a bonnet, long dress down to her ankles and bent over and trying to walk fast. Cotton runs to the back door and yells, "Here comes the witch, here comes the witch." As usual, she wants to know how I'm doing and tells Maw 'bout some little men growing in her backyard. Cotton, Titties, and Slim sit on the back door step listening to every word being said. Cotton hears her tell 'bout the little men in her yard and it gets him mad, and you don't wanta get Cousin Cotton mad. He comes into the kitchen, looks the witch straight in the eye, and says, Maw, I went over to her house to see if it's true, and there's nothing but sunflower plants growing everywhere. I told Uncle Joe, and he said, She just wishes the damned sunflower plants were men so she could get some lovin'. Maw says, you younguns scat, and let me handle this. I leave the room and go outside with my cousins where they're all laughin' but I don't laugh 'cause I'm the one that gets sick. The witch is ready to leave, and says, Mrs. Martin, do you have a wash rag I can borrow? Maw hands her one, and out the back door she goes up the alley in the same direction she came from.

Uncle Joe is waiting for her and I follow him. He goes to the back alley and stays close behind her and begins sprinkling salt on the ground. He's using cuss words I've never heard before in my entire life, and I'm following not far behind and getting an education in cussing. He follows her all the way to the top of the alley where it comes out to the road and he returns. I don't have a fever and I'm playing as usual, and it has never happened before. Uncle Joe's plan is workin'. Maw's not asking questions and he's saying nothing.

I need questions answered in a hurry, so I go to my Uncle Joe. I tell him, Yesterday I heard you cussing the witch a lot; does it mean she can't come back? He tells me, Sure it does, Son, I know just how to take care of her and she'll never bother you again. I learned the ritual from a friend in the Navy while I was stationed at Great Lakes in Chicago, and it does the job. If she comes around again I'll be there to greet her, and your problem is over. I tell him, Thanks, Uncle Joe. I feel a lot better and the rest of the week I'm not sick; the ritual must work.

The following week the witch comes again from the other end of the alley while we're doing laundry. Cousin Cotton sees her and yells, "The witch is here again, she's here again." Maw hears him yelling and goes inside with the witch. I'm not sure what to do, till I find Uncle Joe lying in the shade. I tell him the witch is here again and run back to Maw and Cotton. The witch is yelling and screaming like a wild woman and saying somebody in our house is out to get her for sure, and the little men in the back yard are trying to kill her. Cotton comes in the kitchen, and I can tell he is really mad again. He says, Maw, this witch is crazier than hell, and she's out to get Bid 'cause he's for Jesus. Maw says, Now Cotton, you just stay outta this, and I'll handle it. Cotton says, Maw the old hag just pisses me off real bad, and I'd like to sic Bull on her ass. Maw says, It, sure isn't the Christian way to handle this, Son, and you better watch your mouth or

I'll wash it out with soap. I'm just listening and watchin' the witch and she's not talking till she asks for the wash rag. Cotton and me leave, and finally the witch leaves. Uncle Joe is following her down the alley the same way she came. I follow Uncle Joe and he's cussing again, and I'm listening again. We reach the end of the alley and I tell him, I just wanta be sure what you're saying 'cause I just wasn't sure the first time. He says, If I'd known you was gonna be so close, I'd have let 'cha sprinkle the salt; that way you could gain experience in this sorta thing.

I'm no longer gettin' the fever, and the witch doesn't come to our house. When I ask Maw 'bout her, she says, poor old soul, she don't have nobody, and I'm blessed with my family. That makes me feel good, 'cause I'm part of the family. Before I leave the room, Maw says, don't forget, Son, we need to pray for Mrs. White tonight at the bedside. I'm not sure 'bout that, but I know she will.

I talk to Cotton the next day and ask 'bout Maw washing his mouth out. He says, Bid it's the worst thing you will ever taste in your life and it never gets outta your mouth. I ask how she does it, and he says, Maw grabs a rag, holds your head down over a wash pan of soapy water, and runs the rag around inside your mouth. There's no way in hell you can get away no matter how hard you try. I make my mind up to never cuss. I'll just spell words from now on. That's not cussing.

Things are bad 'cept for certain people working in illegal business, and that's why Uncle Joe is doing fine. He's making money hand over fist in another bootleg joint on the far west-side of Evansville sitting high on a hill over-looking several small farms. He closed his little hole in the wall joint behind the house and is going big time.

It's the middle of the week and Maw's not home. Uncle Joe comes for breakfast and I have questions for him. I wanta know how come he doesn't come home till late at night. I ask, are you workin' late in the new restaurant? He says, Well, it's not exactly a restaurant, Son, it's more like 'The

Greasy,' but a lot better and bigger. I wanta see it so I ask, Can we go now? He says, Sure we can, Son, sure we can; I'll be done eatin' in just a minute and we'll drive there in my new Ford truck. I tell him, Maw's gone to early prayer meeting with some women she knows, and I think they're gonna see 'bout building the church bigger if they can get the money. She won't be back till noon, so I hafta watch out here at home. He knows I like to play the slots, and he shows me how to pull the handle. Dad tells me Uncle Joe is setting the slots just like he likes for pay-offs, and he's trying to figure out how he does it. I just like to hear the bells go off and pick up the nickels or dimes.

We're ready to go to the new restaurant and Uncle Joe puts something in his back pocket I've never seen before. I ask, what's, that, Uncle Joe? He says, It's called a black-jack, Son, but I call it my equalizer 'cause it helps me with bigger assholes who try to get rough. We arrive at the big farm house and I get my first look at his new place. It's like 'The Greasy,' only a lot bigger and there are twice as many slot machines, pretty pictures on the wall of movie stars and lots of tables. He asks if I wanta play the slots and I sure do, but don't want Maw to find out. He hands me a bunch of dimes and says, Play the one on the end, it's ready to hit. I drop a couple dimes in and after a couple pulls, dimes come rolling out, bells start ringing, and I'm looking for my cap to put 'em in. He tells me I'm lucky and I really know how to pull the handle, but I think he knows which one is gonna pay off just like Dad said. He says, Get your money and let's get back before Maw gets home. We head for home in the new truck, reaching home before Maw. I'm feelin' guilty, but Uncle Joe tells me it's better to be rich than poor and not to worry 'bout it.

Uncle Joe asks if I like his new place and I tell him, It's great, especially winning all these dimes. I ask, What am I gonna do with them, now? If I tell Maw, I'm not only in trouble for leaving, but playing slots. He says, Do this, kid, let me have the dimes and I'll buy you some new overalls and maybe a pair of new gym shoes. I agree and say, That's great, Uncle Joe, I won't tell Maw, but I'll probably feel guilty. He says, Don't even think 'bout it, kid, a week from now you'll forget all 'bout it. Saturday morning Uncle Joe brings me a brand new pair of gym shoes and overalls, but I still feel guilty.

Times are tough and family members show up at the house most every morning for breakfast. We talk 'bout politics, religion, families and solve all the problems of the world. Ethnic lines are forgotten and sometimes were joined by Italian, German, Catholic friends and sometimes even Methodist from the nearby church. When they leave, I ask Maw, How come we got all the different people here for breakfast, but I don't see 'em at church and she says, It's called poverty and being poor, Son, and it makes strange bedfellows. I don't know what she's talkin' 'bout, but we have a good time when they're all here.

On Saturday morning I hear laughter downstairs. I half dress, run down the stairs, and sittin' at the kitchen table is a crowd of my cousins, aunts and uncles and they're talkin' and laughin' 'bout Uncle Joe and Dad. Cotton says, I can just picture Uncle Spare jumpin' outta the upstairs bedroom, grabbing his pants, forgettin' his shoes, and leavin' some broad in bed. He sure as hell did it, says Slim.

Aunt Dorie says, I've had a feelin' for some time this was gonn'a happen someday to the two wild ones.
Pat says, what kinda feelin', Mom?
One of 'em in jail and the other on the run, Son, that's the kind of life these two live.
I know one thing for sure, Dad's not home. I go sit in the corner of the room and huddle down. Maw sees me with my head down between my knees and comes to me. She grabs me by the hand and shuffles me outside, and I'm wondering what's going on.

I'm trying to understand what they're talking 'bout when Maw says, Son, something bad has happened now sit here and I'll explain. I can tell she's not happy and almost crying, but everyone else is laughing. She says,

EDUCATION AND HOME LIFE 19

Last night the police raided your uncle's new place and he's in jail; your dad was at the place and got away by jumping out the upstairs window. I haven't heard from him, and I'm gonna get Joe from jail on Monday after I borrow some money on the house. I still don't understand, but Maw thinks I do. I do know Dad's not home, and I don't know where he is.

Maw says, Son, this is a time we just turn those two boys of mine over to the Lord.
That's what you always do, ain't it Maw?
Always do, Son, always do, and it always works in the long run.

Dad comes home, says nothing, and Uncle Joe is out outta jail on Monday. I still don't understand, but I know I won't be going to the big restaurant and play slot machines ever again.

There's no privacy in our house. An elderly gentleman opens the back door and walks into the kitchen and seats himself at the table. I pay no attention till Maw says, Son, this is your Uncle Aden from up the river where I was raised. He's a small man with white whiskers long as Santa, wears a straw hat, overalls and a blue denim shirt. Maw says, Get your uncle some silver ware and let him feed himself at the table. He looks at me, but don't speak, and I know he wants his knife and fork. I might hold 'em till he speaks, but he only talks to Maw and says, Mary I don't suppose you know, but your Aunt Hilda passed away 'bout a year ago. Maw says, Is that so, poor ole' soul, she just worked herself to death I suppose. He comes over, looks at me, picks up his knife and fork and still says nothing to me. I act like I don't see him, 'cause Cotton said it's Christian to treat people the same way they treat you. He did say he only heard it once when he went to Sunday school with Maw two years ago, and she's still trying to make him go again.

I'm still waiting for my new Uncle Aden to say something to me, but he doesn't, and I wonder if he's deaf or cain't see good. He finishes eating, grabs his little suitcase, walks up the stairwell and I still don't know who he is. I ask Maw, Does he know I'm here? She says, Yes, it's not that he didn't see you, it's just he don't talk much and he's been that way ever since he came back from the war. I ask, Was it the same war Uncle Joe was in, Maw? She says, Course not, Son, it was the Spanish American War when he served with Teddy Roosevelt and the Rough Riders. I wanta know a little more 'bout my new uncle, but Maw ain't talkin' much.

I ask, Is Uncle Aden gonna be here long, Maw?
He'll leave when he's ready, Son, just don't you worry your little head 'bout it.
Do you think he even knows I live here?
Yes, he saw you, Son, and he knows you live here; he just ain't the talkin' kind, and if he didn't like you, he sure would have told yuh by now.

I'm not saying anything else to Uncle Aden till he talks.

The next morning Uncle Aden comes downstairs, eats breakfast and takes off again for the day. He's gone all day, comes home before dark, eats his dinner and goes to bed. All my cousins and friends are asking 'bout my new Uncle Aden and I don't know anything to say 'cept, He was with Teddy Roosevelt and the Rough Riders in the Spanish American War. I've gotta problem and I cain't find Uncle Joe or Dad to learn 'bout my new uncle, and Maw won't say much.

Friday morning he eats breakfast, packs his small suitcase and says, Mary, I'm heading home this morning so, I'll make my bed before I go. He says, Lad, you're a good boy keep on helping your Maw, pats me on the head, picks up his suitcase and heads out the door before I can say a word to him. I'd like to know how he's my uncle, but Maw just says for me to call him that 'cause it shows respect. I'm glad he knows I'm here and hope he might come back, and maybe someday Maw will tell me some more 'bout him when she tells me all the other questions I ask her.

Cotton comes to the house and I tell him, Uncle Aden has left. He says, I think I know where he's been goin' every day 'cause one day I went to the movies downtown in the afternoon. My brother and me were walkin' through the Red Light District on our way home and Uncle Aden was walkin' on the other side of the street. I ask, Are you sure it was our Uncle Aden? Cotton says, Yep, I sure am sure, and so is my brother, Slim. We saw some girls pecking on windows at him, and he wuz lookin' back. Cotton is worried Maw might find out 'bout him and Slim going through the Red Light District when they don't have too. I tell him, Don't worry Cotton, it's the last thing I'd ever tell Maw. I've been thinking 'bout what he said going to the Red Light District. I ask, Cousin Cotton, I didn't know you been down there before? He says, Bid, Uncle Joe takes me down there with him all the time, but I don't go 'round bragging like other guys. Heck boy, I'm 12 and almost 13 years old. I tell him, You're big too, Cotton; he's smiling again and acting proud.

He wants to go out in the yard where we can talk privately, and he's gonna tell me something else that's gonna happen. We sit on porch and he starts to explain he needs to ask me something 'bout the Bible that Uncle Joe told him a long time ago. Soon a couple other friends are gathering, and now there's a crowd of my buddies from all over the neighborhood wantin' to hear 'bout Cotton going to the Red Light District. I do too. Slim and Titties, are sitting on the front steps listening and acting like they don't wanta hear, but we know better. They wanta hear what Uncle Joe told Cotton 'bout the Red Light District, the same as we do.

Cotton now has an audience of us boys, and we know he's proud of his experience. He says, Well, it's like this; you all know Bid and me are Uncle Joe's two favorite nephews, and beings I'm the oldest, almost thirteen, he takes me with him a lot. Well, last Friday night I went with him to visit some girl friends in the Red Light District before we went to the movies later. I always sit in the swing outside while he takes off with one of the girls and sometime they come over and talk to me. Usually, I'm only there a few minutes while Uncle Joe is gone and sometimes it may be longer, unless he happens to miss a week. Everyone wants to hear more and questions start to come at Cotton so fast he can't remember what to say.

Slim and Titties are now beginning to laugh, but don't interfere in Cottons' moment of glory and fame. He says, Well guys, it's like this, I know Uncle Joe is having a good time with the girls and some of them are really pretty. There's one named Mary that's not much older than me and she's really nice to me, and sometimes she even puts her hand on mine. Johnny, a neighborhood boy says, What then, Cotton, what then, and another boy hollers, Shut your damned mouth Johnny, let Cotton tell it. Cotton says, Uncle Joe brings Mary out to the swing where I'm sittin' and rockin'. He says, Mary, this is my boy, Cotton; he's like a young bull, strong as an ox and horny as a rabbit. I really felt proud when she looked me over good and I showed her my muscles. Teddy, a neighborhood boy says, Wow Cotton, tell us what else. Does she ever try kissin' you? Cotton says, Not yet, Teddy, but that's gonna come later with a lot more. Another neighborhood kid we call Snotty Nose Lindel asks, Cotton who's gonna pay? Pat says, Wipe, your nose Lindel or you'll hafta go home. He runs his shirt sleeve 'cross his nose and Pat says, Now you can ask Cotton again. Snotty Nose Lindel asks again, and Cotton says, This is gonna be my birthday present from Uncle Joe and when it's over Uncle Joe says I'll be a real man from then on.

Cotton is like a hero to all of us by now and says, Well guys, there is one thing I need to talk to Bid 'bout beings he knows the Bible better than all of us, 'cept Maw, and I sure ain't gonna ask her. Cotton looks at me and says, Does it say in the Bible "*it's better to cast your seed in the belly of a whore than on the ground*"? Is Uncle Joe right 'bout that seed thing being in the Bible 'cause I've never heard anything in my whole life 'bout it before, but I ain't been to church a lot like Bid and Maw, either. I don't know what to say, I'm speechless, but finally say, There's a lot of stuff in the old part of the Bible I don't know, Cousin Cotton, but Maw sure does; just let me find out for sure before you cast your seed. Bob says, No need to worry guys, Bid, knows how to find out, and then we'll all know. Pat says, I don't think Uncle Joe ever lies, but my mom says sometimes he stretches things a little far.

I promise my cousins and neighborhood friends I'll find the answer to Cotton's question. Some of the boys begin to leave and Maw calls me in the house and says, Son, I saw you talkin' to all your friends, and I need to know what it's all 'bout. I tell her Maw, It's 'bout the Bible. She says, Wonderful, wonderful, Son, I'm so proud that all of them look up to you. I really don't think she quite understands and tell her, It's not just that way, Maw, cousin Cotton was told by Uncle Joe something that concerns the Bible and I don't know the answer for sure. Maw wants to know what the question is, and I'm not sure I know how to tell her 'cause it just don't sound right. I'll try it this way, Maw, Uncle Joe is gonna give Cotton a birthday present when he's thirteen, and said Cotton will be a real man then. He said it's in the Bible some place. **"It's better to cast your seed in the belly of a whore than on the ground."** She explodes, and I don't have a chance to explain. She says, What in God's name is that son of mine tellin' you children? I try to explain to her again and tell her I don't believe I ever read that or heard it, unless it's in the Old Testament before Jesus. She says, Son, I've read the Bible backwards and forwards and it's not there, but I know your uncle and he'd like for it to be there, and so would Cotton.

I can tell Maw is getting aggravated, I ask, Maw, what am I gonna tell my friends tomorrow and she says, Well just tell the truth and be sure and tell everyone Uncle Joe would like for it to be in there and you sure can't find it. She walks away muttering My, oh my, what will these sons of mine think of next, they're gonna be the death of me yet. Oh well, boys will be boys. I tell all my friends and only Cotton says he believes Uncle Joe is right and he's looking forward to his birthday present with, Mary.

FRIDAY, NOVEMBER 6, 1931

BOY PREACHER AMAZES CROWD

Just Five, He Shows Thoro Knowledge of Bible

Scores of people were unable to crowd their way into the Market Hall Thursday night to hear the five-year-old evangelist, Arthur McCaffrey, son of Arthur McCaffrey, 3111 Marion-av, preach.

His subject was, "You Shall Be Born Again."

From the time he stepped to the platform until his talk was concluded he amazed the audience by his knowledge of the Bible.

The youthful minister was not embarrassed in the least before the crowd that packed the hall.

Lifting his hands, he asked the people to bow their heads in prayer. And his voice, altho shrill and childish, could be heard plainly as he prayed to God to forgive the people.

Answers Many Questions

During his sermon he pleaded with the congregation to "prepare yourself for the hereafter that is drawing nearer."

"We are God's children and He will protect us," he said, "but let us not deal in crime or give up to sin."

After his sermon, Arthur answered over 100 Bible questions for members of the congregation.

3

THE CHURCH

The church is my life, it's where I find my friends, learn the Bible, hear 'bout saints and sinners, goin' to heaven and how to stay outta hell. Sunday is the day of rest and worship and it begins with Sunday school at nine thirty in the morning, and preaching till noon. We go home for dinner and come back to church at six thirty and listen to the preacher till nine. Wednesday is prayer meeting time and I get to hear all the ladies tell 'bout how things are going at home and all the trials and tribulations they're goin' through. When Dad's living right he's real good at testifying and telling 'bout how his brothers are trying to lead him into temptation, but he always says he's going all the way this time. People like to hear him testify 'cause he can bring on the tears, and some feel sorry the way he's treated. When Maw testifies she only tells how good the Lord is to her and she is so blessed to have such a fine family.

I learn from the Bible all the scriptures 'bout how Samson killed a thousand Philistines with the jaw bone of a jackass, but Maw says donkey. I learn how he was tempted by a beautiful woman named Delilah and later when he lost his strength he pulled down the pillars of a building and God forgave him. I like the story 'bout David and how he killed the giant Goliath and later became king of all Israel. How he fell in love with another man's wife called Bathsheba and sent him out to be killed, but God forgave him when he repented. Maw says, Don't ever forget that, Son, you can always be forgiven unless you sin against the Holy Ghost and right now I'm not sure 'bout what that means.

I like to hear the preacher talk 'bout how Jesus is coming back to earth and it won't be till the Jews all go back to Israel and have their own land. It's all hard for me to understand, but Maw says she's gonna explain to me some day when she tells me 'bout a lot of other things. She says, Don't think about it now, Son, your time will come will come and you're gonna understand it all.

Maw wants me to remember the most important thing of in life. She says, It's the afterlife that really counts and you only got two places to go; it's either heaven or hell. She tells me how Jesus died for every man and woman who will ever live and God sent him for just that purpose 'cause he loved us so much, and the world's problems can be settled by going to the cross. I have trouble understanding what she means. She tells me again, I need to be a little older and then she's gonna give it all to me 'bout Jesus and his love.

I sit in church half asleep with my cousins, aunts, friends and sometimes Uncles and listen to the preacher talk 'bout how some women wear lipstick, dresses up to their knees, and even cut their hair and it's called bobbed hair. He talks 'bout drinking beer and whiskey and how it's gonna send people to hell and I think 'bout my Uncle Joe's places that I've been in playing his slot machines and guys drinking beer, but no whiskey. The preacher talks 'bout how women get men to do things they shouldn't and I think 'bout Dad and Uncle Joe 'cause Aunt Dorie tells me that's their downfall and they'll never lick it. I don't know what it means, but I doubt if they try.

I like the holidays at church 'cause the entire church is always there and there's lots of fun. Easter is the time Jesus rose from the grave. We always have our Easter play showing how he was hung on the cross and some people cry. Dad does especially. We talk 'bout Jesus coming back someday and how he's gonna take us all to heaven with him, and some people really like that part and they start shouting and hollering hallelujah and Dad does it, too.

The preacher says at the end of time when Jesus comes back He's gonna be in Jerusalem forever as King. He talks 'bout good angels and bad angels and how God in heaven has two thirds of all of 'em and Lucifer or the devil has a third and God's gonna throw 'em in hell forever and ever, and that's what our church likes to hear 'cause everybody hollers amen and hallelujah. When the preacher gets done preaching and telling us 'bout Jesus coming back, some of the people go to the altar and beg forgiveness and Dads' usually the first. Maw doesn't go to the altar and we wonder sometimes if she ever sins, but she does pray every night at home, and I pray with her.

The Fourth of July is a real good holiday at church and it lasts all till almost dark. We have our picnic in a park near the church and play every kind of game we know like softball, pitching washers, running races and eat the best home made ice cream there is. Maw always says something 'bout living in the Heartland of America, how we are free from England and how God blesses America above all nations of the earth.

Everybody knows 'bout my preaching and answering Bible questions at the Little Market Hall and when I walk down the aisle at church holding Maw's hand I hear ladies saying, That's Little Arthur, Spare's boy, the one that preached at Little Market Hall. Mrs. Murphy, a member of the prayer group, whispers to Mrs. Davis, I hear Spare's gettin' ready to drag the boy all over preachin' and answering Bible questions, and several others whisper, That's right, that's right, that Spare will do anything to get his name in headlines. I just wanta go sit down and listen to the preacher, and go home and play softball.

Christmas is the best time of the year 'cause that's when we celebrate the birth of Jesus. We talk 'bout how he was born in a manger 'cause there was no room for him at the Inn. We hear how Wise Men riding camels saw a star in the sky and followed it to where he lay with his mother, Mary, and how someday he will be our King of Kings just like the preacher says. Christmas is the biggest day of the year 'cause every kid in the neighborhood comes to pick up a Christmas treat with some candy in a sack, an orange, nuts and some of them we don't see till next Christmas. We don't see any Catholic kids at our church on Christmas, but I see some Baptist and Methodist from my neighborhood. Maw says give everyone a sack even if they aren't Pilgrim Holiness, 'cause that's the Christian way.

The ladies' prayer group wants Maw to bring me to the next meeting and let me answer some Bible questions, but I think they kinda wanta see if I know the answers. Maw says I'm supposed to be clean, have good manners, and do exactly as she says.

Maw's walking fast today as we head to Mrs. Branson's and she's still worried I'll miss some, 'cause she keeps going over some of the same questions and I'm gettin' tired answering. Mrs. Branson tells us to come in and have a seat. I look around the room and there's Mrs. Casselberry, my Sunday School Teacher. The ladies all wear their long dresses, long sleeves, and everyone has hair flowing down almost to their waist; that's the Pilgrim Holiness rule. They come to me, hug me, and tell me how cute I look, and I don't like it. The ladies sit around the room in a circle and I stand in the middle holding onto the Bible and there's a table in front of me. Maw tells everybody to start asking any question they want and that kinda scares me 'cause the Old Testament is hard for me to understand. I'm a lot better on the New Testament 'cause that's mostly what Jesus and his Disciples did.

Mrs. Casselberry says, I've been teaching this boy in Sunday school since he was able to stand straight. Little Arthur, tell us what must one do to be saved. I know this will always be asked and answer, That's the story 'bout Paul when he was in prison and he prayed to the Lord and an earthquake came and shook so bad the gates of the cell opened and the jailer asked him how he could be saved. Paul said, Believe on the Lord Jesus Christ and all shall be saved and thy house. It's in the Book of Acts. Also John 3:16, For God so loved the world he gave his only begotten son that who so ever believe in him will have everlasting life. The ladies look at each other and realize I'm right and start asking more questions, one right after the other till everyone is satisfied. When I finish they come to hug and kiss me on the forehead and wish I was in all their classes at Sunday school. We sit down, they bring me milk and cookies, and Maw punches me on the side, smiles and tells me how proud she is of me. We begin our walk home.

Maw, I've got a question.
What is it, Son?
I've been answering Bible questions and preaching, but I've never been saved like Dad, I know 'bout Adam and Eve in the Garden of Eden and his sin is still on us, now when do I get saved?
Your time will come when you know the difference between right and wrong. Then, you're accountable.
Is that when I am six or seven?
It's not the age, Son.
Are Dad and Uncle Joe accountable, Maw?
I think so, but sometimes I wonder.
Let me know when I'm accountable, Maw, so I can get saved, baptized and sanctified.
You're almost there, Son, almost there.

It's revival time and Dad always looks forward to this meeting, of all meetings, 'cause this is when most regular members are told 'bout their short-comings, why they feel a little guilty, wanta do better and the evangelist is just the kind of person to tell everyone. The evangelist doesn't usually have his own church, but travels from church to church preaching and when he's done he don't hafta stay. Dad tells me that's the kinda preacher he wants to be. Revival time is a time to bring our friends and hear the evangelist and maybe get saved and join our church. It's a time we need extra money to pay the evangelist, and Dad is always in church the Sunday before he comes and makes his pledge.

It's Sunday night before the revival and Dad, Maw, me, and the rest of my cousins, along with Aunt Dorie sit waiting till the preacher asks for money for the revival. At the end of the service Reverend Johnson says, Now, folks I know it's gonna be hard on everyone to give anything to help pay for the evangelist, but it's just gotta be done, and Dad's starting to move around on the bench. The preacher goes on to explain how every church needs to get fired up every so often 'cause sometime we sin and don't go to the altar to get forgiven, and Dad hollers amen, but nobody else does. Now the preacher wants to know if anyone can possibly give five dollars and as usual Dad's hand goes up, and he hollers, I'll give ten dollars, Reverend Johnson. Maw and the rest of our family including all the cousins and Aunt Dorie hang our heads, 'cause we know Dad ain't got ten dollars, and everyone in church knows it, too. The preacher always expects Dad to be the first, and says, Thank you, Spare, for your generous gift, and Dad looks around at the congregation, smiles and sits down. The preacher continues on asking for donations and hardly anyone raises their hand till he finally says, Can anyone give a dollar or fifty cents? Almost the entire church raises their hands.

The service is over and we walk down the aisle and some come to Dad and tell him how happy they are to see him being saved and being so generous, but none of our family believe he's gonna give a nickel 'cause he ain't got it. I know Uncle Orie is gonna get mad 'cause Dad still owes him five dollars for almost a year and Uncle Orie still asks him for it, but he don't get it. When we get home Maw tells Dad she don't see how he's gonna get ten dollars 'cause he's not working, and Dad says, The Lord always provides. I don't understand what he's talking 'bout.

At the breakfast table, Uncle Orie says, Spare, I hear you gave ten bucks last night to the revival would you mind paying me back that five you borrowed a year ago? Dad won't answer and Uncle Joe says, Spare, won't be goin' to church by the time the revival starts anyhow. Dad tells Maw they're persecuting him and Maw shrugs her shoulders and tells Dad to do his best and that's all God expects out of anyone. Orie and Joe finish eating and walk out the door while Dad's in tears. I enjoy listening to everything, till Maw tells me to get ready for school and be sure to wash behind my ears.

The revival comes and the church is full every night with many people going to the altar to renew their faith, and the last night, Dad is at the altar again. He asks forgiveness for all his sins, especially the one 'bout not giving the ten dollars. As usual, several deacons go to him while he's kneeling before the altar begging forgiveness. A deacon says, Spare, why in the world is it taking you so long to get through this time? My cousins and me all know why and hear what the deacon asked. Pat says, I know why and so does everyone else; It's 'cause he didn't give his ten dollars. Maw hears us talking and says, Boys, don't be so quick to judge. Maybe this will do him some good and in the future he won't be so anxious to promise all that money. Pat says, Maw, they never do expect it anyhow, I watched the preacher when Uncle Spare promised, and he didn't even write it down. Maw says, My, oh my, what will these younguns think of next 'bout their Uncle Spare, sometimes they don't show respect to their elders. Dad finally finishes praying through and everyone heads home. I'm thinking 'bout the next revival and hope he don't offer the ten bucks again. Pat says when the preacher comes to the house again he's gonna tell the preacher to not write it down 'cause he's just wastin' paper.

We leave the church and walk outside and there stands Brother Darrell and Sister Faye, two of the nicest young converts in our church. They invite us to their house to spend the night and talk 'bout the Bible. I can tell they like each other a lot 'cause they hold hands and sometimes Darrell kisses her on the neck when Dad's not looking. I like the people we're going home with. He's already a deacon in the church and knows all 'bout Dad. Dad doesn't wanta go home anyhow 'cause Uncle Joe will probably say something 'bout him gettin' saved again.

We sit in their living room, read a couple verses from the Bible, pray, and Darrell and Faye go upstairs to bed while we sleep downstairs below. I know Dad's happy. He's saved again and I'm glad. We talk 'bout what's probably happening at home tonight and now noise and laughter starts coming from the upstairs. It starts gettin' louder and louder and we're just underneath the noise. I can hear 'em talkin' and now it's really gettin' loud.

There's something going on upstairs, and I ask Dad 'bout it. He says, They're just playing games, but it sounds like they're wrestling to me. Now it's getting even louder and I hear Faye holler, Oh yes Darrell, Oh yes, then she stops, for a while and now they start again. Dad's squirming around on the bed and acting kinda crazy and tells me they're still wrestling and I hear it even louder. It sounds like they may come through the ceiling, and we're just below 'em. Dad's not worried, but I cain't sleep for it. I think Faye must be getting the worst of it, but she's not mad 'cause every so often she hollers real loud, Yes darling, yes darling, and that's how I know she likes it and he's not hurting her. I ask Dad again if Darrell is whipping her and he says, Just, shut the hell up, Son, and go to sleep. Dad just got saved and now he's cussing and when I tell him 'bout it, he says, A man can just stand so much, and this has been way too much for me to bear. I don't really know what he means, and just wanta go to sleep if they ever stop the wrestling match. The next morning we get up from bed, eat some fresh peeled peaches with cream and start for the door to go home when Darrell and Faye come downstairs. Darrell asks if we slept well, and Dad says, Oh yes, Brother Darrell, I slept like a log, but I tell Brother Darrell, I went to sleep after the wrestling match got over. Brother Darrell doesn't seem to understand, and Dad shoves me out the door and we head home. Dad won't talk and I don't know why.

Everyone at home is waiting to see Dad and congratulate him on getting saved. Uncle Orie still wants his five bucks, but Dad doesn't wanta talk 'bout it. Maw says she's glad we went to spend the night with such young nice Christian people like Darrell and Faye and wants to know if I enjoyed being at their home. I tell her 'bout the wrestling match, Dad hollers shut up, Son, Uncle Joe and Uncle Orie are laughing and Maw says,

My Oh my, I don't know what's this world is coming to, and walks outta the room and I still don't understand.

4

THE HANGING OF MR. ROOSTER

I've been busy all summer fishing, playing, preaching and going to church. It's autumn time, and the beautiful trees have lost their leaves. The fields are filled with cornstalks stacked upright and we imagine they're Indian teepees, while Bob and me run around pretending to be Indian warriors. The nearby fields are filled with wild game and birds. We're trappers and hunters just as good as Uncle Shave and now we're gonna prove it. We're gonna trap us a rabbit.

It's Friday evening, and we slip outta the house to go place our snare in a place where rabbits run through the weeds like birds flying through the air, and best of all it's the orchard of Mrs. Thelma Brooks, one of Maw's prayer ladies. We're not gonna mention it to her 'cause this is a surprise and nobody will ever know. We place our snare in the middle of her small apple orchard, and tomorrow we'll go grab our big fat rabbit and take him to show everyone.

It's Saturday morning, we slip outta the house early, head for the field, and talk 'bout our future as hunters and trappers, 'cause this is something we're good at. The morning air is cold, the fields are frosty looking and we begin crawling through the tall weeds. Our hands are cold but our prize is gonna be worth it. We can see the long limb and it's raised with something dangling from it. We've got our rabbit and we're gonna be heroes.

Suddenly we're in complete shock. Dangling from the limb is hanging the biggest rooster in the whole wide world; we've got us a rooster we don't want and we still can't talk. I think maybe we're in trouble, and Bob agrees. We need to act fast and Bob says, Don't get excited; just be calm the same way you did when the cops came lookin' for Uncle Joe. We're gonna throw that sucker across the railroad tracks and hope some dog eats him before Thelma finds out he's even gone. Bob grabs him by the neck hands him to me, and he's stiff as a board. I run across the railroad track and throw him in the tallest weeds, and nobody's ever gonna find him.

The trip back to the house isn't what we expected, but we know how to handle this 'cause we been around Uncle Joe a lot, and he never panics like Dad does. We talk some and Bob's got the best idea. We simply act dumb if anyone says anything, we don't worry 'bout it. Bob says, Roosters are the most useless thing on earth and good for nothin' and all they do is strut around the yard, trying to mount every poor little hen that passes by. When they're done with'em, they spend the rest of the day runnin' 'round the yard crowing 'bout it. We did Mrs. Brooks a favor, but we're not telling anybody.

It's Sunday night and we been kinda dreading this night 'cause Mrs. Brooks and Maw always talk 'bout the prayer group and now the service is over, and here comes Thelma. Bob and me start moving back, unless it's not 'bout us. Bob reminds me to act dumb no matter what happens, and let Maw do the talkin'. I can see the look on her face as she heads toward Maw, and it don't look good, it's almost like she's already crying. When I tell Bob she may begin to cry, he says, Thelma, always looks that way.

Thelma says, Mary, my dear, there's been a tragedy in our family and I don't know if I'll ever get over it.
Maw hugs her and says, Was it one of the kids, Thelma?
Oh darling, Mary, it's not the kids, it's Mr. Rooster.
I don't believe I've met him, Thelma.

Oh honey, he's our prize rooster and he's just like one of the family. Some no good for nothing hung him and threw his little body in some weeds, and some no count dog ate part of the poor little thing.

Oh, that sure is a crying shame. I know you must be goin' through some bad times.

Yes, Mary, and I may not be at the prayer group meetin' tomorrow, but have them pray for me that I can make it through these trying times. Times like these sure do test a persons' faith in the human race.

I sure will darling, and I'll have my two boys see if they can find who did this terrible thing, won't you boys?

Bob says, Count on us, Maw.

Thelma just won't shut up 'bout Mr. Rooster and keeps talking to Maw 'bout how he woke 'em up every morning at the crack of dawn and her husband didn't need a clock to wake up for work 'cause he was so faithful. We need to get outta this church building 'cause I don't like being round Thelma. She's saying something 'bout how only someone with a bad heart could commit a crime like this. Now we feel like bad guys or criminals and we only wanted to trap a rabbit. Bob says, Bid, are we bad guys like she says? I don't wanta talk 'bout this 'cause Thelma hears everything. Now she's running over to some other prayer group ladies and telling them 'bout the no goods that hung Mr. Rooster, and I guess we're the no goods. She's all excited and drawing a crowd and talks to Mrs. Robinson, a prayer group lady.

Did you hear 'bout Mr. Rooster, Mrs. Robinson?
No, what 'bout him, Thelma, dearie?
Some no goods hung him right in our orchard.
Tis, a crying shame, Thelma, there's no tellin' what this worlds coming to.
Just pray for me darling that I make it through.
I will, Dearie, and I'll tell everyone else.
I grab Bob's arm and we're heading for the door. Maw can come when she's ready.

We're on our way home and I'm glad to get away from Thelma and the church. I don't wanta hear anymore 'bout Mr. Rooster and I ain't telling anyone. Bob wants know if we hafta get saved, sanctified and baptized for hanging Mr. Rooster and I tell him, Nope, buddy, 'cause that's not a sin, just an accident and Mr. Rooster shouldn't try to act like a rabbit. Bob says, I'm glad to hear that 'cause I wasn't gonna get saved like Uncle Spare just for doing something I never tried to do.

We talk 'bout religion and getting saved on the way home walking far behind Maw, and I tell Bob 'bout how I preached down in Bluff City Kentucky. I answered Bible questions in the morning to a church full of Soft Shell Baptist and the same night to a bunch of Hard Shell Baptist. Bob doesn't know the difference. I tell him the Hard Shells believe like Pilgrim Holiness. If you sin and don't get forgiven right away you go to hell for sure. The Soft Shell Baptist believe, once you get saved, it's forever and you don't need to go back all the time like, Dad. Bob wants to know why Dad doesn't switch to Soft Shell Baptist and I don't know why he doesn't either.

Closer to home and getting farther behind we're still talking 'bout religion and Bob wants to know if Maw ever sins. I know she prays a lot, but I don't hear her ask forgiveness like Dad. I tell him, I don't think she does, but she might make mistakes. Bob says, That's what I thought too till she whacked us a couple times and said it hurt her more than it did us. Now we're kinda worried if she finds out we smoked Indian cigars from catalpa trees, pulled Snotty Nose Lindel from the water, almost drowned ourselves, and what's gonna happen next. I tell him, Don't worry, she'll never find out and we'll never squeal.

Days return to normal and Mr. Rooster is never mentioned again. Sometimes at church when we see Mrs. Brooks coming towards us, we move in the other direction and never look back. We're glad it's over and Mr. Rooster is dead and gone forever.

FRIDAY, NOVEMBER 13, 1931.

CHURCH CROWDED AS BOY PREACHES

Too Many Like the Word of the Devil, Five-Year-Old Evangelist Says

Arthur McCaffrey, jr., five-year-old preacher prodigy whose extensive knowledge of the Bible and public address ability recently has amazed his audiences, spoke before more than 300 persons who jammed the capacity of the Little Market church, Pennsylvania street and first avenue, last night.

"Suffer little children to come unto Me, for of such is the kingdom of heaven," was the text of his sermon.

Arthur declared that everyone should spread the word of Jesus, even small children. "Too many persons like the word of the devil," the boy said, and, pointing to various parts of the assemblage, cried, "You and you and you know that."

The youthful preacher said he intended to be a preacher when he grew older and that he never would desert his calling. He reminded his audience that everything they possessed came from the goodness of God and not through their own efforts.

Before the sermon, Arthur answered a number of questions pertaining to the Bible, asked him by his father, Arthur McCaffrey, sr., 3111 Marion avenue. With two or three exceptions he answered every question correctly.

SPENCER COUNTY SEAL SALE METHOD CHANGED

ROCKPORT, Nov. 12.—(Special)— The Spencer county Anti-Tuberculosis association has organized a mail sale campaign, whereby the Christmas

continued to November 25, bond $1,500.
City vs. William McKenzie, disor-

The Evansville Courier

5

THE PREACHER COMES CALLING

Everybody knows the preacher is coming on Sunday and we're supposed to be like little angels, don't say bad words like Uncle Joe, dress in our best, and we're gonna have chicken and dumplings for sure. Uncle Joe's not coming 'cause he says he don't wanta be around Dad when the sermon comes. I think he's afraid of preachers, 'cause he never goes to church. Bull is headed for the woodshed and cain't come out till the preacher leaves, and any cousin, aunt or uncle who wants to come and listen to the preacher is welcome, but there better not be any fightin' or argueing. Maw is gonna use the same knives and forks her mother gave her. They came all the way from Germany and we might even have napkins to wipe our mouth with.

Maw calls Dad into the front room and tells him to try and not be the center of attention when the preacher comes and I see him frown. He wants to know whose gonna give the blessing at the table and she tells him again; the preacher of course, and he frowns again. I don't think he's happy.

Dad's been saved, baptized, and sanctified again now for almost two months and Uncle Orie and Uncle Joe made a bet. Uncle Joe bet Uncle Orie fifty cents Dad would fall off the wagon and drink some booze before the end of two months. Pat wants to know what falling off the wagon means, and I tell him it means if Dad drinks beer before the end of two months, Uncle Orie is gonna lose his bet. Pat says, Does La Fendrich cigars count the same as beer? I tell him no, just booze, but if Dad sins, he'll probably do both. Dad won't talk to either of 'em 'bout it and only says, I'm goin' all the way this time and I'm praying for my two brothers. Everyone is proud of Dad and when he walks into church, everyone nods and tells him how happy they are he's finally on the right track. I hold his hand and carry the Bible till church starts, then Dad takes it 'cause sometimes he waves it in the air when the preacher talks 'bout sinful women like Delilah who tempted Sampson. The preacher talks 'bout Bathsheba who tempted King David and Dad hollers, amen, Brother, I know whatcha mean. Some don't know what he's talking bout, but I do. Maw just sits and listens and one woman in the prayer group mutters, It looks like Spare is on fire for the Lord this time for sure. I wonder what she means, but I'm not gonna ask. Dad tells everybody he's working on Uncle Joe and Uncle Orie to follow his path and give up sin, but they just cain't give it up. Dads' only got two weeks to go till the bet is up. I hope he makes it.

It's the final week of the two months before the bet ends and I walk down the aisle with Maw and Dad with him carrying the Bible. Everyone smiles, nods, and we go to our seat in the second row from the front. The service isn't long as usual and we start to leave when Sister Murphy comes to us and says, Spare, I never thought I'd see the day you lasted almost two months in your Christian life. You'll never know how much the ladies in our prayer group are praying you go all the way. Dad says, Sister Murphy, I thank you for your prayers, but this is one time sin doesn't enter my mind. She asks if he's tempted to drink or chase loose women like he used to. Dad laughs and says, The urge for that kinda stuff is gone forever, and now that I'm preaching, I'm tellin' everyone how drinkin', gamblin', smokin', and givin' in to loose women can even get the best of us in trouble. Sister Murphy says, I never thought I'd live to see the day I'd hear you say that, Spare. Dad smiles, shakes her hand and she wants to know how Uncle Joe is doing. Dad tells her he's got him on his prayer list along with a half dozen other relatives at home. Sister Murphy says, Keep up the good work, Spare, and walks away. I'm not wanting to hear anymore of this stuff 'cause Dad's not acting right and I'm gonna tell Uncle Joe and Uncle Orie, Dad's got 'em on his list.

At one o'clock, the preacher and his wife arrive and we greet them warmly. Reverend Johnson is a nice looking man of average height, a little plump and a nice friendly personality. He becomes serious in matters of the church and its doctrine and his wife is a small dark-haired attractive lady and very soft spoken. Maw seats everyone and asks Reverend Johnson to offer prayer to give thanks for the food. There's lots of food with the usual chicken and dumplings, and little conversation during the meal. Bob wants to know why hardly anyone's not talkin', and says, When Uncle Joe is here, he's tellin' jokes and everyone is laughing and we're having a good time listening to him. Maw tries to make Bob and me understand that when the preacher comes things get serious and the preacher laughs. He says, Now don't anyone worry 'bout Joe, he'll come along now that Spare and the whole church is praying for him. Dad says, Amen Brother Johnson, I'm glad you said that cause he's got a lot to learn, even though sometimes people here at home make my life hard, I know the Lord will pull me through.

Everyone follows Maw into the living room where she has a small round table in the center of the room with the family Bible on it. All my cousins and me sit on the floor and cross our legs waiting to see what the preacher is gonna say. Maw asks the preachers' wife to say a prayer. Our heads are bowed.

Reverend Johnson reads a couple of scriptures from the Bible explaining how important wives and mothers are leading their children and compares it to Maw. She says nothing, 'cept to thank him for his kind remarks and Dad adds some amens. Finally the preacher is at the end of his message of praise and says, If anyone needs to say something, please do? I know Dad's been waiting for this moment. He stands and says, It's well known my son and me are conducting services everywhere and I will need you to pray for us. The preacher wants to know where Dad will be preaching next and he says, I've got some things goin' over in Kentucky and Illinois, and maybe Indianapolis. The preacher says, Spare, I just hope you preach the truth and nothing else, and Dad tells him, That's what I always do, and you can count on it from now on 'cause, I'm walking down the straight and narrow road. Dad grabs the preachers hand, almost shakes it off, and tells him how much his visit has done for him.

The preacher and his wife decide it's time to leave for home and prepare for the evening church service. He tells us all how much he has enjoyed being at our house visiting, and how proud he is of everyone. Dad says, I'll be in church tonight Reverend, and we stand at the door, shake hands, and hug them as they leave. Later Maw calls us into the house and tells us how proud she is of everyone. She says, I'm especially proud of Bob and Pat, 'cause for once my boys didn't wanta ask a lotta questions and just listened. Bob says, I wanted to, but I didn't wanta embarrass Uncle Spare. Maw don't know what he's talking 'bout, and Bob says, I heard 'bout the bet and I doubt if Uncle Spare is gonna make it, and I think Uncle Orie will lose his fifty cents. Maw tells him to hush up and go get Bull outta the woodshed and feed him the scraps.

Uncle Joe returns home and hears the conversation and says nothing till Bob says, Uncle Spare is praying for you to quit your sinning and is working on you to get saved. Uncle Joe acts kinda mad and says, Hell, Brother Spare can sin ten times more than me once he gets started and nobody will ever stop him. Uncle Joe is still mad and says he's now he's sure he's gonna win the fifty cents from Uncle Orie and Maw still doesn't know what they're talking 'bout. She just walks away smiling, says, Oh my, oh my, what kind of a family am I raising, oh well, I've turned 'em both over to the Lord anyhow.

Dad tells me to come outside and talk, he wants to tell me 'bout our future preaching plans and says, Son, I've decided it's time for you and me to let people know we're just as good preaching as Reverend Johnson. There are some black friends of mine down in Mud Center only a couple of miles from here that wanta hear you answer Bible questions. You know by now that I'm on the straight and narrow way of life, so don't worry 'bout me doing something wrong. I tell him, I've never been in a black church before, but my friend Mel is black and he goes to a Baptist church. Dad says, That's the church I'm talkin' 'bout, Son, so get yourself ready for next Sunday and by the way, we'll be eatin' dinner with them after church. I don't know if it's a secret or not till he says, Tell the world, Son, we're out to spread the word to everyone. I ask, How 'bout Jews? He says, It won't do no good, Son, they won't know till Jesus comes, 'cause they think he's not the Son of God. That sounds like what Maw told me 'bout the last days, so I guess he's right 'bout that.

Bob stands next to me and hears the talking goin' on between Dad and me. Now, he wants to go along so he can get some of the good fried chicken our friend Mel talks 'bout all the time when we play ball. I tell him, Sure, you can go, Bob, 'cause that's what church is for and you can sit on the front row bench with Mel and me. Now, he wants to bring some more of our buddies, and it's gonna be a lotta fun at the black church.

The Sunday morning service begins to a full house and after the introduction, I go to the pulpit and the questions begin. Dad asks me the usual questions, and it's time for the congregation part of the service. An elderly lady dressed in a long flowered dress in the back of the church stands up and says, Young man, I'd like to know who teaches you all these answers to the questions your daddy just asked you? I tell her, Ma'am, I was taught by our preacher Reverend Johnson, my maw, my dad, and I know how to read, and she hollers, Hallelujah, Son, I'm glad your maw taught you some things, 'cause these old sinner men here, don't seem to understand nothing.

I'm enjoying this meeting a lot. An old gray headed gentleman sitting in the front row says, Son, I've never in my life been in a white church, but I know they believe as we do. I'd like to know why white folks don't ask us to come to your church? That's a hard one I'd never been asked before. I look at Dad and down the front row where my cousins sit, and say, Sir, it sounds to me like what Maw taught me when she said some people say one thing and do another. Another nice dressed lady with a beautiful hat on her silver hair rises from her seat and says, Amen, preacher boy, you said a mouthful. Everyone is caught off guard at the answer. Dad says, Brothers and sisters, that's what I've been tellin' them for a long time. Let's sing that favorite song, "Old Time Religion" and maybe that's the answer. Some of the ladies get into the song and it's not long till the music and singing has everyone in a wonderful mood with a lot of shouting and singing of some old spirituals. All my cousins and Mel sitting on the front row are enjoying the singing as much as me, and we all join in, and this is one good meeting.

Dad takes over preaching and I know he's been waiting for this a long time. It doesn't take him long till the sweat and emotions are running high. He has a way of moving all over the podium raising his Bible and crying one moment with lots of tears, and the next moment laughing with glee. This is the greatest day of my life, he shouts and everyone down front yells, Amen, brother, preach the truth. Dad is tellin' 'bout how every man and woman is sometimes tempted to do wrong and it takes lots of willpower to resist, and the only way to resist them is to get the Lord to help you. That's the truth, Brother Spare, yells Mel's dad from the front row and several Deacons holler, Amen, Brother, tell it like it is. Mel's dad shouts again, it's mostly the women's fault, and all the women standing waving their arms sit down and look at their husbands as if they're mad.

The service ends a little after noon-time and we all go outside to a large lot filled with tables and chairs. The tables are completely covered with large white tablecloths, and we have so much food it's hard to imagine The Great Depression is going on. I'm called up front to the head of the table and the church pastor says the blessing. All my friends, both black and white, are seated together and going after the fried chicken, corn on the cob, mashed potatoes and apple pie. Mel says, This is a great day for all of us and we agree, and he wants to know if were coming back. Bob says he sure would like to be here again if his momma lets him, and the rest of my cousins and me all agree.

We're 'bout to leave and here comes a thin middle aged lady looking for Dad, and says, Preacher, I'm Sadie Collins and I'm a member of the Ladies' Prayer Group and I need your help. I know Dad is kinda scared of any ladies prayer groups anywhere. Sadie looks like she's someone who means business, and like she's mad before she even starts talking to Dad. I think he knows it, 'cause he acts like he doesn't hear her. Dad says, Glad to meet you, Sister Sadie, how can I help you, and all of a sudden Sister Sadie is right up in Dad's face, and Dad's backing up. Sister Sadie says, It's just this, preacher, and nothing else. It's just plain orneriness and meanness, and downright bad, that's what it is. Dad backs up a little more, and me and my cousins move in closer so we can hear. Dad says, How long you been that way, Sister Sadie? Me and my son specialize in dealing with that sort of thing. I don't think she likes what Dad said and now she's really mad, and Bob's asking me why she's mad. I don't know what they're talking 'bout, and Sister Sadie says, What, in the hell you talkin' 'bout, Brother Spare, it's not me I'm talkin' 'bout, it's that no good husband of mine; he's home right now down in our basement drinking beer on Sunday and gettin' drunk. It looks like Sister Sadie is madder at Dad than anyone I ever saw.

My cousins come in closer to Sadie and wanta hear more. Dad says, Well, I sure am sorry, Sister, but I feel that's probably something the pastor here oughta look into. Sister Sadie is really getting mad now, and says, It's the same old story, Brother Spare; it's just passing the buck. I can tell Dad don't know what to do or say, so he smiles at her and says, Well, I'm sure sorry you feel that way, Sister, but I will put him at the head of my prayer list. I tell Dad, Let's just put him ahead of Uncle Joe on Maw's list 'cause you were on it, and I think Maw crossed you off 'cause you're preaching now. Dad acts like he's a little aggravated, takes a big gulp, and turns away from Sister Sadie and heads for the road home. We all follow and my pals are wanting to ask questions 'bout why we're leaving, but they don't know Dad like I do in these kind of situations. We walk further down the road, and I don't think Dad is happy like the rest of us, so I ask him, What's the matter? He says, Son, sometimes you just need to keep your mouth shut, especially you should never bring up anything what goes on at home or my past. I'm preaching now and I'm a new man. I don't know what he means, but I still think it was Sister Sadie.

We near home and we're all tired from laughing and begin planning our afternoon. Pat grabs my arm and says, What does 'passing the buck' mean? I've heard it before at home, but never in church. I tell Pat, I think I've got it figured out, if someone asks you to do something you don't wanta do, or don't know how, just tell 'em it's not your job and they should go see someone else.

Maw wants to know if everyone had a good time and if we learned anything new. Pat says, Maw, they do the same thing we do only they seem a lot happier 'bout it and Maw says, I guess they just like serving the Lord better than us. We're all outside playing softball, and Mel and some of his friends come and join us and Bob is still talkin' to Mel 'bout the fried chicken.

When Dad's not preaching he works in a local furniture factory as a spray painter. He tells everyone he's the best in town and some agree. It's hot when Dad comes home from work and he calls me outside to talk after supper. He always calls me outside to talk 'cause he don't want Uncle Joe or Maw to hear and sometime I'm a little leery of what he's gonna say. He tells me we're going over to his new friend's house so get myself ready. I ask, What's his name, Dad, and does he have some kids I can play with? He says, Sure, he's got kids, lots of 'em, 'cause he's Catholic, and his name is Shorty Seibert, and his wife's name is Gertie Seibert.

Shorty's house is only three blocks away and we knock just once and there stands the whole family. Shorty is just what I thought he might be, 'bout five feet five inches tall, skinny, and I can tell he's not the boss of the family. Mrs. Shorty or Gertie is just the opposite, 'bout two hundred pounds, five feet eight, and a big momma and the boss. She pats me on the head and it feels like a hammer. Everyone speaks as much German as English and I like it. There's seven kids and soon I'm playing ball with Hans and his sister Eva in the backyard, kids are running everywhere, and we're having fun. Gertie comes to the back door and yells, Come in everyone, we're having refreshments. That sounds good 'cause everyone is hot and sweating from the ball game. Gertie puts a large pan in the center of the living room floor and says, Gather 'round, and sit on the floor. I look at the pan and it's filled with home-brew with a large piece of ice. Shorty says, Lets pray, and when he finishes everyone gives the sign of the cross, including Dad, not me. I'd never done it before, but I saw the lady across the street do it. Dad picks up the pan, gulps down two big swigs of beer, wipes the foam off his lips, and passes it on. Everyone does the same including my new friends Hans and Eva till it gets to me. I cain't do it 'cause I'm a Pilgrim Holiness and Dad and me preach against drinking beer, and Maw said I'd go to hell for sure if I did. Mrs. Shorty says, Whats de matter, Son, don't you like beer? I don't know how to answer. I tell Gertie, I'm a Pilgrim Holiness, ma'am, we don't drink beer and Dad's not supposed to either, but he does. Dad's face turns red and I can tell he's not pleased. Gertie says, Now, don't you worry your little head off, Son, I fix dat. She leaves for the kitchen and is right back, and places a plate in front of me with two big pickled pigs' feet. I'm not hungry, but I like pickled pigs' feet with crackers and a large glass of ice water, and I soon find out this is good. The pan is making its circle again and again, and Shorty runs to the kitchen to get refills. Dad's gettin' his share of the booze and lots of fun and singing begins. Now, Dad's puffin' on a cigar, and kids run in and out the back door while playing in the yard and I'm eatin' pickled pigs' feet. Hans is teaching me how to count to ten in German and Dad and the rest of the family are singing an old German song I've never heard.

Ach, du lieber Augustin.

Refrain:
Ach, du lieber Augustin,

Augustin, Augustin,
Ach, du lieber Augustin,
Alles ist hin!

Geld ist hin, Mad list hin,
Alles is thin, Augustin!
Ach, du lieber Augustin,
Alles is thin!

Rock ist weg, Stock ist weg,
Augustin liegt im Dreck.
Ach, du lieber Augustin,
Alles is hin!

 A full moon fills the warm summer night sky and now it's time to leave our new Catholic friends. We all hug and say goodbye till the next time and we begin walking down Tunis Avenue. Dad is happy, and begins singing the new German song *"Ach, du lieber Augustin."* I drop a little behind and hope nobody comes along and sees him waving his arms while singing, and sometimes laughing. He's really happy now, and nearing home and he switches to *"When We All Get To Heaven."*

 I've had a good time and now I'm glad to get home. Dad says, What ever you do, don't wake anyone, especially your Uncle Joe. Don't worry 'bout Maw, when she's gone, she's gone, and she snores so loud the roof rattles. I tell him, Don't worry 'bout me 'cause I'll be just like a little mouse and I'll tip-toe through the kitchen to the upstairs. Dad says, That's my boy, that's my boy, I know you can do it, but whatever you do, don't wake your Uncle Joe, 'cause he's the one that causes me lots of problems when I only have a couple beers. I ask Dad if he's worried 'bout Uncle Orie losing his bet and he acts like he doesn't know 'bout it, but he does. I stop in the kitchen, find the coal oil lamp, and move up the stairwell to the upstairs, and now it's his turn. He's having some trouble on his way and making lots of noise and finally makes the top. He reaches for the door handle, looses his balance, and falls back down the steps and lies at the bottom, groaning and begging for help. Uncle Joe hears the noise and comes running to the top of the stairs and sees Dad at the bottom. I know he's not gonna help, 'cause Uncle Joe doesn't show pity, unless it's some woman, and I cain't help 'cause I gotta hold the lamp.

Dad says, Help me, brother, help me, I think I broke my back.
Uncle Joe doesn't believe Dad and says,
You're drunker than hell, Spare, now get your ass up here and get to bed, 'cause I need some sleep. I'd really be on your ass, but you just made me fifty cents.
I'm going to bed, and later Dad makes it up the steps.

Maw calls Dad three times before he comes to breakfast and when he finally makes it, she looks at him and says, You don't look so good, Son, I guess you're just an ole' sleepy head. Dad tells her she's gonna have to get him another mattress to sleep on 'cause that's why he doesn't sleep good. Uncle Joe starts laughing, I smile, and Maw cain't figure out why. The next day I tell Maw 'bout Dad drinking beer at Mr. Shorty's.

She says, Sounds just like your Dad, but you knew better, didn't you, Son?
Sure did, Maw. I don't wanta go to hell.
Son, it's time you get saved. Sunday night you go to the altar, and from then on, you're accountable.

Sunday night before the entire church I go to the altar and get saved. Saturday afternoon I walk out in the deep water of the big Ohio River and our preacher and Brother Salvatori put me under the water, and I'm wondering if they'll ever let me come up. They probably don't know I cain't swim or they'd let me up sooner. On Wednesday night I'm at the altar again getting sanctified. I am now accountable. Now, I gotta go tell Bob, and he can get accountable.

It's Monday morning and Uncle Orie is here for breakfast with Dorie, Pat, and Evelyn. I think he's mad at Dad, 'cause he won't even look at him, and Dad acts like he doesn't wanta look at Uncle Orie. Uncle Orie throws two quarters on the table, Uncle Joe picks 'em up and Dad wants to leave, but they tell him to stay while Maw and me just watch. Aunt Dorie says, Spare you've finally done it this time, and after our prayer group had so much faith in you. Dads' head falls lower and I see a tear or two. Dorie says, Spare, how in the world could you get drunk and smoke after Sister Murphy got up in church and testified 'bout you being an example to all the other sinners in church? Dad still won't answer and Maw's not saying anything. Uncle Joe starts laughing and says, Brother Orie, that's the easiest money I ever made, and Uncle Orie isn't smiling. Finally Dad tells Maw he's goin' to the altar Sunday night, and she shakes her head and says, Will it ever end, will it ever end?

6

BEGINNING THE EVANGELISM

Dad is teaching me some signals we're gonna use when he wants to talk to me, or when he wants me to just shut up. He just pokes me in the side with his elbow once if he wants to go outside, then he goes to the door and nods for me to come outside. Most of the time it's probably a secret he don't want the rest of the family to know 'bout. If he pokes me twice it means to shut up what I'm talking 'bout and just listen, and if it's more than two pokes I better look out 'cause he's not liking it. I ask him how he learned the signals and he says it comes from his military experience in the cavalry.

It's Sunday at dinner and Dad gives me one poke on my side, gets up from the dinner table, goes to the door, nods so nobody can see him, I get up and go outside and nobody knows we gotta secret. He tells me 'bout some preachers who heard me preach at the Little Market Hall. They want us to come to their church near Mt. Vernon, Indiana and Mt. Carmel, Illinois and hold a couple night church services. I ask Dad if it's a secret and he says, Not this time, Son, but it might be the next time. He tells me we need to talk 'bout this more so we're gonna take a streetcar ride this afternoon and see the city while we make plans for the meeting.

The streetcar heads for the east side of Evansville and it's not long till he begins explaining his plans. Dad says, I've come to the conclusion you have a special gift in remembering the Bible and we're gonna be doing a lot of preaching and saving a lot of sinners' souls. Dad says, he's gonna be looking out for me from now on and not Maw, and that kinda bothers me. He tells me he wants to raise me proper, and not like Uncle Joe wants to, by hanging around with sinners all the time and anything he does for me is for my benefit, not his. Dad wants to know if Maw is trying to turn me against him and I tell him, Maw says I should always obey you 'cause she knows you have good intents. Dad says. Well, that sure surprises me. He shows a big smile, and now he looks happy.

The streetcar reaches downtown Evansville and Dad says, Son, instead of riding, let's walk down Main Street and look in the store windows and that will give us some time to talk 'bout our plans. He knows I like to look in the windows even though we don't buy anything. He says, We're gonna be staying with a family who own a garage along the highway between Mt. Vernon and a small community called Solitude. They're a real nice family and they liked your preaching at Little Market and I've got some big things lined up for us, though you're too young to understand. Dad says I can rest assured that he's gonna be there looking out for me. I tell him, If, you don't, Maw will. Now he's frowning again.

Son, please don't lose faith in your dad. I've got enough to contend with just trying to keep my family from interfering in my life.
I won't, Dad.
Thanks, Son.
I have no idea what he's talking 'bout, but I'll do it.

We walk down Main Street and look in every store front till, we come to Montgomery Ward. Inside the big front window sits the prettiest balloon tired bicycle I ever saw. In my eyes, it's a fantasy 'cause the price is almost twenty dollars and that's unbelievable. We both stand and look at the bike and Dad tells me someday he's gonna buy it for me when the long-green comes rolling in, but I don't know what he means. He says, When we get to preaching all over it's gonna happen and there is nothing better than having the long-green. Dad says I hafta do a better job of preaching and answering Bible questions and when I do we'll get the long-green, the bike, and the Lord will provide. I wanta know how the Lord is gonna do it and Dad says, I'm absolutely sure your gifted reading the Bible and preaching and the Lord wants us to have the best of everything. It sounds good to me, but I doubt if the Lord is gonna do it like he says, and I know Maw and Uncle Joe don't believe I'll get the bike preaching.

Heading home, Dad says, Son, I want you to realize this is just the beginning of our career and you need to listen to me good when I tell you the kind of preaching I want you to do. The most important thing is to preach like I tell you, not what Maw says, do you understand? I tell him, Sure, I do, Dad, but you change a lot and Maw never changes and I don't know who's right. He says, Maw's just not educated like I am, and she doesn't understand the situation and circumstances like I do. When we get down to this church near Solitude and preach a couple nights, we'll be heading for Mt. Carmel, Illinois for a few nights preaching. Dad wants to know if I understand our plans and I really don't, but I tell him I heard on the radio that's where they're having floods and he says, Son, there you go again worrying, worrying, and I just told you the Lord's gonna provide and from now on you just gotta show some faith like me.

We're on our way to Mt. Vernon via E&OV Bus Line. This is a good time to talk 'bout the coming church service and Dad is preparing me how to greet people. He says, Son, if you were far enough along to know how to deal with people like I do, I'd let you do some of the greeting, but you've got a lot to learn. I'd even let you talk more without me having to poke you all the time. Most of the time, Son, just keep your mouth shut and above all remember your manners when you're around these people, and don't let me catch you eatin' fast. I tell him, Maw gets on you all the time at home for eatin' fast and Dad says, That don't count 'cause the rest of the family does the same thing. I'm just gonna eat like Maw told me when she said, Just eat normal, Son.

The bus stops at the station and a couple is walking towards us and they ask if we are the preacher and son team coming to hold the two night revival. I can see they're just like my folks at home and feel at ease. They look to be 'bout forty years old, well-fed and both red-headed. He says, I'm John Mitchell and this is my wife, Gloria. He reaches out to shake hands with me instead of Dad. I shake his hand and tell him, My name is, Bid, and this is my dad, and at home they call him, Spare, but at church when we preach everyone calls him Reverend McCaffry. Dad acts like he's upset and grabs Mr. Mitchell's hand, and almost shakes it off. Dad says, Brother Mitchell, sometimes my son gets a little anxious to meet people like you so I hope you understand. He says, I sure do, Spare, and it shows you're training your son the way it should be. Dad says, Thank you, Brother, I try to do my best, beings he ain't got no mother.

An old Ford truck waits for us and heads down the highway toward home with three adults in front and me in the back. After 'bout three miles, we pull into a drive off the highway and we're home. The house isn't big, but it has a garage attached that serves as a workshop where John works on cars and does small welding jobs. A sign on the garage says, 'Heaven's Highway Garage' and underneath reads 'You're always welcome and we fix it.' This sounds friendly and I already like the family 'cause they're just like my family at home. I go inside and meet two boys and two girls and now it's even better.

After supper, everyone gathers in the living room and we begin telling 'bout ourselves, and what we're doing along with some plans for the future. The night wind has picked up and a fire is roaring in the fireplace. John begins telling how he got in the garage business. He says, I was farming till I just couldn't make it anymore and the last thing in the world I ever dreamed of doing was running a garage like this, and the darn seed is costing more than what I can sell it for. Right now, corn and wheat are selling for 'bout fifty cents a bushel. I cain't make payments to the bank, and the best way to get money is get me a garage and I feel the Lord is gonna help me make the payments. Dad says, Don't worry 'bout it any further, Brother John, let's get down on our knees and pray that the Lord provides your needs, and your problem is gonna be solved. John's not so sure, but tells Dad he believes in a man of faith and wants to try, and Dad smiles.

Everyone begins praying and Dad's leading. When it's over, we all sit down and now it's Dad's turn to tell 'bout himself. He says, It's like this, folks. I was a little young and restless and the first thing I thought 'bout was joining the Army when I was seventeen. I ended up in the cavalry down on the Mexican Border right after the World War, and the only fighting we did was chase 'bout a hundred Indians and Mexicans back to Mexico. Gloria is listening to every word Dad speaks and really liking it. She says, I'll bet it was really something down there on the border wasn't it, Brother Spare? Dad says, Oh, it was just in the line of duty for us cavalry men; not a lot of glory as they had in the big war with Germany. It had to be done and we did it. One of the kids hollers, How 'bout tellin' us 'bout chasing the Mexicans and Indians, sir. Dad says, Its' a long story and something I don't take a lotta pride in, but when they began raiding our peoples' ranches and taking cattle back across the border, that's where the cavalry comes in.

John says, I guess we could sit here all night and listen to some of your stories, Brother Spare, but we better get to bed and start worrying 'bout how we're gonna get to church. Further down the highway water is over the road five feet deep and there's no truck goin' through that kinda water. I can tell Dad still wants to talk 'bout his cavalry career, but it's late and the kids beckon me to follow them to the bedroom, and everyone heads for dreamland.

The next morning we head for the shop and everyone is talking 'bout the weather 'cept Dad. We wonder who might be going to church tonight and if it's possible to make it by auto. The radio blurts out a news report the water isn't going down and it could possibly rain again. John says, Well, brother Spare, I guess that takes care of the meeting tonight and I'm real sorry to get you and your son down here. There's no way in the world can we get to the church tonight, cause when Big Creek starts overflowing the highway, it's time to get outta the way. I can tell Dad's not liking what John's saying, and he says, Listen to me, John, if that meeting on the other side of the highway is for tonight, I feel it's my duty as a man of the Lord to let Him lead us over there. John doesn't quite understand what Dad's talking 'bout, and I'm hoping it's not what I think it is.

Dad says, John, my friend, what did we have before cars? There's your answer.
If you're saying horses, Brother Spare, I ain't got that kinda faith.

Dad don't like John's attitude 'bout the water. He goes to the other side of the garage and sits down, and mutters something soundin' like, 'Help us Lord.' He comes back to John and says, The problem's solved, Brother, the Lord wants us to go through the rising waters 'cause I may be able to help someone tonight. I can tell John doesn't exactly feel like Dad and he says, Well, if it's O.K. with you, Brother Spare, I'll just guide you down to the water and let you go conduct the meeting yourself. I can tell Dad doesn't like what John's saying and he says, John, my friend and brother, you just gotta have a little faith. They don't look at each other and Dad wants to pray again.

It's not that I don't have the faith, Brother Spare, but the Lord didn't tell me.
What 'bout you, Bid, are you gonna ride through the water?
Well, I just do what my dad thinks best, sir, unless Maw tells me different.
Now, Son, I've never told you wrong, have I?
Not lately, Dad.
Well, it's settled then, Son, you'll be riding just behind your old dad.

John says, I'm not gonna let some six-year old evangelist boy have more faith than me, so count me in tonight. The kids clap their hands and John says, There is one thing for sure though, kids, you're not goin' with me, so don't get so happy, I've got faith but it only counts for me. Brother Spare I guess that settles it, I'll be with you tonight riding through the waters and I sure wanta pray before we leave. Dad is all smiles and says, I never once doubted your faith, Brother John, I knew all along you'd go with me. I ask Dad if the Lord told him and he says, It's simple faith, Son, simple faith and John says, Spare, I sure am glad to meet a man of your faith and I hope it works tonight. A big smile lights up Dad's face after hearing John admire his faith.

After an early supper, we take off from the house riding two well-groomed horses John brought from the farm. The family waves us good-bye and a couple of cheers come from the kids. In 'bout twenty minutes we see the water covering the highway, and the closer we get it's easy to see the strong back-water rushing across the road. The full moon lightens the sky and makes the water in front of us easy to see. John says, I believe the water is just a little stronger than I thought when I was praying, how 'bout you, Spare? Dad says it don't bother him one bit, but now John wants to know how I feel 'bout it and I tell him again; I just do what he tells me, unless Maw tells me different. Now I remember something I hadn't thought 'bout. I cain't swim. I ask Dad, What should I do if I fall off? He says, Try dog paddelin', Son, and hang on to the nearest tree. I cain't dog paddle, so I tell him again, and he says not to worry 'bout it, 'cause he cain't swim either. Dad says, Don't worry 'bout a thing, Son, the Lord is looking out for all of us.

John's listening close and it's getting dark and suddenly he says, Well, if we're gonna do it, then let's do it and get it over with. He gallops off down the road and plunges into the water. Dad yells, Hold on, Son, here we go. I grab him around the neck and shoulders and off we go. It's only a short distance into the water till the horse is swimming and headed for the distant shore 'bout a block away. Water is up to my waist and it's ice cold. John reaches the other side and is waiting. He yells, Come on, come on, come on, and it isn't long till we touch pavement. John says, I'll hafta be truthful, Brother Spare, I almost chickened out at the last moment, but I guess the fact I knew you had experienced this in the cavalry gave me some courage. I knew it was almost nothing to you and now that it's over, I'll probably have the courage to do it again. How 'bout you, Bid? I'm shaking from the cold and finally able to say, I've got to tell the truth, John, I was scared, and I'll probably be scared going back. I was a little scared before we started and when we got across, I felt better. I really didn't think I could dog paddle in the current if I slipped off, and that that kinda makes me worry 'bout going back.

Everyone feels better that we're on dry land. The horses are put in a stable and Dad begins telling me some things 'bout what the service is gonna be like and I need to get ready to answer questions, and I'm still cold from the water.

We arrive at the small country church and gather in the back room. I'm drying off, and I can hear the preacher beginning to talk. Church begins and when I look out towards the audience I can tell these people have had it worse than others. Their faces look weather worn, their hands look cracked like leather, and the men dress in bib overalls. The women's long print dresses seem worn by time and hard wear. The pastor introduces us to the congregation and remarks how we had to swim the horses to get there and says, This is an act of devotion. This proves to everyone that this father and son and our own Deacon John are people of great faith. Dad and John stand up, bow to the crowd, and there's lots of amen's. After a couple of songs, the pastor says, I'm sure many of you have heard or read 'bout the young boy, so let's make them welcome here tonight. Undoubtedly there would be far more people here tonight if the weather permitted, and I doubt if anybody dreamed they would make it across the highway. I sure didn't think they would make it, and no doubt the Lord was with them. Dad smiles and says, You're right, brother, you're right.

The preacher makes some other remarks concerning the church and urging a little more tithe giving if possible. The hat is passed around and it's evident these are hard times. Several persons reach into their pockets and pull out a few nickels and dimes and drop it in the offering. When the offering is brought forth to the pastor, he says, We, don't have any money left today folks, but we got the faith, and several holler amen.

Dad's now in charge of the service and grabs his Bible in his right hand and waves it at the congregation and says, Tonight Brothers and Sisters we're here to do the Lord's work and does everyone agree? All the hands go up and he brings me to the front and says, You, folks can ask this boy anything 'bout The Bible you wish, and he will give you an answer. There may be times he just doesn't know, but feel free to ask. He doesn't understand or know everything in this Holy Bible, but he knows a lot and you'll see. I look straight forward and hold the Bible in my hand and remember the times Dad drilled me over and over and I know exactly how this is done. I see some older person dressed in bib overalls and a long-sleeved shirt in the very last row of the church. He stands up and says, Young man, first of all, I'd like to say you gotta lot of guts to ride through the flood-water, but you got more guts to stand up there before this bunch of sinners and let 'em quiz you. I ain't a Christian, but if you can tell me why I should be one, then I might turn into one tonight. I look across the pulpit at Dad and the minister and try to think how to answer the man. This sounds like one of the questions Maw's prayer group asked, but this guy is no prayer group person. I'll give him the same kind of answer. I tell him, Sir, the decision is up to you, but I do know the Bible says that God so loved the world He gave His only begotten son and whosoever believeth in Him will have eternal life. I'm thinking 'bout how many times Reverend Johnson said that every Sunday night and now I'm glad I stayed awake long enough to hear it.

The man in the back is still standing and everyone in the church is glaring at him. This guy looks kinda mean. He scratches his head and looks for words, and finally says, Young man, you got me there 'cause I never read the Bible, but my mother told me that years ago. I need to answer him, so I'll say another Bible verse or something 'bout Jesus, 'cause it's the truth, and Maw says always speak the truth and you cain't be wrong. I tell him, Sir, I know He died on a cross outside Jerusalem and three days later rose again. He says, Pastor, can I come down there now and ask Him to forgive me and say I believe? The preacher is jumping around on the pulpit and hollers, Come on down, Fred, we've been waiting for you for years, and this is what we been hoping you'd do someday. Everyone is stunned and Dad's saying nothing for a change. There are no more questions, but a lot of praising God and singing and the meeting's over early.

People come to the pulpit and wanta talk 'bout Fred. A middle-aged lady comes to me and says, Son, I don't know what in the world brought Fred to church tonight, he's been the meanest and orneriest man in the whole county ever since his wife died 'bout three years ago. You surely said something he finally understands. Our preachers tried to talk to him 'bout his meanness for a long time and he would just laugh at 'em. The Lord works in mysterious ways. She seems to be happy for Fred, and I tell her, He sure does, ma'am, that's what my maw says. She laughs a little and walks away talking to herself.

Dad doesn't get to preach and John cain't get over the fact he talked with Fred and says, The Lord sure works in mysterious ways. I remind Brother John, I know that and so does the lady leaving the church talking to herself. We walk outside and I can still feel the cold. People come and hug me and tell me how happy they are Fred finally came to the Lord. I'm starting to shiver from the cold and a couple boys holler, Have a good swim, preacher boy, you don't need to worry 'bout taking a bath tonight. It's not funny to me.

The trip home isn't as exciting as going. John and me aren't making remarks 'bout drowning or falling in the water as the horses began to swim. When we finally hit pavement on the other side, we all take off galloping for a while and begin to laugh. Dad says, Now, John, you must understand people need to have faith instead of fright and John says, You're right there, Spare, but don't ask me to ever do it again. We weren't laughing before, but now we can, and soon were home telling the story to the rest of the family.

Additional church services are planned at the little country church, but the weather isn't suitable. After having a great night seeing the county's biggest critic come forward and ask forgiveness, and the pastor cancels the remaining nights. Dad's planning our next meeting farther west in Mt. Carmel, Illinois. John wants to talk 'bout a planned meeting in Mt. Vernon next summer at the Coliseum, and he's gonna have things lined up for us to get with a couple other ministers and church people. He wants to know if I'm gonna be ready to do my answering questions and preaching. Dad says, Sure can, John, that boy of mine is always ready. I'll have plenty of time to make him understand this is gonna be a lot bigger than anything we've been to yet. The Coliseum will hold lots of people and with other preachers helping we'll have us a good old time Bible talkin' good meeting. John says, It's a deal, Spare, the meetings are on and I'll write you later 'bout our summer meeting.

The river has dropped and Big Creek is almost back in its banks. Traffic is moving up and down the highway in front of the house. Friday morning we have prayer, hold hands, and hug each other. The bus pulls up in front of the garage and we board. The family is waving goodbye and I feel like I'm now part of their family. I wanta see them again.

We're on our way to Mt. Carmel and I know Dad's gonna tell me what I did wrong at the meeting. We settle in our seats and he says, Now, Son, you just gotta pay a little more attention to what I'm trying my best to make you understand. I tell you and tell you 'bout calling me Spare and for some reason you keep doin' it. Don't you know you embarrass me when you're always tellin' people to call me Spare? For God's sake, Son, show a little respect to your old dad. I don't understand why you just don't get it, or is it something my family at home puts you up to? I don't know what he means, but that's all I ever hear at home, and I ask, Dad, What's wrong with Spare? He says, Ministers of the Lord should be called pastor or brother and surely not, Spare. I promise Dad I'll try to remember, but Uncle Joe, Uncle Orie, and all my cousins' call him Spare. Dad says, When Reverend Johnson comes to the house everyone bends over backwards to be nice and call him Reverend, but not to me their own flesh and blood. I guess he's talkin' 'bout himself. I promise him I'll try and remember from now on, but it's gonna be hard. It's' almost like not cussing when I get around Uncle Joe and Cotton.

I'm enjoying my talk with Dad and now I can ask him 'bout some of the things he keeps telling me that I just don't understand. I tell him, Dad, you always say you're being persecuted all the time at home and Maw don't ever say it, how come it's you and not her? Dad says, This is the first time in your young life, you've asked me a question that I'm glad to answer, and it's simply 'cause Maw and all of my brothers and sisters are the ones persecuting me. When you're living for the Lord and preaching as good as I do, it's just a burden I'll have to carry for the rest of my life. It's even gonna get worse before the Lord comes. I've never heard that before either and we continue our talk. Dad says, Son, I've already got my first sermon planned, so if they want you to speak remember to make it short and sweet. I ask him what he's gonna talk 'bout, and he says, It's an old favorite of mine, it's gonna be 'bout Samson and Delilah and how men have to be on guard for women who are out to snare us for the devil. I'm gonna tell the world what temptation is 'cause I go through it every day of my life, and it's hard to bear.

I like to talk 'bout Samson and Delilah and remind him how Samson's great strength was gone when he give in to Delilah, and later got forgiven and pulled down the pillars of the building. Dad says he's just like Samson, and there have been times that even he has to be forgiven and that's why I see him at the altar a little more than some other people who aren't tempted as much as him.

I talk low, 'cause I don't want people to hear.

Dad, you say you get tempted every day, how come?

Sure I do, the old devil really goes after me 'cause he knows I'm a preacher.
What's the biggest temptation you ever get?
Probably smokin' and drinkin' beer.
How come smoking cigars and drinking beer is a sin. Catholics do it.
We're not Catholics, and our body is a temple of God.
Uncle Orie says it makes you crazy.
Dorie thinks so too, but they're jealous of me.
What 'bout goin' with loose women?
Lots of men have a problem with women, just like your Uncle Joe.
That's when Maw turns you over to the Lord.

Dad, have you ever thought of becoming a Catholic? You could drink beer and smoke cigars all yuh want, and you only have to tell the priest. Dad wants to know how I know 'bout priests. I tell him 'bout Mrs. Sierdorf who lives across the street and I go buy her camel cigarettes at the drug store. She gives me a nickel every time, and I take the nickel and buy me a popsicle. Dad says, Son, do you mean that good lookin' red head 'cross the street that never talks to me when I say Hi? Dad's right she's a red head and married to Fritz, and he's big as a giant. They come from Germany. Don't talk much 'cept 'bout going to confession. That's what we call getting saved. She said, Fritz, I'm gonna go to confession today after what you caused me to do last night and you need to go too; Fritz said he ain't gonna go 'cause she was part of the sin. Dad, I think I should tell you what Uncle Joe told Uncle Orie one day. What is it Son? Dad asks. Well Dad, Uncle Joe said her husband Fritz would twist your ass into something looking like a pretzel if you even come close to Mrs. Sierdorf. Dad acts like he doesn't hear me and turns his head away. He wipes his forehead and says, Son, Just 'cause your Uncle Joe says such vulgar things doesn't mean you should repeat 'em. He wants me to find out what she did, but I'm not gonna tell him 'cause Maw says, it's sacred and just between her, the priest, and God.

Dad says, Son, if you'll just find out maybe I can help the poor soul get right with the Lord and she won't need to go see the priest. He still doesn't understand, so I tell him, Dad you better remember what Uncle Joe said 'bout Fritz, and I know she's gonna go see Father Schoenbacher at Sacred Heart and nobody else. Dad's not happy, and says he knows what it is to fight the devil. I can tell he doesn't wanta talk 'bout Fritz, but Uncle Joe is right. Fritz is a mean looking guy and nobody fools with Fritz. Sam Gander the ice-man is afraid of Fritz, and he's plenty tough. I tell him, Aunt Dorie said, That, Spare, is just full of the devil. Dad says he knows everyone is against him when he's trying to do right and he wants to know if Aunt Dorie says anything else 'bout him. I tell him, I remember one thing she said real good, 'cause I had a hard time figuring it out. She said one time, Spare, is out for the almighty dollar and any split-tail able to walk. Dad's a little upset and tells me to drop the subject and he is only trying to help some poor soul deep in sin.

7

MEETING ELMO

The bus stops in Mt. Carmel and we are met by the Yancey family. Mr. Ralph Yancey is a middle aged man with dark hair, 'bout five foot seven, a little paunchy in the middle, slightly over weight and friendly from the start. He says, Preacher, this is my wife, Mary, my half brother Lloyd Thomas Yancey, and our pride and joy is my son Elmo T. Yancey. We are pleased to meet you and your son. Mary is a light blond lady, nice looking, well endowed, and looks ten years younger. Lloyd is 'bout six feet two or three, blond and rather handsome. The pride and joy is 'bout seventeen, tall, thin, and blond.

We become friends immediately and it seems as if we have known each other for years. Dad laughs 'bout the trip to the church in Mt. Vernon and tells 'bout swimming the horses through the water, and how the biggest sinner in the county got saved. Elmo likes to hear Dad and hollers, Hot damn, brother, that's what we need here in Mt. Carmel 'cause we gotta lotta them kind, don't we Uncle Lloyd? Uncle Lloyd doesn't answer right away, but finally says, I guess so, Elmo, but we don't talk 'bout 'em. Elmo says, I do Uncle Lloyd, I know every damned one. Mary says, Please, Son, quit your cussin' or the preacher and his son won't think good of us. I tell Mary, If your pride and joy was at our house, Maw would wash his mouth out with soap, and Cotton said that's the worse thing in the world to happen to anybody. Dad isn't liking what I say, I can tell, but it's the truth and Maw says, always tell people the truth. Dad says, Folks, that's what I'm good in, helping the sinner and hard to get kind, ain't that so, Son? I nod yes, and say, At our house, we talk 'bout sin all the time, and Maw reads the Bible while she turns 'em over to the Lord.

I really like these people, especially their pride and joy, Elmo. They drive us to their house and show us our room and Mary fixes us a real good dinner. Before we offer thanks for the food, Mary asks, Can our pride and joy, Elmo, offer the blessing 'cause he's been looking forward to this and he's practiced all week? Elmo looks proud and begins his lengthy prayer, and gives thanks for almost everything on the farm. At the end of his prayer, he asks special help in his trapping business catching muskrats and fox. I like Elmo even more now 'cause Bob and me used to be trappers till we caught Mr. Rooster. When he finishes for good, Mary hugs and kisses him on the cheek and says, I'm the proudest momma in the world to have a boy so blessed, while Elmo smiles from ear to ear.

We dress and head down the road to a small Baptist church not far away. This is a farm church and the people are of every age and German and Irish descent. I can look in their eyes and see struggle and pain and people who never give up and I hear 'em talk 'bout happier days when they had some money till the banks went down and they lost everything. Maw told me we didn't have that problem 'cause we didn't have nothing before The Great Depression, and probably won't when it ends. These people seem to be happy, even if they did lose their money.

After the introduction, everyone begins singing "**Rock of Ages**" and follow with "**When the Roll is Called up Yonder.**" I like both songs 'cause we sing the same thing at the Pilgrim Holiness where I belong. The singing is over, we're introduced, and Dad takes over on the podium. Dad says, Tonight I'll show you some of my son's ability to answer questions pertaining to the Bible and when I'm finished with a few questions, it's gonna be your turn. He begins asking question after question concerning the life of Jesus, the disciples and their names, their deaths and ages, and other questions 'bout the preaching of Jesus. The audience is quiet and attentive and when it's over they look at each other and stand up. Now, I feel welcome here.

I come to the edge of the pulpit and I'm dressed in a dark wool suit with shirt and bow tie and look straight at the audience. I remember exactly how Dad told me to act. I tell 'em, I haven't been doing this long, but I do a lot of it at home; they laugh and I don't know why. A lady dressed in a long gown like I've never seen before asks me where my momma is and I tell her she's dead, but I got a real good grand maw. She sits down, and acts like she shouldn't have asked the question. I don't know why, but it's true. Now the people seem friendly and some from the back move forward. They wanta know 'bout different scriptures in the Bible, mostly 'bout the disciples and Jesus and that I know good 'cause that's all Maw and me talk 'bout at home. I kinda wish they'd ask me when Jesus is coming back, but they never do. Maw and me know all 'bout that.

There's an old guy in the far back waving his arm off and wanting to ask something and Dad finally sees him. The guy says, I've gotta question for you young fella. What kind of fish swallowed old Jonah when he wouldn't do what God told him? I've heard that story hundreds of times, but nobody ever said what kinda fish, 'cept large fish. I tell him, Sir, it was a big one. The audience is thinking 'bout it and they begin laughing. A man sitting close to me in the front row mutters something real low sounding like, I sure as hell thought it was a whale, and I don't wanta answer him. I just act like I don't hear and he says no more. I finish and Dads' got the pulpit and starts preaching fire and brimstone, telling them if they don't straighten up and quit their sinning ways, they're headed straight for hell. His remarks don't seem to hit the audience well, 'cause most of the congregation are already saved, baptized and that means forever, just like the Soft Shells down in Bluff City Kentucky where I preached.

It's time for the altar call and one elderly lady 'bout seventy comes forth. She looks as if life has really been rough to her and she cries without stopping. She says, I know I've been to this altar a lot, preacher, but I still sin a lot. Dad knows how to handle this 'cause he told me he's real good at it. He says, That's what we're here for, Sister, to save the sinner and I'll stay here all night with you if necessary to help get those sins taken away. The altar call is over and several ladies come forward to pray with her and it isn't long till she stands up from the altar and says, I want you all to know this is the last time I'm coming to the altar, 'cause this time I'm sincere. Several yell amen, and one Sister says, it's 'bout time. The minister dismisses the church and everyone leaves.

We arrive home, and Elmo says, Preacher, I'm a trapper and I'd like to take Bid with me in the morning when I go run my traps, is it O.K. with you? Dad knows I'm good with animals, but he does wanta know if we'll be getting in the water and Elmo says, No need to worry, Brother Spare, I'll be with the preacher boy all the time, and I'm a damned good swimmer. Dad says, It's not you I'm thinking 'bout Elmo it's my son, the preacher boy. They don't need to worry 'bout me cause I've been through lots of water and I sure would like to go run traps with Elmo. Finally Dad says, Take him with you, Elmo, and be careful 'cause the boy cain't swim. Please don't wake me up from sleeping 'cause I had a bad day on the bus coming here trying to explain the Bible to the boy.

We head out across the fields 'bout daybreak and I ask Elmo, Where are the traps? He says, Preacher boy, I've got traps everywhere around this farm and it's almost three hundred acres, but this morning we're goin' down to the back-water and run muskrat traps first. Elmo says, I want you to be real careful, Bid, 'cause you're gonna be sitting in the back part of the boat and back-water is real swift, so don't get up and start moving around a lot. He don't need to worry 'bout me moving 'round 'cause I cain't swim, but I'm not sure 'bout dog paddling.

We come to the edge of a large flooded area covered with trees of all sizes, and I can see a row-boat tied near the bank. Elmo says, Shove it in the water, Bid, I'm gonna show you how I get them suckers. The water looks deep and the current is strong, and small trees with limbs bend over hanging in the rushing waters. I ask Elmo if he thinks it's safe and he says,

Heck, Bid, I do this every time the water comes up and floods this place and believe me, that's where I get the big ones. We shove off into the swirling waters and Elmo has a long pole guiding the boat from one brush covered tree to another and now he's starting to get excited.

We check a couple of traps and find what we're looking for. Elmo says, Hold on, we got us a dandy this time, preacher boy, your gonna learn how it's done this time 'cause I'm the best when it comes to catching muskie rats. I'm not sure what's gonna happen and we're having a hard time getting through the brush. Elmo grabs hold of tree branches and reaches in the brush and pulls out the biggest muskrat I ever saw. Elmo is hollering, I told you so, Bid, I told you so, over and over, and I'm hoping the boat doesn't sink 'cause the current is swift and trying to send us backwards. The steel trap is around the muskrat, and Elmo pulls him free, and puts the trap back in the brush as we head for another tree. It's not long till we end up with a bag full of muskie rats; that's what Elmo calls 'em, and he's the best. Elmo says, Preacher boy, these suckers are gonna bring me seventy five cents for every one and that's for sure. I tell him he's the best trapper I ever saw and he starts telling me 'bout all the other things he catches and says if I stick around him very long he'll teach me everything there is to know 'bout trapping. I know I cain't, 'cause I'm gonna be preaching with Dad and that may be a long time.

Elmo wants to head to the barn where he keeps all his hides and as we walk, he starts talking 'bout his family and I like to talk 'bout families, too. Elmo is real proud of his family. I tell him, Elmo, you sure got a nice farm here and you're lucky to have a nice uncle, dad, and mother. He smiles and says, I sure am, Bid, and a lot of people say I look more like my uncle than my dad. I know he's right 'bout that, so I tell him, Elmo, if you looked like your dad, you wouldn't be tall and blond like your uncle. Elmo says, Yep, I'm just lucky, I guess; I sure wouldn't wanta be like Dad 'cause he's only five foot seven and I'm already five foot ten and still growing. Everyone says I'm the spittin' image of Uncle Lloyd, and he's six foot three. I guess we're just one happy family even though we ain't got any money, and some people say we're a real close knit family. I know he's proud of his family and so am I. He probably wants to know 'bout my family so, I tell him, You gotta close knit family, Elmo, and we are too at my house, but nothing like yours. I wanta be friendly with Elmo and learn more 'bout his family and ask, How far did you go in school? He says, Clean through the sixth grade, then I had to quit so I could do the trapping and help pay some of the money my dad owes the bank. Elmo wants to know how I learned to read and write so early 'cause he couldn't write till he was in the second grade. He's good at it now, and can do some spelling. I tell Elmo, It comes easy for me, but that's all I ever hear at home.

I'm surprised when we get to the big barn where Elmo keeps his hides. High above our heads hang row after row of animal skins on boards waiting to be taken to town and sold. Elmo says he's caught every kind of critter that can walk, crawl, or swim and he's got 'em all in this barn. He's got fox, mink and coon skins that he's proud of 'cause he says, that's where the big money comes from. Now he's feeling real proud and says

I don't suppose you ever met anyone who could catch varmints like me, huh, Bid?
My best friend and me caught a rooster in a rabbit snare, but I ain't talking 'bout it.
I don't wanta catch a rooster and don't wanta hear 'bout it, anyhow.
I've learned a lot from you, Elmo.
Yeah, Bid, I guess I'm kinda gifted, just like they say you are.
Elmo, is there anything you would like to do, but can't?
Yep, there sure is, preacher boy, I'd like to skin a bear.

I don't know 'bout bears being around here, but maybe Elmo does, so I ask, Where's, the bears, Elmo? He says, Mom says I'd hafta go all the way to Tennessee to find a bear, but I doubt if I'll ever get to Tennessee, how 'bout you, preacher boy, what would you like to do some day? That's not a hard question so I tell, Elmo, I'd like to ride a big red bicycle like the one I saw in the window at Montgomery Ward in downtown Evansville. Elmo says, How 'bout your, dad? I know Dad cain't drive a car or fly an airplane yet, so I tell him, He wants to drive a car and fly an airplane. Elmo says, I kinda think your dad might be able to drive a car someday, but I have doubts 'bout a preacher flying an airplane. Your dad does look like the kinda guy that might try flying an airplane, if he can find one.

We near the house and talk more 'bout home life. Elmo says, Bid, our family shows a lot of love and affection like huggin' and kissin' each other before goin' to bed, is your family like that? I don't know what he means 'bout everybody huggin' and kissin' but I don't wanta act different so I tell him, Not exactly, Elmo, but Maw sometimes gives me a hug and kiss before I go to bed, but the rest of the family may fight and argue more than kiss and hug. Heck, one time Uncle Shave and Dad got in a fight while eating dinner, spilled beans all over the floor and Maw made Dad clean 'em up after they finished fighting outside. Elmo acts surprised at my remarks 'bout my family and wants to know if Maw got mad when they spilled the beans. I tell him, Maw doesn't get mad 'cause that's a sin, but she does get aggravated. Maw's a Pilgrim Holiness and been saved, baptized and sanctified the same as me. Elmo seems to be hearing things he knows nothing 'bout and I'll drop the subject. When we get back I tell Dad how we had a good time running traps and how much I learned, and he's glad I never fell in the water. I don't ever worry 'bout it 'causes Dad says he's always there lookin' out for me.

We arrive at church on Saturday night and I'm surprised to see the church filled. The pastor does his introduction, and someone in the middle of the audience raises their hand and asks to make an announcement and the preacher says, Sister if it's important, please, tell us your announcement. She says, Well, pastor, I got news before coming to the meeting tonight that Ellie Mae just passed away at home this afternoon, so don't count on her being here tonight. Pastor says, That's the most remarkable thing I ever heard of 'cause she was just here at the service last night and got saved again. Someone in the audience remarks, Well, I remember her saying when she was gettin' saved last night this would be her last time, I guess she kept her word. Another lady wants to say something and the preacher says, Go ahead, Sister Miller, and she begins saying, Well I guess I was Ellie Mae's closest friend 'cause she didn't have too many close friends; the poor old soul talked 'bout a lot of people, but the Lord forgave her I'm sure. The preacher says, Let's all bow our heads and remember Ellie Mae, I'm confident she's gone on to glory and is in that sweet by and by.

The service is long and I do the usual preaching and answering Bible questions, and it's time to give the altar call. The pastor raises his arms and points to the audience with tears streaming down his face and says, Folks, any of you who have problems like Ellie Mae need to think 'bout it. I'm sure you don't wanta end up like her without first gettin' some things straightened out with the Lord. Several ladies in the back look at each other and walk forward, kneel at the altar and the preacher adds, This is wonderful folks, are you sure there's not something in your heart that's bothering you like Ellie Mae had hidden in her heart? The entire congregation are looking at each other and several more come walking down the isle, kneel at the altar, and now we got an altar full all 'cause Ellie May died. I'm thinking what Maw's gonna say when I tell her 'bout this. The service ends and Elmo says, Old sister Ellie Mae sure got a lot of sinners saved tonight, didn't she, Bid. I look at the altar, and its empty now, but we had a lot of 'em tonight and I tell Elmo, Ellie Mae 'caused it all.

The next morning, it's time for us to return home and the family drives us to the bus drop and we bid them farewell. Ralph says, Sure has been a wonderful couple of nights at the church, but I doubt if we would have been so successful if Ellie Mae hadn't died. Elmo says, The Lord works in mysterious ways. We all hug, cry a little and they wish us farewell and a safe trip home and plan to meet us in Mt. Vernon. I love these people, especially, Elmo the trapper, 'cause he's their pride and joy.

I'm greeted by cousins, uncles, and friends wanting to know 'bout my preaching and Maw wants to know if I was treated well, and I tell her, It was swell, Maw, and I sure learned a lot. I tell Uncle Joe 'bout the old guy getting saved and he says, It's 'bout time Spare got someone saved besides himself. I tell Bob 'bout the muskrats and now he wants to skin a squirrel. When Maw asks what I preached 'bout, I tell her 'bout everyone getting saved. She's pleased and says, Preach that way, Son, and you cain't be wrong, 'cause that's what it's all 'bout. I tell her 'bout the old lady getting saved at the last minute and she says, That's exactly what I been trying to tell your Uncle Joe all these years.

Everyone is gone from the house 'cept Maw and me, and I notice she's just not acting right, and when I ask her if she's sick she says, I'm not sick, Son, just worried 'bout your Uncle Lloyd whose in Boehne Camp Hospital 'bout to die with tuberculosis. Now, Son, you get ready 'cause were goin' to see him before he dies. I know a lotta people go there and don't come back, and when you get T.B. you're a gone sucker; that's what Uncle Joe told me. I gotta get outta this trip for sure, so I tell her, He's not my uncle, Maw. Uncle Joe said he's Lige's boy before you and him got married, and he's not a McCaffry like us. Uncle Joe said he was mean to him and Uncle Orie. Maw says, Don't, you dare talk that way, you know nothin' 'bout what went on, and keep your mouth shut 'bout such things, especially coming from, Joe. She's gettin' kinda aggravated, so I gotta be careful what I say. She says, Lloyd, is part of our family whether he's a McCaffry or not, and you stop tellin' those stories your uncle teaches you. Now, you get dressed and maybe you'll learn something when you see how the other half live. I ask what other half and she says, People that don't have it near as nice as you. Now I feel a little better, but I still don't wanta go. I'll go, but I ain't gonna be happy.

How we gonna get there, Maw?
Walk, of course, how else?
She's getting aggravated again, so I better shut up and get ready.

Boehne Camp Hospital is 'bout a mile away and she's dressed in her long print dress almost down to her ankles, a blouse with long sleeves, and a bonnet covering her long hair. I'm wearing a pair bib overalls with a short sleeved shirt, a pair gym shoes with the toe out and she's almost dragging me. Maw's tall and I'm short and when she's gotcha by the hand there's no way to get loose even if I know I might get T. B. and die like Lloyd. We don't talk the entire way to Boehne Camp Hospital and the sun is blistering down us, and Maw's not happy.

We arrive at the hospital entrance 'bout an hour later and go inside. We walk down a long hall and there's cot after cot lined up on each side of the hall. Every cot we pass sick men are lying on 'em and I don't like it here. I've heard 'bout morgues and this might be one, but they just ain't dead enough yet. I tell Maw, I need to get outta here, but she just holds my hand tighter and says, I don't like it either, Son, but you're gonna stay and see what it is like to be in this condition. I guess she means this is what the other half looks like.

We find Lloyd at the end of the hall, lying in bed and he's nothing but skin and bones, coughing his head off and looks pale as a ghost. Nothing covers him 'cept a pair of B.V.D.s like Uncle Joe wears all summer long and I feel sorry for Lloyd and all the other people, but I sure don't wanta get near any of 'em and neither does Maw. I stand back a little distance from his bed and Maw walks over to talk and I hear her say, The Lord will take care of you, and she bows her head and prays. I'm not praying, unless I hafta pray to get outta here. I'm getting sick from the smell of piss and guys gagging and letting farts and there's an odor that smells like dried piss from the sheets and B.V. D s. When I tell her I'm gonna vomit for sure, she says, Hold it, hold it just one more minute and try holding your nose at the same time. There's no way I can do that, 'cause it's hard to just keep from vomiting. Some of the guys are spitting in wash pans and that makes me sick, and I'd like to faint, but she won't let me.

Lloyd gives the sign of the cross, and Maw walks away from him.
I ask, What's that mean? I saw Dad do it at Mr. Shortys' house.
Lloyd's Catholic, Son, and it's 'cause Jesus died on the cross.

I didn't know we had any Catholics in the, family.

Lloyd turned Catholic some years ago, but I know he's saved and will go to heaven. There's gonna be Catholics in heaven, the same as us as long as they believe in Jesus dying on the cross, and ask forgiveness of their sins.

Finally it's over and we leave the hospital; I run across the road to a wooded area and puke my guts out. Maw says, I knew you could hold it if you tried. We begin our walk home and I'm feeling better as we talk 'bout other things, but mostly the Bible. She always wants me to learn and I need some questions answered.

Maw, are you still worried 'bout Lloyd?

No more, Son, but I am worried 'bout your dad and Uncle Joe.

Why, Maw, are they sick, too?

Well, I'd just like to see 'em find some nice Christian girl and settle down.

How 'bout, Flossie? Her Mom's even in your prayer group.

Not Flossie, Son.

Is she wild, Maw?

And then some, I'd say.

How, 'bout, Pearl, Maw? She goes to our church and Uncle Joe likes her and Dad likes her, too. I heard Uncle Joe say, Spare, if I ever catch you foolin' 'round with Pearl I'll kick your ass clean up to your elbows.

I've told you before, Son, don't use vulgar words.

O.K., Maw, I'll just spell it from now on like A.S.S.

That's better, Son, much better.

My new Uncle Lloyd is dead a week later. Everyone goes to the funeral 'cept me and I still remember the smell of dry piss at Boehne Camp Hospital.

8

REVIVAL TIME IN KENTUCKY

It's the day before graduation from the second grade and my teacher, Mrs. Bethel, tells me to stay after class 'cause she needs to talk to me. I'm thinkin' of everything I've did wrong and still cain't figure out what's so important to stay after class. All my friends know 'bout me staying and they don't know either 'cept maybe Big John. He says it might be 'cause I told him some answers on the math test.

Mrs. Bethel says, Sit down, Arthur, I just want to talk to you about your coming year in the third grade. That's a relief, and now I feel better. She is a real nice teacher and almost as pretty as Miss Strupp who I gave the chocolates. When Mrs. Bethel says something, you better listen, 'cause she doesn't say it twice, and then she's not so nice. She talks slow and she calls it precise, and says some things I have a little trouble understanding 'cause we don't talk exactly that way at home.

She says, Arthur, I want to commend you on your grades and try and prepare you a little better for your future here at Rheinlander school, and that's why I asked you to stay. I feel a lot better now. She says, I notice you have nothing but Es, which stands for excellence your first two years in school, and that is something to be proud of. I tell her, Thank you, ma'am, Maw tells me to do my best. She says, I know a little about your background because it has been in the paper. I feel there may be some things in your education that I might be able to encourage you to do better. Now, Arthur, I want you to try and understand what I'm trying to tell you may be important, and it will affect you in the third grade, our next school year. I tell her, Thank you, Mrs. Bethel. I'm hoping she's gonna finally tell me what it is I did wrong, but nobody at my house talks as good as her.

Mrs. Bethel says, Arthur, the way you read and write is excellent, but the way you talk is not impressive and I think you need to improve your vocabulary.

She's using words I've never heard at home, but I do know what they mean.

I ask, How, do I do it, Mrs. Bethel?

Well for instance, I hear you say the word eating and you call it eatin'. I want you to start sounding your vocabulary all the way through as you speak. After you sound it through, then I want you to start using the word in your vocabulary the same way. Do you understand, Arthur?

I know she's right, but that's how everyone talks at home and all my buddies speak the same way. I do a lot better than most of the family.

I know you're right as usual, Mrs. Bethel, and I'm gonna try and do better.

Well, that's wonderful, Arthur, and from now on say, I'm going to, not gonna.

She got me already, and now I've gotta watch and sound 'em out as I speak.

Arthur, does your grandmother still provide for your welfare and educational needs?

That's a tough one, and I need to think before I answer. I tell her, Yes, ma'am, she does and so does my aunt Dorie, my Uncle Joe, my Uncle Orie and my dad.

She looks a little confused, but I think she understands.

Arthur, I just want you to know you can always come to me if you desire to know something concerning your education. I am aware of your traveling throughout the area preaching and answering questions concerning the Bible, which I'm sure it will benefit you in the future. I do want you to improve on your language and the way you pronounce words during the next school year, and I'm sure you will. I thank her again, and I'm gonna be watching my every word from now on.

She says, I hope you understand my interest in you, Arthur, and I will be keeping notes on your progress in the future years here at Rheinlander Grade School. Now you may leave, and when you get home you may wish to inform your grandmother of our discussion.

I'm getting outta here right now, and I ain't saying nothing to Maw 'bout this, or nobody else. I'm gonna start watching my vocabulary, or what I call talkin' from now on, 'cause someday I wanta talk like Mrs. Bethel.

I'm seven, eight, and nine years old and Dad is preaching by himself a lot, but people wanta see and hear me, the boy evangelist display Bible knowledge. Dad has a letter from a small town in southeastern Kentucky, near Providence, inviting us to hold a revival. He's glad to accept 'cause the money and expenses are great. We're gonna be staying at one of the deacon's house for one week. Things aren't going well with Dad at home, President Roosevelt shut down all the bootlegging joints, booze is legal, and speakeasies are closing, but not Uncle Joe's.

It's the middle of July and it's hot. I'm playing baseball every day with friends and Dad gives me the poke in the side, nods for me to come outside, and tells me to be ready to go preach in Kentucky on Monday morning. I tell Maw and Uncle Joe I'll be gone for a week and she tells me to look out for my father and to wash behind my ears before goin' to church. She wants to know what kind of church I'm goin' to, and I tell her probably Baptist. She says, Baptist are good people and serve the Lord, but some of the old Kentucky grand maws are known to sit on their porches, rock in their chairs and smoke corn-cob pipes. I ask her if they'll go to hell, and she says, No, son 'cause they've been saved and the Lord hasn't shown them it's a sin yet. I ask 'bout Dad smoking cigars and Maw says, That's different 'cause he knows better and still does it, and may end up in hell if he don't change. I ask Maw if I should preach on smoking corn-cob pipes. She says, No, Son, the Lord will put 'em under conviction for their sin when it's time. I'm a little confused 'bout the word conviction 'cause Uncle Joe told me he was convicted of vagrancy in Georgia and put on a chain gang. When I ask her 'bout it, she tells me it's a different kind of conviction and for me not to worry 'bout it just now. She kisses and hugs me and out the door we go to the bus station.

We arrive at the terminal and soon on our way to Kentucky. Dad tells me this is gonna be some big time preaching and he wants me to just answer questions and make my preaching short and sweet so he can have plenty time to do the big stuff. He tells me this is a Soft Shell Baptist church and they believe in once in grace, always in grace. I tell him, It sure sounds like the same Baptist we been preaching to at other churches. He says, Well, Son, not everyone believes like Maw and the Pilgrim Holiness where you go to hell for just having one little beer or cigar. I tell him he should join the Soft Shells and he gets kinda aggravated like Maw does sometimes. Then he tells me we just got done preaching to Soft Shells in Solitude, so don't worry 'bout it. Dad says sometimes I get kinda insulting for a kid, and I need to watch what I say. I'm enjoying this talk with Dad and learning 'bout Soft Shells.

Were rolling along and making good time while sometimes picking up some more passengers at every bus stop. Dad tells me he's gonna hold a baptismal service at the church before we go home. I tell him, I'm not baptizing anyone cause I cain't swim. He says, I wouldn't let yah do any baptizing, anyhow 'cause you're too short and might drown. I remind him what Maw said 'bout him not being a regular preacher, just an evangelist. He doesn't like what I said, and looks out the window, like he usually does when he doesn't like something. I still need to get some things straightened out, so I tell him

Maw says you cain't marry people, cause you're not ordained.

I don't need to be ordained to baptize people. I'm just gonna give 'em a good dunkin'.

You, cain't swim.

I don't get in deep water; now shut up and let me worry 'bout the baptizing.

You better never baptize in the big Ohio River, Dad, it's deep.

We arrive at the bus station and are greeted by Mr. and Mrs. McDowell. Mr. McDowell is a deacon in the Baptist church where we're gonna preach and they look like real nice people. She's real pretty like Maw, but seems younger than Mr. McDowell, whose hair has already turned grey. Dad gets in the front seat of the truck and I jump in the back, and we head towards their home. Dad's already got 'em laughing and he's talking 'bout how he enjoyed educating me on the way to their house. He tells 'em he doesn't wanta ever see the day his son could live like some people he knows, and I don't know who he's talking about, unless he means Uncle Joe.

I've been looking at every house and barn we pass for old Kentucky women who sit on their porches, rocking in their chairs and smoking corn-cob pipes, but haven't seen a single one. We're heading in their long drive to the house and Dad is telling 'bout his past preaching. They wanta know how much I'm gonna be a part of the revival 'cause I'm, what they're looking forward to see and hear. Dad says, Oh the boy is there for your disposal and you can use him to answer Bible questions anytime you want, and he does preach some. We're only here to bring you the word of the Lord.

The country lane to their house is beautiful with long lines of trees on each side, and horses and cows stand inside a fenced area that makes it even more beautiful. They ask Dad how long he's been preaching, and he tells 'em he really became convinced he was called to preach when he got out of the cavalry, but when his mother encouraged him to follow the Lord, he knew it was where he belonged. I didn't know that. Now they wanta hear 'bout his cavalry career and after dinner we're gonna talk 'bout it. I'm trying to do my very best in speaking like Mrs. Bethel wants me to.

The huge house looks like a mansion. Mrs. McDowell says, Follow me, Son, and I'll show you your room. Dad is still talking to George. They're patting each other on the back and George says, I sure didn't know you had all the experience preaching, so you just go ahead and plan on being part of everything, including the preaching. Dad looks happy now, and pats him on the back again.

We go in the house and, they show us around and everything is beautiful beyond belief, and I tell Mrs. McDowell, This is what heaven must look like only the streets ain't paved with gold. She laughs and says, I see one thing for sure young man, you know the Bible 'cause that's the way heaven is going to be. She wants to know who taught me all 'bout the Bible. I tell her, I go to church a lot and listen to Reverend Johnson, and at home Maw teaches me, Dad teaches me, and I can read real well and next year I'm headed to the third grade. Dad's listening to her and I kinda think he may not like it. Now she wants to know 'bout Maw and Dad's really frowning, and I think he may come over and give me the poke. She says, Son, you sure know a lot 'bout heaven, and what it's gonna be like.

I'm thinking she must be just like Maw and tell her, Maw says, We gotta all be sure we get there and she laughs again, but Dad kinda frowns and doesn't look pleased. I like Mrs. McDowell a lot and she says, Your Maw must be a wonderful person, am I right? Before I can answer, Dad begins shaking his head back and forth, and grabs the suitcases. He says, Well, Son, I guess we better get to our room and get ready for church and I don't get to answer her. Inside the room, Dad's real upset and says, Now, Son, I've told you ten times, don't mention Maw, and you've already done it. What in the world is wrong with you, cain't you even do one thing I tell you without bringing up Maw or Uncle Joe? I try to explain, but he just doesn't understand, I tell him, It just kind of slipped out. I can tell he's still upset, so I promise him again I won't mention Maw till I get home, and that's gonna be hard. Remember that promise, Son, no more Maw, or I'll hafta put my foot down, Dad says.

Our bedroom is unbelievable with a beautiful bedspread, nice white curtains, a dresser with a mirror, and a chiffrobe with four drawers at the bottom. There's a nice big rocker to sit in, and I try it out. I look at a big Bible on the dresser, but Dad won't use it 'cause he's got his own marked with all his favorite text to preach 'bout. He pulls it out of his suitcase and begins going over it 'cause the revival starts tonight. There's a knock on the door and Mr. McDowell says, Dinner's gonna be 'bout 4 o'clock and after dinner, we'll go down to the church. When you're ready, come on down to dinner and I'll introduce you to the other part of our family. Nobody mentioned anything 'bout other family members. I'm still looking 'round at all the fancy stuff in the room and tell Dad, They even got a big pretty bowl on a wash stand to wash your self, and when you're done just throw it in the can and you don't even hafta throw it out the back door like we do at home. I'm still looking how pretty this room is and tell him, These people must really be the richest people we ever met and, he says, For once, Son, you're right, now don't you say something like you do at home and have them think we're not used to this, just act natural and enjoy it 'cause you may never see it again like this in your entire life.

I don't want Dad worrying 'bout me saying something wrong. I tell him, Don't worry 'bout me, I'm gonna wash real good in this big wash bowl, comb my hair, put on my best pants and tie and after all that, I want you to check my ears. I remind him, Maw, said she hoped you wouldn't eat fast while staying with these people. He's frowning again.

Son, you've did it again quit reminding me what Maw says day and night, I only eat that way at home and that's 'cause the rest of 'em don't eat slow either.

I'll be watching you, Dad.

I hate to say this, Son, but sometimes you almost drive me nuts.

I heard Uncle Orie say the same thing 'bout you, Dad.

We go down the stairs to eat dinner at four o'clock and there's seated two of the prettiest young twins I've ever seen. I know a couple twins in my school, but they don't even look much like each other. I cain't tell the difference and it's almost like I'm seeing double. They dress alike, talk alike and one says her name is Norma and the other says her name is Naomi and this is gonna be hard to understand. Dad's looking at 'em real good and he still cain't talk. They're telling him to sit down, and I don't think he can hear 'em, 'cause he just keeps staring. The girls are blond, 'bout nineteen or twenty, and pretty as dolls. Norma says, Preacher or reverend beings you're gonna be here for the week can we call you something other than reverend? I tell her, Just call him, Spare, 'cause that's all my folks at home ever call him. Mrs. McDowell told me to just make myself at home, so his name fits just like home. I think this is pleasing, Dad, but he doesn't look happy and now he's frowning again. Dad says, We're all brothers and sisters in the sight of the Lord, so just call me Brother Spare here at home. Mr. McDowell says, Amen, brother, amen; that's good to hear, I like a man like that. It puts us all on equal footing and after all, we're all serving the Lord, ain't that right? Dad says, It, sure is brother, it sure is, and that's what we're here for.

Dinner is over and Brother McDowell says, Tell, us 'bout your time on the Mexican border chasing that Mexican bandit, Brother Spare. Dad says, Sometime it's really hard for me to talk 'bout that part of my life, but I'll do it. He pulls a couple of pictures out of his coat pocket and passes them 'round for everyone to see. Mr. McDowell says, I see your cavalry buddies are dressed almost like you, but not wearing a gun. Dad says, I always carried my gun 'cause I wanted to be ready for action at any time. I never heard any of this before and I know Uncle Joe didn't. The girls sit and stare at the pictures and look at the forty five pistol strapped on Dad's waist and move closer to him as he continues. Dad tells how everyone was close, just like family, and when someone gets in trouble everyone is there for each other. Now, he starts to choke up, like he cain't talk any longer. He seems to be sad, and finally says, I don't know if I can go through with this, but I'll try. Now he's got me interested and I never heard it before.

Mr. McDowell says, What's wrong Brother Spare, what's wrong and Dad says, Sometimes when I see this picture, it really gets to me 'cause that's Jimmy, my best friend, and he didn't make it back from one of the raids. Dad's almost in tears. He finally continues and says, Mexicans were hiding out on the other side of the Rio Grande River. One night around midnight, we made a raid across the border and went charging in on 'bout fifty of 'em while they were asleep. It was almost like a massacre at first till some of the lookouts came into the fight, and there was lots of shooting and fighting all around. I saw Jimmy being cornered by three Mexicans and rode my horse between them, and that's when he got it right between the eyes. It was something that will live with me forever, and that's how I lost my finger. I couldn't fire my rifle and the army never needed me anymore so I came home to take care of my mother. One of the twins asks, Brother Spare, do you think you'll ever forget? Dad shakes his head no, and says, I doubt if it will ever end, it's probably a burden I'll hafta carry for the rest of my days. Now everyone feels sorry for Dad, 'cept me, 'cause Maw didn't say Dad came home to help her. Dad's still telling his story and says, It, broke my heart to leave my buddies, but let's not dwell on my life. Let's think 'bout the revival and get to church. I'm trying to forget all that killing.

We're ready to leave and I need an answer. I give him the poke and nod signal and he follows me outside. I can tell he's kinda angry, and he says, How come you give me the poke and nod signal, I never gave you permission to use our signals? I tell him, I thought it was for both of us, and I gotta ask you something. How come at the revival meeting in New Harmony, you said there was a hundred bandits down in Mexico and today you're saying fifty? Dad's not happy again, I can tell. He says, What, in the hell's the difference in fifty or so Mexicans, Son, who cares exactly how many there were, only you care, nobody else, just you. Sometimes, you get me aggravated with all your questions, and you've got a bad habit of sometimes questioning your elders and that can be a sin. I'm walking away wondering, was it fifty or was it a hundred?

We head for church with the twins and Dad's in the back and I'm in the front between Mr. and Mrs. McDowell. Mrs. McDowell says, Bid, enjoy yourself here on the farm 'cause I'm gonna' see that you have a good time while you're here. I thank her and I know Dad's gonna have a good time. We've gone a short distance when Brother McDowell says, Brother Spare, I think it is only fair I tell you that the main reason we called you for this revival was because of the boy. We read a couple of articles in the paper 'bout him and felt we needed someone like your son for this revival. It's not that we don't want you to preach, it's just that we didn't know your background and how much experience you have. Now that I find you're well qualified, just make yourself at home and speak as you wish. I'm sure the other deacons will feel the same way after they meet you. I can tell Dad is surprised, and he says,

We're all in it for the glory of the Lord, Brother, and that's all we're here for.
Right you are, Brother Spare, right you are.

We arrive at the church and I'm surprised to see the place is crowded with people. Brother McDowell ushers Dad and me to the front of the church and stops now and then to introduce us to certain people in the church. Everyone is friendly and I like these kinda people around me. We're seated on the podium side where everyone can look us over good, and they do.

Brother McDowell gets the meeting started with one of the old favorite songs, "**When the Roll is Called up Yonder** "and follows through with another old favorite, "**The Old Rugged Cross**." The twins step forward to sing a special song, and they're good. Now it's time to take the regular offering. Before it's taken, Brother McDowell says, Money needed for this revival has been raised but if someone wishes to offer more, feel free to give more. He offers a prayer and Deacons move down the aisle passing the basket. I see a few persons put paper money in the basket, and back home many have nothing but nickels and dimes to give.

A warm welcome is given us by the audience. Brother McDowell informs the congregation he has discussed several issues with the evangelist and he can't be more pleased. He says, I'm placing a couple of Brother McCaffry's pictures about his background here on a table. After the service, if anyone wishes to come up and see them, feel free to come forth. Dad tells the church how happy he is to be in their presence and deliver the word of God. He brings me forward and I say a few words to the crowd and Dad says, Please don't be afraid to ask my son any question in the Bible, and if he's not sure, he's gonna tell you. There may be times you may disagree with him, but everything said and done should be in the will of God so everyone will have a better knowledge of the scriptures.

The questioning begins. There are questions such as, Is Jesus the only way to heaven, baptism, is there a hell, what will heaven be like, are there any unforgivable sins, when will Jesus return, will the Jews ever recognize Jesus as the Messiah, all the disciples and prophets and how they died, how old they were when they died, etc. I always answer and usually quote the scripture. There are some people who question me further on the subject, but are polite, especially to a young boy like me. They're impressed with my knowledge and when I finish, Mrs. McDowell comes to me and guides me over to sit with the twins in the front row. Now it's Dad's turn, and he's always ready.

He takes off his coat and loosens his tie, and begins to preach 'bout the coming of the Lord and how everyone better be ready. He moves wildly back and forth across the podium with the Bible in his right hand and you can see his missing trigger finger. He waves the Bible in the air, and the sweat begins rolling down his brow. Dad's good at it, and it's not long till he has everyone crying as much as him, and he's real good at bringing on tears. He describes Jesus hanging on the cross for a bunch of sinners like us and everyone feels the same way, and he makes the altar call. They begin playing one of his favorite old time religion songs **When We All Get to Heaven** and several people come forth. They kneel at the wooden altar and others gather 'round to assist them. He gives a final call for people to come forward and when it's over, he announces a baptismal service on Saturday afternoon at a nearby lake.

The congregation is pleased and come forward to congratulate him and Brother McDowell. Dad likes this kind of meeting and he's happy again. When we arrive back home he gives me the poke and nod signal and we go outside and he says, Now, Son, please don't ruin this meeting by saying anything 'bout what Maw might say or do. I promise I won't and tell him not to worry 'bout it, but he still looks worried and I want Dad to have a good time, but he always looks worried when I talk 'bout home.

I'm having some cookies and milk and Sister McDowell sits with me at the kitchen table while others are talking 'bout the meeting in the living room. She's gonna take me all over the farm tomorrow and show me everything. I tell her, I've never seen a home as nice as this before and the only one I ever saw outside was the mayor's and the guy who owns Fendrich Cigar Company. I sure hope they like my preaching and answering questions. She says, We sure do, honey, and that's one thing you needn't worry 'bout. We get up at six a.m. here tomorrow morning, so I think it's time for my husband and me to get off to bed. I'm tired too, so I head up the stairs and Dad's in the living room with the twins explaining certain verses in the Bible. I hear one of the twins say, Brother Spare, will you be there for sure to baptize me tomorrow? Dad says, Girls, there's nothing in this whole wide world I'd rather do, 'cause I'm only here to do God's work. I close the bedroom door and hear nothing more from Dad and the twins.

The next morning Dad and the girls seem to know each other a lot better with laughing and kidding going on between them. We all enjoy the conversation and for a change, it's not 'bout the Bible. Sister McDowell wants me to give thanks at the breakfast table and when it's over one of the girls says, For a little boy you sure offer a fine blessing. I tell her, I've had a lot of practice at home. Dad frowns 'cause I mentioned home and I hope he doesn'tgive me the poke, 'cause I'm not leaving breakfast.

Mrs. McDowell and me take off for the barn. A guy is milking some cows and she tells me he works for them. She also says they sell some of the milk and give the rest away. We walk to the edge of the large woods and she says, Here is where all the wood comes from and some of our furniture is made from it, and some is used for the fireplace to furnish heat. She's teaching me just like Maw and I like it. We walk all over the farm and I see Dad walking down the dusty lane holding hands with a twin on each side of him. I guess he's explaining the Bible to them. We go to the house and Dad comes in laughing with the twins. We're all happy.

The second night of the revival, I'm called to give a sermon after the usual question and answer session. My sermon is, "You must be born again." and I know it well 'cause it's the same sermon I preached at Little Market Hall when I was five. The people like my sermon and a gentleman down front hollers, Tell it like it is, son, tell it like the Bible says. My message isn't long, and when it's over, I go down in the audience and join the twins on the front row. Dad closes the meeting by holding an altar call and nobody comes to the alter 'cause they're once in grace, always in grace Baptist. Near the end of the revival, few come forth to be saved, but the church is packed every night.

The meeting is a success and it's time for the baptism on Saturday afternoon at the lake. Saturday morning, the McDowell's ask if anyone needs to go downtown with them to get supplies and I gladly volunteer. Dad doesn't wanta go 'cause he says he needs to stay and pray for the baptism, and the twins are staying at home so they can get ready to be baptized. I have a great morning and when we get home the twins are dressed out in their baptismal dresses. One says, Spare has been such a help to us explaining the importance of baptism. The other twin says, Brother Spare has been such a blessing to us I don't know how we could do with out him. I've never heard that before and I wonder what she means.

Early in the afternoon, the baptismal service begins. The lake is small, nothing like the big Ohio River, and men, women, and children are standing all around the bank. Mr. McDowell calls everyone to prayer and explains how Jesus was baptized by John the Baptist and was put under the water and we need to go under the water just like Jesus. He talks 'bout how important it is 'cause that's when we get cleansed by water. Mr. McDowell and Dad go to the water's edge to begin the service and Dad offers prayer for the service. Everyone joins in by singing," **We Shall Gather at the River.**" The twins are first in line at the water's edge and their father and Dad are standing out 'bout twenty feet from the bank, Water is up to their waists, and I'm watching in the shade of a big elm tree. This is old stuff to me 'cause I was baptized in the big Ohio River when I was six years old by Reverend Johnson and Maw was there to watch, but I ain't gonna tell nobody 'cause Dad doesn't want me to talk 'bout home.

The twins walk into the lake and reach Dad and Mr. McDowell. They dunk 'em good and they both come up wiping water from their face, shouting, and crying out loud, "Praise the Lord, I'm now saved for good." I need to talk to somebody, and I go sit under another big oak tree with Mrs. McDowell. I always like talking to her 'cause she's a lot like Maw. She says, I always wished I had at least one boy to go with my girls and if I did, I'd like for him to be just like you. That makes me feel good and I tell her, Ma'am, if I didn't have my Maw, I'd sure like nothing better than to be here with you, 'cept maybe to see my Uncle Joe and Uncle Orie once in a while. I see a tear trickle down her face, and she says,

Your, Maw, and uncles must surely be some kind of wonderful people.
I love 'em a lot, ma'am, and they're the only ones I've got.
Son, you have your father, don't you?
Yes ma'am I do, but he's away a lot.

I guess he's out preaching the gospel, is that right?
I guess so, ma'am.

Norma comes to us and says the baptism is almost over, and we get up and prepare to leave with a crowd of people still here, while Dad and Mr. McDowell are still dunking 'em under the water.

Before church, the McDowell's ask if we can stay till Monday morning. They want us to hear the new preacher who is coming on Sunday and Dad is glad 'cause he says he might have some advice for the new preacher. Dad says, Saturday night being the last night of the revival is usually the best night 'cause that's when you can look over the week and ask yourself a question. Did I do any good, and if the answer is yes, it's successful; if no, it's worthless. Brother McDowell says, You're right, Brother Spare, you hit the nail on the head.

Saturday night Dad begins his preaching part of the service by expressing his thanks for being with them and hopes he did some good. I'm brought forward and the audience applauds. Dad is becoming emotional and tears are streaming down his face, and he says, Folks, you mean so much to me you're just like family, which I love so much. Norma and Naomi begin crying with him and he's getting even more emotional now and says, I want all of you to be faithful till the end as I'm gonna do and wherever I am. I'm gonna be praying for you dear folks for the rest of my life. Dad loves this part of the service and by nine o'clock it's over. Everyone stands outside the church after the service and enjoy each other's company, and for us evangelists, it may be the last time. I'm surrounded by young teen age girls asking questions 'bout my life, and I like it a lot. They're a lot older, but lots of fun.

The next morning we join the McDowell's attending church and meet the new minister. Dad has some advice to offer him and begins saying in a fatherly way, Young man, I've seen it all. I've seen good days, and I've seen bad days, and the only advice I have for you is make them the Lord's days.

He walks away from the young preacher and he looks puzzled 'bout what Dad said. During the ride home, both of the twins are holding Dad's hand in the back seat and having lots of fun 'bout something I know little 'bout. It doesn't worry me, 'cause I'm going home tomorrow to see Maw and Bull. I remembered all week long what Maw told me 'bout old grand maws sitting in their rocking chairs on the front porches smoking their corn-cob pipes, but didn't see a single one. I thought 'bout it a lot and I wonder if maybe she meant Tennessee where Elmo wants to go someday. This has been fun, and I've met some wonderful people at a small Soft Shell Baptist church in Kentucky. People I will never forget.

Arthur (Spare) McCaffry & Buddies
US Cavalry Brownsville Texas 1919

9

RETURNING HOME

Monday morning, we pack our suitcases and prepare for the trip home. Mr. McDowell and his family drive us to the bus station and wait till the bus arrives. Mrs. McDowell comes to me in the waiting room and kisses me on the cheek and puts a five dollar bill in my hand and says, Son, you've been a joy to me and I'll always remember you, and walks away with a couple tears coming down her face. It brings a tear in my eyes, but I wipe it off before I join the others. She's a wonderful lady and I know it. The twins give Dad a big hug and he gives them more than a fatherly kiss. The bus is here now, and the McDowell's are in the car while the twins wave wildly. I tell Dad, They're still waving, and he says, I know, Son, but after all this time, I still can't tell one from the other till I hear 'em say something.

I know, Dad, I never even tried. I just called 'em girls.
That's good thinking, Son, wish, I'd thought of that, 'cause I got mixed up a couple of times.
Dad, you'll probably never see the twins again.
You're right again, Son, right again.

We're going home and Dad says, he don't see any sense in using bus fare to travel in luxury, so we're gonna get off at the next stop and hitch-hike the rest of the way home. That's fine with me 'cause he's gonna have a little more money when we get home. We get off the bus, grab our suitcases and head down the dusty road till we arrive where a big oak tree is shading the highway. Dad likes these kinda spots, so he can sit in the shade while I wave my hand and point my thumb in our direction. I've done some hitch-hiking before and know just how to stand and wave at every passing car. Dad tells me it's better with a young guy like me doing the thumbing, 'cause we stand a better chance of getting picked up a lot sooner than if he was doing it. I've got a question for Dad that's causing me trouble and sometimes he gets aggravated. I ask, Dad, Now that you're not preaching this week, does it mean people will stop calling you Brother, Reverend, or just plain Spare. He says, It really doesn't matter, but it's probably Spare, and don't ask me any more of such foolish stuff.

Hitch-hiking might take a while to get a ride, but after 'bout ten or fifteen minutes, the problem is solved. I'm watching an automobile coming towards us and I can see it's an old friend of Dad's, the township trustee, drugstore owner, and politician named Mr. Hunter. He's probably the richest guy in our neighborhood, but sometimes Mr. Hunter and Dad don't get along too well. When they do they're really happy, and they both like cigars. Dad's still sitting under the oak tree till he sees it's Mr. Hunter and now he starts waving his hand. Hunter sees us, backs up, and says, Spare, what in the hell are you doing walking down the road in the middle of nowhere? Dad tells him he's just been out spreading the gospel like he always does. Hunter says, Spare, you and your boy can ride with me in style, 'cause I just got a new Ford. I've been down on a farm I own and I'm on my way back to Evansville, so you just sit your ass down in the front seat.

This is wonderful news 'cause he lives just two blocks from where we live. I jump in the back seat with both suitcases and Dad gets in the front with the trustee. Mr. Hunter is a man we've known for a long time as a druggist and politician, and he's important in the neighborhood, and Dad knows it. The trustee is a short, roly-poly sort of guy 'bout forty years old and like most politicians and preachers, he wears a hat and tie most the time no matter how hot it is. Today, he has on a short-sleeved shirt, no tie and it's nearly one hundred degrees in the shade and he's still sweating.

We don't go far down the road till Dad and Hunter begin telling each other stories and start laughing hysterical like, and I'm wondering what in the world they're talking 'bout till Hunter says, Well I'll be damned, Spare, I never knew she'd do that. I still don't know what they're talking 'bout, but it's probably some woman. Dad tells the trustee 'bout something he enjoyed and Hunter yells, Spare, you devil, you devil, I sure never dreamed you had it in you. I've heard that before. The trustee whops him on the head with a newspaper and I'm watching and hoping he don't run off the road. Hunter wants to know 'bout some widow in church he knows and when he hears the answer, they both begin laughing wildly again. I don't have the slightest idea what what's going on 'cept a couple of times Hunter gets upset and starts cussing Dad. The cussing doesn't last long and now they're laughing again.

Hunter pulls a cigar from his shirt pocket and throws the band in the back seat. It's a King Edward cigar and Dad only smokes 'em when he can't get, La Fendrich or Charles Denby his favorite brands. Dad's watching Hunter puffing away on his King Edward and I can tell he's wanting one real bad. When he can't stand it any longer, he says, By the way, buddy, do you think you could spare one of them smokes? Hunter reaches in his pocket and hands him one, and Dad looks at it kinda dissatisfied. He says, Well this really ain't my favorite brand, old buddy, but I'll smoke it anyhow beings I cain't get me a LaFendrich or Charles Denby; King Edwards are kinda cheap. I can tell Mr. Hunter is peeved and he shouts, Spare, dammit, you're never satisfied no matter what in the hell I do for you or what I give you. You're a fine one to complain 'bout a cheap cigar; hell you ain't even gotta cigar. You come in my office and ask for something and it's never enough till you get every damned thing I got. Hunter's mad and he keeps cussing, but not as bad as Uncle Joe did when he got rid of the witch. He says, Spare, you go tell people I'm tough on you and now I'm wondering what in the hell's wrong with you? Hunter continues ranting, but I can tell Dad, doesn't care 'cause he just keeps on smoking his King Edward, and looking out the window as he always does.

I'm enjoying this and laughing my head off, but I don't wanta let Mr. Hunter see me laughing. Uncle Joe would say it's like a show and I laugh so hard I start coughing. Hunters' still mad 'bout the King Edwards and says, I don't know who in the hell nicknamed you, Spare, but they sure hit the nail on the head. I know who named Dad Spare. I tell, Mr. Hunter, Maw said Uncle Orie named Dad, Spare, 'cause he always wants to know if Uncle Orie can spare him some change; Uncle Joe says he won't loan Dad 'cause he won't pay back. I touch the trustee on the shoulder, and tell him, It all started over a cigar, didn't it, sir? I'll tell you one thing, Mr. Hunter, my dad can get you a whole box of cigars from my Uncle Orie if you want 'em. If he can't get 'em I can, but please don't tell Maw 'cause she'd say it's a sin. Hunter wants to know how I can get cigars, and what in the hell I'm talking 'bout. I look at Dad and he's shaking his head no, no, but I'm gonna tell him so he quits getting mad all the time and don't kick Dad outta the car. I know Dads' wanting to give me the poke, but he cain't 'cause I'm in the back seat. Mr. Hunter says, Go on boy, go on boy. I tell him, Uncle Orie is a boss at Fendrich Cigar Company and Dad takes me there sometimes to get the best cigars there are. Dad says, Sure, buddy, I'll get you the best Charles Denby or Fendrich cigars they make; they're called defects or seconds; I can get fifty for fifty cents a box. Hunter, old buddy, if I get you some, does that square us? Hunter seems happy again, and lights up another King Edward. Dad's happy again, and Hunter says,

Sure it does, Spare, I wasn't mad at you anyhow.
I touch him on the shoulder again.
Mr. Hunter, you sure fooled me, I thought you might throw Dad outta the car.
Oh no, Son, that's just how me and your dad have fun; we really like each other.

The hot summer sun in the open car hits us in the face all the way home. We stop at a couple of gas stations on the way to fill up and use the restroom, and finally we're home 'bout four o'clock in the afternoon. Dad and the trustee are still having their laughs and Hunter wants to know something 'bout the coming election. Dad says, Hunter, old buddy, you know I'm behind you, haven't I always worked my ass off for you? Hunter says, I'm gonna be honest 'bout it, Spare, I never could tell just which damned side you're on. Dad says, Hunter, my pal, sometimes you can hurt a man by saying such things, and looks out the window as he always does when he just don't care to listen. I can't keep from laughing, 'cause I've heard the same remark to Uncle Joe and Uncle Orie lots of times before.

Maw greets us at the door and I see tears streaming down her face and it doesn't stop; something is wrong, and it must be bad. She says, Sit down here at the kitchen table, and we need to talk seriously. I know by the way she's crying, it must be 'bout Uncle Joe. She says, Joe has been arrested for bootlegging and is goin' to prison at Pendleton, Indiana for six months. Dad's not saying anything and I ask, What happened? She says, Police raided his place pretty close to the river on the west-side and broke up everything and they had pictures of it in the paper. I'm crying and take off running for the front room and finally gain control of myself. Maw comes and hugs me and says, It's all gonna be fine, Son, the Lord knows how to handle these kind of things. Dad wants to know if someone turned him in and Maw says, I don't know what happened, but he's in jail for sure. Dad says, It doesn't seem to matter how much praying I do for my brother, he just won't straighten up and go to church. I'll do what I can for him so I guess I better go tell Pearl 'bout my brother being in prison. She might get worried when she doesn't see him around, and I'll do my best to console her. He grabs the suitcases and heads upstairs to his bedroom. I stay with Maw and try to keep her from crying. She's full of grief and taking it hard and this bothers me a lot. It's hard to watch her cry and wipe away her tears, and I wanta help her, but I don't know how.

I sit with Maw in the living room while she rocks in her rocking chair reading the Bible and I put my arm around her and offer her the five dollars Mrs. McDowell gave me. She says, Son, You know I've tried to make him and your dad live a way of life these kind of things just don't happen, but it just hasn't worked. I turned both of them over to the Lord sometime ago, but I guess He's just taking his time to do something 'bout them two. There is a saying, you can lead a horse to water, but you can't make him drink. I've showed them the way, and they haven't taken it. There's another saying, 'bout young people just hafta get out and sow their wild oats. Maybe some day they'll settle down, but I wonder how long it's gonna take. I tell her 'bout the new baby horse I saw on McDowell's farm jumping up and down kickin' it's hind legs in the air. Mrs. McDowell said he's just too young to have any sense, but he'll learn someday. I ask Maw if that's how Dad and Uncle Joe are, and she says, Exactly, Son, but the Lord's gonna sure bring 'em 'round someday 'cause it says so in the Bible. I tell Maw, Dad's got some money now and Uncle Joe's not here, so you better get the board from him now before he gets outta the house. She says, I'm glad you told me 'cause I'm gonna need every penny to survive. Dad comes downstairs a few minutes later and says he's gonna feel sorry for Pearl when she hears the bad news, but he'll try to help the poor girl the best he can. Maw gets the board and sticks it down her sock.

I visit Cousin Pat and Aunt Dorie to tell 'bout my preaching in Kentucky. In the kitchen sits an old grand maw rocking in a cane chair, smoking, huffing, and puffing on a corn-cob pipe. She looks exactly how Maw described her to me. Aunt Dorie says, Bid, this is my mother, Mrs. Schumacher, and she's come to make her home here with us till she dies. I nod my head to Mrs. Schumacher, but she just keeps rocking, smoking and puffing on her corn-cob pipe. I ask

Where's your momma from, Aunt Dorie?
Philpot Kentucky, Bid, just a few miles across the river.
Does she go to church?
She's been in church all her life, she's a good Soft Shell Baptist, but now she's a St. James Methodist.
How come she turned Methodist, Aunt Dorie?
Closer to our house, Bid, and we take her every Sunday.

I look at her momma again before leaving and she still hasn't looked at me. I'm thinking she might be from someplace where Uncle Aden lived 'cause he didn't speak either. I tell Maw, I met Mrs. Schumacher and she's a Soft Shell Baptist, but now she's going to St. James Methodist. The church is closer and she looks just like the one you told me 'bout before I went to preach in Kentucky. Maw says, That's her, Son, the one I was telling you 'bout that sits on her porch smoking her corn-cob pipe and rocking all day. I met her at Dorie's prayer group 'bout a month ago. I'm still confused, and I'm gonna drop the subject, 'cause I don't think she even heard me say she turned Methodist.

10

UNCLE JOE AT PENDLETON

When Uncle Joe was sent to the Pendleton State Penitentiary during the heat of the Depression it left a big gap in my life. Everyone in the neighborhood knows bootlegging is illegal and felt Joe should have stopped when all the other bootleggers stopped. They still feel compassion for violators 'cause there's still no jobs and working people are desperate for work. They forgive him for his mistake.

Uncle Joe has served 'bout three months of his six-month sentence in prison. Mrs. Salvatori, a member of the prayer group offers to furnish the car and her husband will be the driver to visit him. I'm hoping to go along, and after a lot of pleading, Maw finally says, Joe will be wantin' to see you I'm sure, so get ready to go. Those are wonderful words to my ears and I begin thinking 'bout what I can take him. I've got some money saved from selling junk to Happy Jack, the ragman, and I was gonna buy him some Bull Durham tobacco no matter what she says, but if Maw catches me I know she thinks I'll go to hell and I'd hafta go get saved like Dad. Everyone in church would pat me on the back and say, Come through, Bid, come through, we know you're guilty, and I sure ain't gonna do that. I'll just slip him the dollar and he can get what he wants. I heard Uncle Joe say once if he didn't have a package of Bull Durham he'd go nuts for sure. Maw is taking him some food, soap, a Bible and some religious tracts from church to read. Some of the other ladies in the prayer group are sending Christian material along with a few other small gifts. Dad's not sending anything, but told me he's praying for him and he's got him on his prayer list. I didn't know he had a prayer list, but I know he's on a lotta others.

The trip to Pendleton begins 'bout five o'clock in the morning and the distance is 'bout two hundred miles, and we need to get back the same day, 'cause the next day is Sunday. Mr. Salvatori, works for the L&N Railroad and the car is new. We're breezing along all day 'bout forty miles an hour and the weather is great. Sister Salvatori and Maw say a few prayers for my uncle kinda low now and then, while Mr. Salvatori says a few amens. We stop only two or three times, and arrive at the prison just before lunch. Mr. Salvatori is a big Italian gentleman with a heart of gold, plays an accordion in church and is loved by everyone. Mrs. Salvatori is a beautiful dark haired lady who plays the piano and sometimes they sing specials in church, and when they finish there are a lot of amens and hallelujah shouts from our members. We arrive at the gate and the guards let us pass into the prison. It scares me. They tell us we can see Uncle Joe before lunch and we all wait.

We sit in the waiting room and Uncle Joe is brought in wearing his prison clothes. He doesn't look proud. Maw says to the Salvatoris, Go ahead and say something to him if you wish, and Bid, and me will go over and talk to him later. They finish soon, and it's our turn. I'm already feeling sorry for him being locked up with all these other guys that look like murders and bank robbers for sure. He sees us coming and I see a couple tears in his eyes, but he doesn't show his emotions as I do. Maw says, Joe, I brought the boy along 'cause he misses you a lot. He says, I expected that Maw, I miss all of you a lot, and I'll be glad when my time is up in this joint. I hand him the envelope and hug him, but don't cry. Uncle Joe and Uncle Orie don't believe in crying 'cause it shows weakness. Maw says, I turned you and Arthur over to the Lord, so He will lead you. Uncle Joe has his head down and says, Yeah, yeah, I know you did Maw, and when I get home, things will probably be different. You know, Maw, this is the third time I've served time; first Georgia, then Evansville, and now this for six months. Maw says, I'm glad your brother, Spare, isn't in this place 'cause I believe it would kill him. I believe Dad would try to escape, but Uncle Joe says, Nobody can escape from this place, and the only way outta here is if they carry you out in a bag. I ask him if the food is good and he says, You eat it and don't leave it, and it's nothing like you're gettin' at home.

We talk for a short time, and the guard comes over to us and says, Time is up. He's not smiling, and carries a billy club that looks something like Uncle Joe's black-jack, and he looks like he should be the one in prison, instead of Uncle Joe. I tell him the guard looks mean and he says, Every damned bull here is mean and they'll hit you in the head if you look cross-eyed. I ask, Whats a bull, are they named after dogs? He says, they're a lot like cops, but a helluva lot meaner, 'cause you cain't fight back. I guess that's where my dog gets his name, but he sure ain't mean like these guys. I hate to leave Uncle Joe here and I know he hates to stay, but there's nothing we can do. Maw wants to pray more and the Salvatoris agree, so everyone is praying while the guard looks on. When we finish the guard gives the sign of the cross, and he wasn't even praying. Maw looks at me and says, You better not dare say a word, 'cause he's probably Catholic. Uncle Joe tells us how much our visit means to him and when he gets back things are gonna be better. He asks 'bout Dad and I tell him, Dad's praying for you, and you're on his new prayer list. He laughs and says, I'm praying for him too and I've got him on my list. We hug him again and the guard leads him away. Maw and me are crying, but nobody knows it and soon we're on our way home.

Maw and the Salvatoris' talk 'bout everything, but not one word is bad 'bout Uncle Joe. Maw's not talking much, and I can see she's sad and worried the same as me. The Salvatoris' talk 'bout church and how things are gonna get better now that President Roosevelt is in office. They say everyone is gonna get a job, and there's gonna be plenty food for everyone and the banks won't be taking peoples farms and homes. I wanta make her feel better and tell her, I know one thing for sure, if anyone can take it, Uncle Joe can. He's not very big, but he's tough and they never caught him in Georgia, and that was bad with all the cotton mouths and alligators down there. Maw says, I'm not worried, Son, the Lord will take care of everything, and that's one thing I'm sure of. We arrive home, and Maw still has to cook Sunday's meal and by the time she gets to bed, it's far past her bedtime. Night comes and we sleep well, 'cause Uncle Joe is safe in jail.

It's not long till Uncle Joe is due home. I've been doing a lotta Bible learning from Maw, and Dad's had me in several churches around the area answering Bible questions while I'm still going to church with Maw. Besides all that going on, I still have a good life with my many cousins and friends playing and enjoying life. Dad's doing his usual on and off religious life, but everyone accepts it from him.

Maw is gathering the family together 'bout a week before Joe's homecoming and says, Children, Joe has been in jail for six months and he's gonna be coming home next Saturday. We need to celebrate his return just like the rich man in the Bible did for his Prodigal Son who went away and wasted his life. We'll plan a picnic in the park for next Saturday afternoon and I want every member of our family at the reception for him.

It's mid-summer, hot, and everyone is overjoyed at the thought 'cept Dad. I can tell Dad doesn't like the idea of celebrating Uncle Joe's return.

He says, I sure hope everyone would do the same thing for me if I was locked up.

Orie says, Spare, you're probably the one that belongs up there instead of your brother; you've did a helluva lot more things than any of us, and got away with it.

It looks like Dad's feelings are hurt 'cause I see a tear.

He says, It seems like I'm always the black sheep in the family, and nobody appreciates the work I do in the church.

Cotton says, It's 'cause you don't stay in the church long enough, Uncle Spare.

That really hurts me, Cotton, it almost breaks my heart, but I'll still pray for you.

I can tell Dads' feelings are hurt again and he leaves the room. Cotton says, Uncle Joe's gonna go see his girl friends for sure, and he may want me to go along.

I'm sure Cotton's gonna be with him, and that's for sure, too.

The following Saturday Uncle Joe is home, and Orie drives him to the local park where we all await his return along with Reverend Johnson and the church people. Instead of returning in shame, he's welcomed as a son who has gone astray and comes home like the Prodigal Son in the Bible. Dad puts his arms around him, and a few tears show in his eyes and he says, Brother, brother, you will never know how much I've missed you, and the long hours I've spent praying for you. I'll always love you even though you go astray and I'm not one to give up on someone. Orie and Dorie burst out laughing and Joe says, Sure Spare, I've been praying for you too, and I've got one question to ask you. Dad looks kinda puzzled, and Joe says, Have you been calling on any of my girl friends since I've been gone? Dad looks shocked at his question, and says, Brother, brother, you know I wouldn't do that for nothing in the world, especially not to my own brother. Now, everyone is laughing 'cause we all know he's being seeing Pearl, and I told Uncle Joe during my trip to the prison.

11

FISHIN' AT HART LINES

Uncle Joe has to find some work and there's no work anywhere that's legal. He cain't go back to bootlegging or he'll go to jail forever, so we're all goin' fishin' at Hart Lines River near Griffin, Indiana. The area is well known for tornadoes and bad weather. Dad isn't going 'cause he's working on some places to go preach and he's gonna be taking me along. He tells me he's got big plans for us to preach at lots of different places and one place he's looking forward to is Mt. Vernon, Indiana. He wants me home from our fishin' trip in time to go over some Bible questions and what I'm gonna be talking 'bout. He won't tell me what kinda church it is and that makes me feel suspicious of him. Maw wants me back before Sunday 'cause it's church time at the Pilgrim Holiness, and I'm not 'bout to miss church for no fishin' trip.

We gather our fishin' supplies and look forward for Monday morning. Cotton, Slim, Titties, Uncle Joe and me will be going. I'm having a hard time convincing everyone my dog, Bull, needs to go along for our protection. Most everyone has a good opinion of, Bull, 'cept cousin Titties who seems to think he's just a little too eager to chase someone. I've got him well trained and he's a good dog at heart. My pleading is finally over and everyone agrees on the condition; if he gets someone by the ass, I'm gonna answer for it.

Sunday is Maw's day, and we head for church dressed in our best clothes. We walk down a couple of streets and other kids from the neighborhood join us including my best friend, Bob, his sister, Sissie, and brother, Charlie. By the time we arrive at the church for Sunday school, there's a long line of us all following, Maw. All morning long, I'm thinking 'bout the trip tomorrow and everyone wants to go, but Uncle Joe says there's no more room.

Sunday night, Bob and me are back in church sitting next to Maw in the second row from the front as usual and the preacher's talking 'bout adultery. Maw's trying to keep us awake, but having a hard time as we stretch out on the bench. She knows we played hard all day, and Dad had me in the house for 'bout two hours questioning me on Bible questions and showing me how to speak from the podium.

The evening service ends, nobody goes to the altar, and it's time to head home. A couple of the prayer group women come to Maw and talk 'bout the next meeting and we take off for home. We walk behind her so we can talk 'bout our problems. Bob's got a question for Maw.

Is the preacher and his wife coming to the house again, Maw?
Sure is, Bob, why do you ask?
Why do preachers always eat first?
It's just plain sense, Bob, just plain sense.
I tell Maw, Dad eats before everyone, and once even forgot to say the prayer.
That sounds like your dad, always thinkin' of his self, nobody else.

Monday morning finally arrives and everyone is excited 'bout the trip to Hart Lines. The old Ford truck is loaded with food, drinks, fishin' tackles, Bull, and five boys between the ages of seven to sixteen. We are given our final lecture from Maw 'bout behavior. Joe is driving and warns everyone the radiator is leaking, bad. It's at least forty miles to the river and traveling at least thirty-five to forty miles an hour, we might make it in 'bout two hours.

We begin our trip, Maw's waving goodbye, Bull's barking, and Titties is yelling at him, Shut your damned mouth! We travel seven or eight miles, and the radiator begins to heat up and we need water. A nearby pond supplies the water, but the leak doesn't stop and Uncle Joe yells, Be on the look out for road apples. I don't know what they are and Cotton explains to me they're nothing but horse shit, and he's already saw a lot of it. Down the road we find plenty of road apples, drop a few in the radiator and take off for Hart Lines with no more trouble.

Bull's tongue is hanging out after 'bout an hour and he's lapping up the pond water used for the radiator. The sun's shining brightly and we finally see the river. The only way to reach the river from the road is to travel over Farmer Toms' lane and that's 'bout a quarter mile from his house. Tom is a tall, slim man 'bout forty years old, wears a big brimmed straw hat, no shirt and sometimes no shoes. Tom drinks beer all day and sometimes all night, if he hasn't passed out. There's no way of getting around Tom, however, 'cause he owns the farm, the fishin' boats, and we need food from his farm. What Tom needs from us, is the beer that Uncle Joe brings to trade.

Joe greets Tom like a long lost relative, and gives him a quarter to use a boat and another quarter to pass over his land. Tom is a business man and Joe is a trader. I didn't know we had beer in the tubs and I ask Uncle Joe how he hid, it? He says, Son, sometimes you just have to out figure Maw, and this is one of those times. I just put it out in plain view, cover it with soft drinks and she doesn't look twice. Uncle Joe always knows how to handle things like this, but I know I'd never try something like that 'cause she'd catch me for sure, and I'd feel guilty for the rest of my life.

Tom is looking our truck over good and I know he's looking for the beer. He says, I see you got a dog, whut's his name? I tell him, Bull, sir, and he's my dog. Tom starts to pat him on the head, and Titties mutters, Oh, shit all hell's gonna break loose now. I have him by the collar and I'm not 'bout to let him nab, Tom. Tom says, Is he a Brendal Bull, I hear that's the best there is? I never bothered before to worry 'bout what brand of dog he was, I just figured he was a dog with small ears and no tail that we call, Bull Dogs. I tell him, He must be, sir, but that really doesn't matter to us. Tom's still looking everything over in the truck real good and says, I think I need to warn you 'bout my old mother pussy-cat called, Midnight, cause she can get pretty mad if some dog comes near her kittens. I know he thinks 'bout his pussy-cat the same as I think 'bout, Bull. I tell Mr. Tom, You needn't worry 'bout, Midnight, sir, I don't think Bull would bother a hair on her head if she's got babies. Titties and Cotton begin to laugh and I cain't figure out why.

We arrive at the camp and it's not long till the supplies are unloaded. Bull is running 'round in circles. Joe tells me to tie him up 'cause he's already pissed on every tree and he's still looking for more. I know Bull is having a good time, but everyone else thinks he can't be trusted if Tom comes around. I'll watch him so he doesn't get into trouble, but they don't seem to understand he had to hold it for two hours. Titties says, If Tom shows up, Bull's gonna go after his ass for sure, and we'll all be in trouble and Bid, you're gonna hafta answer for it. Cousin Titties can't seem to understand that Bull is a good dog at heart.

I've trained him to be watchful, Cousin Titties.
You sure have, Bid, he's too damned watchful. I trust him just as far as I can see him. Besides that, he's got every dog in the neighborhood afraid to walk in front of our house.
You're right, Cousin Titties, I may have him a little over-trained. Maw sure likes Bull and says, he's just like one of the family and there's never no need to worry 'bout getting rid of the garbage 'cause he eats everything she throws out.

Bull doesn't bark when he's chasing varmits like most dogs and I find him running through some tall weeds with his nose to the ground. Slim says, Bid, I kinda like what you said 'bout Bull to my brother. I don't know why he's afraid of him, 'cause he's always been friendly and playful to me. I'm glad Slim likes him even though some people just don't understand him. Cotton likes my dog too and says, Don't let it bother you, Bid,

I like him a lot, and I like it when he's after somebody's ass, as long as it's not mine. After all he's just like most dogs that like to eat, drink, piss and try to mount 'bout everything they see. Cotton's just like me, he understands dogs.

We gather firewood, clean up the camping area and everything looks great. Sundown comes and Tom comes trudging down the lane towards camp. Joe, tells us to keep our mouth shut 'cause he's known him for years and knows how to deal with him. He says, Let me handle this, 'cause sometimes he gets crazy ideas and sees things that ain't really there, especially when he's drunk. Tom says, Is everything all right, Joe, I see you've got some home-brew over in the tub, how 'bout letting me sample it for you? I can tell Uncle Joe don't trust Tom when it comes to home-brew, and Cotton told me he gets in it when Joe's not 'round.

Joe says, Sure, Tom, I sure will but first I need to sample some of your corn and vegetables and maybe a couple of chickens, is it agreeable?
Joe, we've been friends for years, now pick what you want, grab a couple fryers, but don't let the old lady up at the house know anything 'bout this, now where in the hell is the opener for this bottle of home-brew?
Yep, Tom, it's a deal.
Tom agrees and says, Joe, it's that way till the beer runs out or you leave.

Tom is happy with the deal and takes off with a couple bottles of brew in his hands and sits down near the water's edge. He makes a few more trips to the truck for beer and nobody sees him till the next morning lying in some weeds passed out. Later he gets up, walks home and is back the next evening.

Hart Lines isn't a big river, 'bout thirty yards 'cross at any place, but it's clear, clean water and full of fish. The following morning everyone is anxious to fish and I wanta explore the woods and see the wildlife. Uncle Joe has been on the river all evening with Cotton and Titties placing trout lines in the water. He calls everyone together and says, Now, listen to what I have to say and I'll only say it once. We're down here to have fun and I don't want anyone gettin' in the home brew, 'cause that's for Tom. If we don't have food we'll be leaving for sure. Things are going well and Bull's having a good time running in and out of a nearby thicket. Titties, seems to understand him better now.

I'm trying to get Bull to come with me when he grabs something off the ground, shakes it around a few times, brings it to me, and lays it at my feet. Cotton is watching and says, he wants to know what he's got. I look down and there's the biggest toad frog I've ever seen. Bull looks up at me, kinda like he's smiling, with slobbers all 'round his mouth and trying to wag a tail he doesn't have. He's so proud of himself and offers me something wanting to please me. Bull must be the best trained dog in the world, even though he's bug-eyed, has hardly any ears and no tail. He's mine, and just the kinda dog I like. I bend over to pick up the toad frog and Cotton screams at me.

Whatever you do, Bid, don't pick up the toad frog or you'll regret it forever.
What do you mean, Cotton?

Toad frogs can put a curse on you, Bid. They did it to a good friend of mine, Warty McGee. If they piss on you, they'll give you warts and you 'cain't ever get rid of 'em. Hell, Bid, Warty was the best baseball pitcher my team ever had. We called him, Lefty McGee, till he got warts. Now he cain't pitch, cain't hit and still has eight big warts on his left hand. We kicked his ass off the team all 'caused by a damned toad frog. Just like that, his whole baseball career was over.

What 'bout dogs, Cotton?
Nope, not dogs, just people.

It's the third day at camp and after a wonderful time in the open air, I decide early in the morning to cross the river and fish on the other side. Uncle Joe and a couple of my cousins are out in the river baiting trotlines and using the boat. The only other way to cross the river is to use a nearby railroad trestle 'bout fifty yards down-stream and that's what I'm gonna do. I tie Bull to a nearby tree gather some fishin' gear and head for the trestle and a train passes over the river. I stop to listen and decide nothing else is coming, especially this early in the morning.

I begin to walk across the bridge and look down at the cross-ties while glancing down at the deep clear water far below, and my heart flutters. Walkin' 'cross the trestle isn't as easy as I thought. I begin to pick up my pace and quit looking down at the water and I hear a distant rumbling of something I've heard before; it's exactly what I don't wanta imagine. The rumbling is much louder now and no doubt 'bout it, this is a train coming at me. I see the smoke billowing from the locomotive and hear the long whaling of the whistle, and I know I'm in trouble. I hafta go back or go ahead before the train reaches the trestle, or I'm dead for sure. I'm scared as never before, can't pray, and my legs are shaking so bad I don't know if I can run.

I've gotta act fast. I glance at some bushes near the bank on the other side and run as fast as my legs will take me. This is no time to worry 'bout falling, and my heart pounds hard and fast. The big coal burning locomotive is in plain view and I see the engineer with his head stuck out the window of the engine. The black puffing engine seems to be roaring like a bull coming straight at me. I'm near the end of the bridge and look down, and there below is nothing but small trees and brush. I jump and land on top of the brush as the train passes over. I'm a little scratched around my face and hands, and somehow, I make it safely. Now, I hafta get outta the brush and find my fishin' gear. It's scattered all over the river bank. I fish for a while and get myself back to normal, and now I'm ready to go back to the campsite. Cotton is out rowing the boat a little down-stream and comes to pick me up and he takes me to the campsite. I'm saying nothing to Cotton 'bout what happened and all I wanta do is see Bull. He licks me 'round the face a couple times, I'm still shaking, and I'll never again try walking 'cross the bridge.

I tell Uncle Joe 'bout my close call crossing the trestle and he says, Son, you're just gonna hafta be a little more careful. When you get a little older, you'll learn not to take those kinda chances; did yuh lose your fishin' gear? I explain, I saved my fishin' poles, but almost got killed, and he says, That's fine, but if you go across again, be a little more careful. I untie my dog, pat him on the back, and take him for his morning walk and a romp in the nearby woods. I'm finally calmed down, but when trains roll across the bridge, I still remember what happened.

Sundown is here and we're prepared for the night. Our large bonfire sends flames high in the air and we eat catfish and carp from the river, chicken, tomatoes and corn on the cob from, Tom. Nightfall is here and Uncle Joe is on his third home-brew and Cotton's kinda upset 'bout something. He says, Uncle Joe, how come I cain't even get a swig of beer to wash the fish down and you're on your third? It just doesn't seem fair that you get the beer along with Tom. Uncle Joe doesn't like his attitude and says, Cotton my boy, I made the beer and I make the rules. Cotton thinks 'bout what he said, and says, I understand now as long as it's in the rules. Uncle Joe tells me to take it easy on the carp 'cause its filled with bones so small you cain't see 'em and if one gets caught in my throat I'll choke to death before I can get to a doctor.

A large snake goes slithering across some wood piled nearby and I tell Uncle Joe, It's probably a Cotton Mouth Water Moccasin and he says, Don't pay any attention they're all over this damned place. He has another beer while he lies on the blanket, smoking his cigarette and begins to hum a tune I like, and I ask the name? He says, It's my favorite song,' DANNY BOY" but it makes me sad when I hear it. I tell him he shouldn't sing it if it makes him sad and he says sometimes he likes to be sad so he can remember things better. I sure as hell don't wanta feel sad, says Cotton.

I watch the fire and feel sleepy when off to the side I see another large snake slither towards his blanket and I yell at him to look out for the snake. He acts kinda disgusted at me; then he knocks it away with a stick, and lays back down on the blanket, and says,

It sure as hell would be nice to be in Ireland, where there's no damned snakes crawlin' round botherin' me when I'm trying to sleep.
Who told you there's no snakes in Ireland, Uncle Joe?
Your grand-paw, he came from Ireland.
How come there aren't snakes in Ireland, when there's plenty here?
Saint Patrick, Ireland's patron saint ran 'em all out to protect the people.
I think it was a Water Mocassin, Uncle Joe.
You're right, this place is covered with 'em.

Bull lies by my side and is being a good dog just like I promised everyone. Out of the bushes from nowhere comes a big black momma cat and she looks exactly what Tom described. Just like Titties said, all hell breaks loose. Bull, lunges at the cat and up the lane they run towards Tom's house. This must be momma, Midnight, 'cause she's one big pussy-cat and Bull's not gaining on her as they head towards the barn. Titties says, Our ass has had it now, Bull's gonna kill the cat for sure. Uncle Joe says, Bull may get more than he can chew this time, 'cause that pussy-cat is one big, bad lookin' momma. I'm not gonna worry 'bout it, 'cause the cat came to our territory, and Bull wasn't the one that started it. I hope Tom understands, but he's probably gonna be drunk anyhow.

It's morning and Bull hasn't come back, and I'm beginning to worry that I may hafta go look for him. Cotton says not to worry 'cause he's one dog who can handle anything. I look down the lane and Bull's coming back, but kinda slow. The closer he gets, I can see he's just not normal. He comes to me and lies down, and his face is scratched and bleeds. He's covered with mud, and looks like he could cry, but dogs don't know how to cry; they can whine and Bull's doing a lot of it as I pet him on the head. Titties, says, Well, this is really something. Bull, sure as hell found a real mean pussy-cat he couldn't handle. I guess he means, Midnight.

Everything is going great. Lots of fish are being caught and Tom is supplying plenty of food, but the beer is starting to get low. Tom hasn't seen a sober day or night since we arrived. He's in the boat with Joe running trout lines and suddenly stands up, steps out of the boat and goes under the water. They're under the bridge and the water is at least fifty feet deep. He comes back to the surface and Joe grabs him and pulls him back into the boat and I hear him calling Tom worse names than he did the witch. They arrive back at the camp, and Uncle Joe is still cussing him. He says, Tom, where in the hell did yuh think you were when you got outta the boat? You gotta be the craziest bastard I ever saw in my whole life. Tom is hanging his head down like Dad does sometimes at home, and he's trying to dry himself off around the campfire. He says, Joe, do you know what happened to my straw hat? I've had that old hat for ten years and I sure would hate to lose it. We're sitting around the campfire listening and we talk 'bout how Tom could have drowned for sure. Cotton says, The damned guy thinks more of a straw hat than his own life, but we'll be outta beer by tomorrow night, and that'll be the end of Tom. If we stayed another day, he'd drown himself for sure.

It's Thursday, everyone is tired, we smell like fish more than humans and we need baths. Joe tells us to get our ass in the truck and we'll drive up the road and scrub off in a pond. I grab the soap and a couple of towels. Everyone ends up in the water including Bull. He loves the water till I begin putting the soap to him. The rest of Thursday goes well, but night time is coming and the sky is beginning to have a different look. Darkness has arrived while the campfire is blazing and all of a sudden out of the sky comes loud thunder and lightning flashes all over the area. The wind begins to pick up and just as suddenly the heavy rain comes pouring down.

The atmosphere has changed completely. This is no ordinary storm. Bull is up against my side, frightened, and shivering as the lightning and thunder gets worse. Joe shouts, This ain't no time to be out here in the open, so head for the old barn on the other side of the railroad trestle and get your ass out of here fast! Cotton wants to know 'bout all the fishin' stuff and food and Joe yells, To hell with it, just get your ass moving. It's a foot race to the barn with Bull leading the way.

This old barn isn't a pretty place to be, 'cause it's half full of hay, farm materials, and dark 'cept for a lantern Cotton is carrying. We're soaking wet, the wind is howling, the sky is filled with lightning. Trees are bending over touching the water and falling into the river. The lighning and thunder is loud and deafening and we're not talking. Titties is lying on the hay next to Cotton and begins to laugh when he sees Bull cowering and shaking under my arm. His head lies buried half way down in the hay, and Titties says, That's something I never dreamed I'd ever see, Bull's actually afraid of something. Bull shakes every time the thunder roars and lightning goes through the sky and I'm trying to calm him. We bed down for the night and soon fall asleep till a freight train comes roaring across the bridge waking everyone. Bull jumps up and begins barking, and runs over near Titties and Cotton; he hikes his leg and pisses on an old farm plow. Titties yells, Damn you, Bull, you almost pissed on me just when I was trying to believe you're a good dog, and if you ever do it again you're a dead dog for sure. Cotton must think it's funny, 'cause he doesn't stop laughing along with Uncle Joe.

The next morning after a rainy night in the hay, it's bright and all new. The fields are filled with water and the campsite is nothing but a sea of mud and water. Uncle Joe surveys the damage and says, Boys, there's no way in hell we can get this place cleaned up so let's get ready and head for home. We look at each other and we're glad he said it, 'cause this place will be unbearable for a couple of days. Everything is picked up and the fishin' trip comes to an end. Everyone is happy and ready to go home and even Bull seems pleased to go home, and he's the first to jump in the truck. Bull is barking, Titties is cussing Bull, and the rest of us are laughing as we take off for home without seeing Tom.

Maw says she's surprised to see us home so early and hopes we got our fill of fishin' and wants to know if I had a good time. I tell her 'bout Bull catching the toad frog and how Cotton saved me from having a hand full of warts the rest of my life. She says, Well that's fine, Son, Cotton's always there looking out for you, not like your dad. I tell her 'bout almost getting killed by a train and she tells me to be a little more careful the next time I cross a trestle. I tell her 'bout the storm and she says, Well I'm glad there wasn't any boozing goin' on or you might not made it. Maw takes things real easy and nothing excites her. I finally tell her 'bout Tom almost drowning and she says, Well, I'm glad the poor man wasn't drinking or he may not been so lucky.

I'm not saying anything else to Maw 'bout the trip. She hands me a sack full of scraps and says, Take this to your dog, he must be famished by now. I don't hafta go far 'cause Bull's at the back door waiting. Maw takes a look at him, and he's still looking kinda pitiful. She says, I cain't remember ever seeing Bull lookin' so sorry, what in the world happened to him? I don't really wanta tell her 'cause this is the first time he ever got whipped good. He knows Maw always thinks good of him. I don't know how to explain it, so I just tell her what Titties said. I think he just got hold of a pussy-cat he couldn't handle, Maw, and I think she understands. Now I gotta go tell all my friends 'bout the wonderful time I had at Hart Lines and how Warty Mc Gee ruined his baseball career.

12

<u>CROSSING THE OHIO</u>

It's hot and humid in the afternoon and me and Bull are romping in the backyard playing beneath an apple tree. Slim comes to see us and says, Uncle Spare, how 'bout you and Bid goin' with me this afternoon on a trip 'cross the Ohio River? Dad wants to know how Slim's got a boat on the Ohio and Slim says it belongs to his friend Bootsy Davis who lets him use it anytime he wants. Dad's not preaching today or tomorrow so he says, Let's get to goin' Slim, I like the water a lot. I know Dad cain't swim, but it sure doesn't scare him like it does me 'cause I cain't swim either. I wanta take Bull, but Slim says, No way Bull's goin' in a row-boat with us in the big Ohio River, hell, he'd get us all drowned, and he'd be the only one able to swim across.

Slim and Dad are good buddies, and have been close to each other while taking some short hobo trips to southern Kentucky and western Illinois to have fun. Dad is Slim's Uncle and Maw thinks he kinda looks up to him for some reason, but she doesn't know why. I heard her tell Slim one day, Slim you need to find you someone else to look up to besides my son, Spare, 'cause he's got his own problems. Uncle Joe said he thinks Slim might be a little bashful 'cause Dad's not, and they both like girls a lot. Maw said she thinks he's bashful 'cause he's been raised 'round mostly boys. Dad is always preaching to Slim 'bout getting saved, but Slim doesn't go to church, 'cause he feels just like Uncle Joe. Most of the family feel like Dad isn't setting a good example for Slim.

We walk 'bout a mile to the river down near the power plant and there is the boat rocking in the big Ohio River, and there's two oars for us to paddle our way to the sand bar on the other side. The breeze causes a few waves in the water and I know there's some swift current, 'cause this is the same place I got baptized last year and the entire Pilgrim Holiness church watched as the preacher dunked me good.

Slim and Dad are more anxious to get started than I am, 'cause I'm not so sure 'bout getting in the boat with two guys, and one of them cain't swim. Dad takes off rowing, and Slim sits at one end, me at the other, and now I'm glad Bull's not along. They're real happy, singing sailor songs and laughing, but I'm not singing. Dad's bragging 'bout how he can paddle the boat all the way to Henderson, Kentucky if Slim wants to go, but I sure don't. I put my feet in the water, it feels good, and Dad tells me there are some big fish in the Ohio that can probably swallow me. I gotta remind Dad of something.

Dad, remember I told you I can't swim.
Sure, I do, Son, and I told you I cain't either.
Well, I still cain't swim and this place is deeper than the back-water.
Don't talk that way; you're gettin' me upset.
Can you swim all the way 'cross, Slim?
Don't talk that way, but I don't think I can.

Dad's rowing and Slim is standing at the end of the boat when outta the blue, we hear a loud horn billowing not far down the river from the south. Suddenly a huge steamboat comes roaring around the bend of the river and smoke billows from its smokestack. Slim says, I'll be damned if it ain't the Delta Queen, the biggest darn steamboat on the Ohio River, and Dad says, It sure as hell is, hell's fire, I don't know which damned way to go. Dads cussing again and now he'll hafta visit the altar again for sure. Slim says, Back her up, Spare, so we can have some fun riding the waves of that son of a gun, this is gonna be one day we'll remember forever. Now, I'm getting worried.

Dad begins rowing with all his strength, but we're going the wrong way. Slim is standing and hollers, Dammit, Spare, you're takin' us to Kentucky, go back to Indiana. Dad's really confused and doesn't seem to understand, and I don't like the looks of things, cause the Delta Queen is coming closer. Slim yells again, Dammit, Spare, you're goin' the wrong way; head for Indiana, not Kentucky. I don't think Dad knows which way is Indiana.

Spare, what in the hell are you doin', do you know how to row this damned boat?
Hell no, Slim, I was in the cavalry, not the damned navy.
Get the hell outta the way, Spare, let me handle this.

Slim takes the oars and turns us around just as the Delta Queen is 'bout on us and I'm feeling safer. I'm still learning and now I just wanta get away from these two guys before we all drown. I know both of 'em oughta go to the altar, 'cause they been cussing like sailors.

Slim begins heading back towards the Indiana side, and water is starting to fill the boat, I'm bailing out with a can and they're laughing. The Delta Queen is almost directly in front of us and I can see people yelling and waving at us from the top deck. The calliope is playing loud music and Dad and Slim are waving and shouting to the passengers standing on the deck. The little row-boat is bouncing straight up and down and Slim says, Here, Spare, now that I've showed you how to row this baby, you can take over. Dad starts rowing back towards Kentucky behind the Delta Queen. Slim yells, Get closer to the paddles, Spare, get closer. I sure don't wanta get closer 'cause I'm getting sick. The closer we get, the higher the boat goes in the air and drops back down with a big wallop. Water is spilling in the boat as it rocks backwards and forwards, and I wanta feel some land. I'll say something to turn 'em back. This always works on Dad.

Cousin Slim, are you saved?

What in the world are you talkin' 'bout, Bid, asking me if I'm saved out here in the middle of the Ohio River?

Well, Cousin, if the boat sinks you might not make it to the other side and you'd drown for sure. Maw says if you ain't saved, you know where you'll be going next.

Well, I can swim, but I don't know 'bout making it to the other side.

Dad says, Come to think of it, I'm not so sure I'm saved this week either.

Dad wants to get away from the waves and head to the sandbar and Slim says, I've only been to church twice with Maw and never got saved either time. She did tell me though she hadn't given up on me and was still praying. I want Slim to feel better so I tell him, I don't think that's going to help, Cousin Slim, but I do know you're number five on Maw's prayer list.

It's not long till we head for the Kentucky side and soon Dad and Slim begin having fun running up and down the bar, playing ball, racing each other to see whose the fastest, and I'm building an Irish castle looking just like one I saw at school. Later we head back across the river and arrive home early in the evening.

Maw's in the kitchen cooking the Sunday meal. She asks her usual question 'bout if I enjoyed myself and I tell her, I sure did, I had a great time. I found out cousin Slim's not saved and Dad's not sure. She says, What in the world you talkin' 'bout, sometimes you sure get me confused trying to figure out what's on your mind. I tell her, Well, it's like this, Maw, when we ran into some pretty good size waves, I thought maybe the boat was gonna turn over. I thought 'bout Jesus on the sea with Peter and the disciples. I asked both of 'em if they were saved. It took'em a while to answer, but they decided it was time to quit riding the waves behind the Delta Queen. Maw acts like she's a little confused and says, Well, I really don't know what you're talkin' 'bout, but I'm still praying for your cousin, Slim, and your dad never knows from one day to another 'bout his relation with the Lord. I'm sure you and I do, but he's my biggest concern. I ask her if Cousin Slim is still number five on her list and she says, He was, but now I'll make him number four.

I begin helping Maw with the cooking by doing some dishes and the conversation moves on. She's in a good mood, so I'll ask her a question. Maw, My Aunt Tessys' five boy cousins and one girl are all 'bout the same age, how can that be? I asked Uncle Joe one day and he said there's only six years between the six of 'em. He said we may have a record of having six kids in six years and none of 'em twins. Uncle Joe said to the best of his knowledge she didn't miss a year having kids for six straight years. Is Uncle Joe right 'bout that, Maw? Is that a record, Maw? I'd sure like to know so I can tell all my other cousins and friends. I don't think any of our neighbors can beat our record.

She's not looking happy and turns around and removes her apron. I've seen this look before, but this time it looks serious. She says, I've told you a thousand times not to ask your Uncle Joe anything before you come to me, and now I'm tellin' you one more time and this is the last. Come to me first. Do you now understand? I'm also tellin' you that if you don't shut up 'bout such questions, we'll be taking a trip outside and you know what that means. I tell her, I sure do, Maw. Bob and me both don't like to see you wanta go outside with us. Sometimes when you say the paddling is gonna hurt you more than us, well, maybe that's not just exactly right. We don't think you sinned, but you may have made a mistake. Sometimes you just get aggravated. She's still not happy and I know she's not gonna answer my question. She says, I told you Son, I don't wanta hear any more of your questions today. I know it's time to shut up 'cause Maw's patience is 'bout to run out. Cotton warned me when her patience is running out it's time to get away. We finish the cooking, she hugs me and kisses me on the forehead, and I go romp in the grass with Bull. I'm not gonna test her patience.

Dad received a letter from Ralph Yancey, our friend in Mt. Carmel. It reads:

Dear Brother:

Sorry to send you some sad news 'bout our plans in Mt. Vernon. Our son Elmo was running his traps down near where the back water was and stepped into one of them. He's on crutches, his ankle is cut and swollen, and is only able to hobble around. I have to run his traps.

Go ahead and take care of the meeting at Mt. Vernon with the other Deacons and preachers and I'll see you later when Elmo is O.K.

Your friend in Christ,
Brother Yancey

P.S. Elmo said be sure and tell Bid the trap he stepped in is the one he couldn't find when they were in the back waters. He also said he got $416.25 selling furs.

I go with Dad to the Coliseum meeting. I answer Bible questions before a full house, but don't enjoy the service. It's a foot washing service with lots of other preachers and deacons on the stage floor. There's a lotta singing, preaching, and sweating going on. Women fill dish pans with water and Dad washes a great big guy's feet, then spills water all over the stage. I don't wash feet. I tell Maw I don't wanta go again, and she says, Son, you don't hafta go if you don't wanta, I'll handle this matter with your Dad. I don't go, but Dad does. He says nothing 'bout the meeting, won't talk, walks away and acts hurt.

13

MOUNT VERNON PENTECOST MEETING

There's a lot of interest from other churches and ministers inviting us to come and hold revivals after the appearances at the Farmer's Market Hall in Evansville, Mt. Vernon, Mt. Carmel, Illinois, and Kentucky churches. All of a sudden Dad's life is changing 'cause I know the Bible. We're invited to hold a two-night meeting at a very popular Pentecostal church in Mt. Vernon, Indiana. Dad says the pastor's name is Reverend Mills, a very devout person with a faithful following. The church is well-known for its belief in speaking in tongues and frowned upon by many churches such as Baptist, Methodist, and others. Maw's church, the Pilgrim Holiness, is strictly opposed to speaking in tongues. It's been only a short time since we returned from preaching in Kentucky, but it's too much for Dad to turn down. He knows I wanta enjoy some free time with my buddies and dog, but it's important for him and he can't do it without me.

Dinner is almost over Dad gives me the poke and the nod. I'm not done eating yet, but I get up and go anyhow 'cause lately I've been telling him that I don't feel the poke. This poke is a good one. We go into the living room and Dad says, Listen to what I have to say, Son, 'cause it's important. You know how your old dad is always looking out for your interest, don't you? Well, it's like this, Son, we've got this wonderful opportunity to speak in Mt. Vernon and I don't see how we can pass it up. I ask him if he's talking 'bout the Holy Roller Pentecost church in Mt. Vernon and he says Uncle Joe and Maw are telling me things I shouldn't know and are working against him by putting thoughts in my mind. Dad says all he wants to do is preach the gospel. I try to make him understand it might be the devil's work when people start talking in unknown tongues, and I ain't wanting any part of that. He keeps saying, I know they put you up to this, didn't they, Son? I have no idea what he means.

I guess I'm kinda afraid of something like tongue talking, 'cause we've never had it in the Pilgrim Holiness, but sometimes they do get happy, run down the aisle hollering amen and hallelujah while waving their Bibles, and I'm used to that. We talk some more 'bout the preaching in Mt. Vernon and I finally tell him, I'll go and do whatever you say. Dad says he's always doing things for my benefit, but I just don't understand. I wanta go outside and play ball with my buddies, so I tell him whatever he wants, I'll do it, and now he's happy. Dad wipes the sweat off his forehead and says, Thank God that's over.

Dad is still wanting to talk 'bout the Mt. Vernon meeting and says, There's gonna be a lot of people at this meeting, Son, and I've got some swell ideas how I can really make some good money. I want you to take a look at these pictures I have of you holding the Bible. I look at the picture, and it's only me holding a Bible and I don't know how he can make money of me holding a Bible. Dad says, I'm gonna sell 'em, Son, they're good for a dollar a piece. I tell him it just doesn't sound right, and he acts disgusted, shakes his head, and says he needs the money, and for me to shut up 'bout it. I think we should give it to 'em for coming to church, but Dad says I'm crazy to even think such a crazy thing. Dad says, This is his one time I'm gonna make some honest money and you come up with the silly idea of giving away your own picture. Son, you gotta realize you're some kind of celebrity. Hell's fire, Son, it sounds like something Maw would say. I tell him O. K., Dad, I'll do whatever you want. I wanta get outta this room and go play ball with my friends. Dad says, Thank the Lord this is over, and leaves the room.

I return from playing ball and Dad still wants to talk to me. He says, Son, there's one thing you should understand by now. My family's been against me from the start of my preaching career and that's for sure. They're jealous of me 'cause I've got the brains in the family and they know it.

Uncle Joe says it's just the opposite, he's got the brains.
I'll tell you one thing for sure, Son, when this meeting is over, I'm really gonna put my foot down on some things they keep tellin' you 'bout your dad.
What's putting your foot down mean, Dad?
It means I'm running the show, no tellin' how far we can go preaching the gospel.

We're on our way to Mt. Vernon and Dad wants to talk 'bout meeting Reverend Mills and what I'm expected to do during the night's meeting. He says, Now listen, Son, this is one time I definitely want you to keep your mouth shut 'bout my name being Spare, 'cause I cain't afford you making mistakes. I'll probably be doing most of the preaching and you will be mostly used answering questions 'bout the Bible. When I place the pictures of you out front of the podium, I want you to stand back and watch. Your dad will handle the money and pictures. This is good experience for you, now do you understand, Son? I nod my head and tell him, Sure, I do Dad, I don't wanta be around anyone talking in tongues anyhow.

He seems kinda worried and says, Stop it, Son, stop it, I don't wanta hear anymore 'bout speaking in tongues, we'll worry 'bout that later; I just wish Maw and them wouldn't poison your young mind 'bout other churches. I thought he was a Pilgrim Holiness or Baptist and now he's talking Holy Roller stuff. Dad says, Son, it kind of makes me jittery when you say you understand and I don't know what Maw said to you before we left. I don't want Dad to feel jittery, so I tell him, Don't worry, Dad, Maw said people should understand each other when talking and she don't trust people who might be possessed of the devil. She told me to have a good time and tell the people the truth. Dad seems worried now, and I wonder what he means by some of the things he tells me.

After my nice heart to heart talk with Dad, we arrive in Mt. Vernon and walk to Reverend Mill's house. We are greeted at the door by the Reverend's wife, a very friendly, nice looking lady with a beautiful smile showing her pretty white teeth. The Reverend is a business type person and different than what I expected. He's friendly, wears glasses, a little paunchy and a little older. He's not much like his wife with her pleasant personality. He says, Lets' get down to business, Spare, tonight is gonna be big and there's a lot of people gonna be here to see your son. Are you ready for it? Dad says, I'm always ready, Brother Mills, and by the way, who told you I'm called Spare? Mills says, Don't worry 'bout that, when I introduce you in church it's gonna be Brother McCaffry, and I can understand why a man wouldn't wanta be called, Spare. There's gonna be some other preachers here tonight to help liven the place up, so don't be surprised if they wanta add something. Dad says, It don't bother me at all, 'cause I'm only here to spread the gospel.

Reverend Mills wants to know if being around people talking in tongues will bother me, and I tell him, It's not gonna bother me at all cause Maw told me not to pay any attention to it 'cause I'm a Pilgrim Holiness. Dad's acting real nervous, like he's got the jitters he talks 'bout, and says, My boy is usually around Baptists and Pilgrim Holiness, Brother Mills, but he knows all 'bout Pentecost. Mills says, I hope so, Spare, for the revival's sake.

Inside the church people are beginning to gather and soon it's filled to capacity. The small wooden church with the big bell hanging from the front on the outside is a place of high activity on this hot summer night. Dad and Brother Mills are enjoying every minute of the gathering crowd and people stand outside in the street hoping to get inside. A couple of other preachers have joined Dad and Brother Mills on the podium along with a couple of ladies with tambourines. A piano is on one side of the podium and another lady has begun practicing. I move towards the back of the podium and a couple church ladies wanta know if I'm gonna be preaching or just answering Bible questions. I tell 'em, I always do what Dad tells me, unless Maw tells me different, and they pat me on the head and kiss me on the forehead. One of 'em says, I would just give anything in the world if my kids were that way and other lady says, All my kids ever do is sass me back.

One big ceiling fan is operating full blast, but with the hot night and with the large crowd, a lot of sweating is going on. It's hot and humid and most of the ladies wear long dresses with long sleeves. All preachers on the podium have on white shirts, and remove their ties, and I'm the only one who hasn't worked up a sweat. This reminds me of Pilgrim Holiness women, but there's one here and who uses a lot of rouge, lipstick and everyone knows it.

Exactly at seven p.m., the meeting begins with Reverend Mills calling for everyone's attention with a couple of usual announcements, and then introduces Dad and me. Dad seems relieved when he calls him Brother McCaffry. A couple of good old-fashioned gospel songs ring out and the church immediately becomes alive with the sound of the piano music and two well dressed young ladies are banging away on tambourines. The podium shows a lot of enthusiasm with a couple of the visiting preachers moving back and forth across the front.

It's time for the collection and several men walk into the crowd and pass the offering plate. With The Great Depression in full swing, it's evident these people might be a little better off than the average church people. One of the visiting preachers comes forward and gives a short prayer saying the money will be used to carry on the church work and expenses.

Another song is sung and Reverend Mills comes forward and introduces us to the large crowd. He tells 'bout my preaching in Mt. Carmel and riding through the back-water at Big Creek, and turns the meeting over to

Dad. That's what Dad likes. He grabs his Bible in his right hand, takes over the meeting and says, We're all here tonight to praise the Lord, and anyone who isn't, better get ready to get saved. Me and this boy will show you what it takes is a good old case of The Old Time Religion. I hear a lot of amen's throughout the crowd. An attractive young lady sitting in the middle of the crowd gets a lot of attention when she jumps up and yells, That's, the kind of preaching I like preacher. She draws more attention for her painted face, short hair, and wonderful endowments and people look at her more than Dad. A gentleman sitting close by yells, You're right, Ruby, you tell 'em, kid. Dad's looking at Ruby, still holding his Bible in the air, and saying nothing.

Ruby sits down and the attention is again on the podium, Dad introduces me and begins the question and answer session. Now it's time for the audience to begin firing questions at me, and they sure do have a lot. Question after question comes to me and most of my answers are correct. Once in awhile as usual, someone brings up something in the Old Testament that causes me to say, I just don't know. People understand and many don't know the answers either. When the question and answer session is over, I give a short sermon on Adam and Eve explaining how it was the first sin ever. I follow through with how all humans there-after are born in sin from Adam's downfall and need the blood of Jesus Christ to take away sin. People believe it and know it's true and there is no shortage of amens and hallelujahs.

Dad begins his sermon preaching fire and brimstone and again the young lady down front becomes the most emotional person in the crowd. She leaves her seat when Dad says, We, have all sinned and come short of the glory of God and everyone begins singing **Give Me That Old Time Religion**. People are overcome with emotions throughout the church including those standing along the aisle and some begin talking in tongues and I don't like this part at all. Some of the women dressed in the long dresses and with the long hair wave their song books in the air and begin talking in tongues and the ladies are banging on tambourines. Dad's waving his Bible wildly in the air, sweat's pouring down his forehead, and his shirt is soaked with perspiration.

I move to the back of the podium when I see how emotional everyone has become, and wish I'm back in a Baptist church instead being with a bunch of Holy Rollers Maw warned me 'bout. Suddenly several people come running down the aisle waving their arms and heading towards the altar before the call is made, and I know Dad's not gonna like this 'cause he likes to give the altar call. Brother Mills sees it coming and takes over. Dad moves back towards me and says, Now, don't be afraid, it's just the way they worship in Pentecost churches, and I tell him I don't like it and I'm telling Maw 'bout this for sure. He don't answer 'cause he's watching the young lady, Ruby, running towards the altar waving her hands and yelling something sounding like **Kaseeniki, Kaseeniki** over and over, time and again. I ask Dad if she is speaking in tongues and he tells me he don't know, but it must be 'cause he cain't understand it either, and this is no time to bring it up.

The entire building is wild with singing and shouting and talkin' in tongues. Some are running up and down the aisle. Ruby lets herself go limp in front of the altar and falls on the floor wiggling back and forth with her arms stretched out high over her head. Her black free flowing skirt is up to her waist and she lies on the floor moving back and forth babbling the same words I heard before; **Kaseeniki, Kaseeniki**.

I'm standing back away from the altar, but notice Ruby's skirt is still up to her waist. I run to Dad and tell him, Ruby's bloomers are showing and you better go tell her or the whole church is gonna see it. He tells me he can see it and for me to not worry 'bout it. Dad says, Son, Just let me handle this matter, and they're not called bloomers, they're called panties. Dad moves to the floor where Ruby lies, holds her hand, and says, I'm with you, Sister, I'm with you, now cover yourself up and pray through. Dad should have covered her 'cause some of the other preachers are still looking at Ruby and finally Reverend Mills is pulling her skirt down.

Dad's at the podium and I tell him, Maw's never gonna let me come here again, I know she won't. She said if they don't know what each other is saying, it could be of the devil and I ain't wanting no part of that. Son, just shut up for once and please quit talkin' 'bout what Maw's gonna do and let me sell these pictures. I need the money bad, so don't interfere with my business, he says.

We're back to near normal, and Dad places my pictures on a table and people file by buying them for a dollar each. It's not long till all the pictures are gone and people want more. Dad says, There will be more tomorrow night, folks, just be here early. Ruby is up and walking around in the audience and giving inviting glances to Dad and he smiles at her glances eagerly. I've saw that kind of glance before and Aunt Dorie told me it's Dads' sheepish-look, and he has it just before he gets ready to sin real good. The meeting ends and we go outside the church. Here comes Ruby. She grabs Dad's arm and says, Preacher, you did a lot for me tonight and I'm on the straight and narrow path from now on.

Don't worry Sister Ruby, I'm gonna be there for you from now on.
Preacher, I've had some problems in the past.
That's my specialty, Sister, solving problems, be here tomorrow night and you'll see.
I'll be here, preacher, and you can count on it.
Ruby gives another inviting smile, wiggles her hip, gives Dad a hug and I don't like it.

We wait for Reverend Mills to come and close the church and out of nowhere I hear a kind of hissing sound from down near the end of the building. I see someone over in the shadows making a motion for us to come. Dad says, Do you see what I see, Son, over near the building? I tell him, I sure do, Dad, and he wants us to come over to him. Do you think we should, 'cause Uncle Joe says some guys don't think of your preaching too kindly? Dad says he's not worried 'cause he doesn't know anyone here in Mt. Vernon, 'cept the preacher. The man leans against the side of the building and we move to him after looking around for other guys. He says, I'm Howard G. Wilkens and I need to warn you 'bout something. Howard is a tall person 'bout six feet, very thin, and gaunt. He's dressed in a pair of bib overalls, a short sleeved blue denim shirt, and wears a big straw hat.

Dad looks him over good, and says, What, in the world seems to be the problem, Howard G? You look like you haven't got a friend left and I'm known to help a lot of people. Howard won't talk. I think he might talk to me and say, What's the G for Howard? He says, The G is for Gary, preacher boy, my dad wanted me to be named after his brother and my mother wanted me named after her brother, so they called me Howard Gary. I tell him, That sounds like a swell idea and I'll tell Maw and she may wanta do the same thing for one of us someday. Howard says, I really don't care for my Uncle Howard very much, but I really like my Uncle Gary. I'm gonna change it to Gary Howard. I like the idea of changing names and tell Howard. You sure are a smart guy. Howard says. You're smart as a whip preacher boy and you're one person that understands me. Dads listening, but not talking till he says, Brother Howard, I need to warn you 'bout my son, whatever you tell him, he's gonna tell Maw.

Dad gets closer and Howard comes out in the light where we can see him good. Howard says, I heard what went on here tonight and almost went up to the altar and I bought one of the preacher boy pitchers. Dad says, Howard my friend, why didn't you come to the altar, I could have solved all your problems right there? Howard says, That's the problem, preacher; when I was headed that way, I saw Ruby lying on the floor and she's my real problem. Dad says, What in the world are you talkin' 'bout, Howard Gary, that woman was praying through and I was helping her.

Howard's getting upset and walks further out in the open and says, Preacher, you just don't understand. That woman Ruby is like a wildcat and no man is ever gonna tame her. I've been trying to tame her for three months and I've lost almost everything. I used to weigh 'bout a hundred and eighty-five and now I'm down to one hundred forty-five. Howard is almost crying and looks rather pitiful. He keeps talking and says, You know, preacher boy, my own dear mother said, Howard, you're sure beginning to look like nothing but a stack of skin and bones, what in the world is happening to you? It really hurt coming from Mom. I feel sorry for Howard.

Howard, I know what you mean 'cause my Maw never says anything bad 'bout Dad, but my uncles make up for it.
Thanks, preacher boy, some of my friends are calling me Skinny and it's plumb embarrassing.
Don't let it bother you Howard G, Skinny ain't bad, I've got a cousin like you and we call him, Slim.

Dad says, Son, you stay outta this and don't call him Skinny. It's a matter of preacher and sinner. Howard says, Preacher, when I got down there near the altar and saw Ruby with her skirt up to her waist I knew there was no way I could handle it so I left. I tell Howard, I saw her bloomers and he says, Them ain't bloomers, preacher boy, they're real silk panties and they came all the way from China. Dad don't wanta hear any more 'bout Ruby 'cause he's gonna try and get her straightened out.

Howard is holding his hands on his head like he's in pain and says, I don't know what in the world I'm gonna do. I've gotta wife and four kids on a farm down in the river bottoms, and I just don't know which way to turn. I thought 'bout bootlegging, but the new President Roosevelt is gonna make booze legal. I don't want Howard to get in trouble so I tell him, Don't, do that, Howard, 'cause my Uncle Joe just got out of Pendleton Penitentiary for bootlegging and he was in there for six months and the food was bad. When he got home we treated him just like The Prodigal Son and we all forgave him. Howard says, I'd like to be treated like The Prodigal Son account of what me and Ruby did, preacher boy, but I don't think it's gonna happen with my mom.

Dad says, Howard, I've got your problem solved. You don't have to worry no more. You just go home to your wife and kids and I'll take care of that woman, Ruby. I'll try to see what her problem is, and rest assured I know how to solve it now that she's saved. I'm wondering what in the world he's talking 'bout. I'm not so sure 'bout Dad solving her problem and tell him, Dad, it looks to me like she might be one of them women like Delilah or Jezebel Maw talks 'bout. He says, That's my problem; not yours, Son, and I'm gonna solve Howard's problem. Just remember this, Son, there's no woman with a problem your old dad can't handle.

Reverend Mills closes church and we stay the night with him and his family. The following night begins like the previous night and even more people stand outside waiting for me to answer Bible questions and preach. The meeting begins as the night before with emotions, talking in tongues, wild flailing of arms, and some running up and down the aisle. Ruby sits in the front row and Dad greets her with a couple of hugs. She is dressed like a movie star with rouge and lipstick on her face and her short bobbed-hair makes her stand out amongst the crowd. She crosses her legs and her short skirt expose more than normal while other preachers watch with Dad.

I do my usual questions and answers, preach on the coming of the Lord and how everyone needs to be ready. Dad gives some more fire and brimstone comments and the service heats up with a lot of amens and hallelujahs, and the altar call is given. I look to see if Howard Gary is around, but he's evidently gone home to his wife and four kids. I tell Dad, Howard Gary ain't here, so don't forget what he told you 'bout Ruby being a wildcat. Dad says, I'm keeping my eyes right on her and I've told you before not to worry 'cause I know how to handle her for sure. Ruby is starting to talk in tongues again and I ask Dad if he understands what she's trying to say. Dad's not happy again, and says, Listen to me, Son, I've told you before I don't understand tongue language or whatever it is. If they wanta talk that way, I just don't care, now let's forget it.

All the pictures sell out again and several people come forward and kneel at the altar. The meeting ends, Reverend Mills needs to get home earlier than usual. Everyone thanks us for being there for the two nights, and other preachers come to us and shake hands and everyone takes off for home.

A car is parked and waiting for us; when I open the door I get a surprise. There sits Ruby in the back seat and a driver in front. She says, Hello there, Sonny Boy, my name is Ruby. She don't need to tell me her name, everybody knows Ruby. She's the one who runs down the aisle yelling and talking in tongues. I tell her, Howard Gary told me 'bout you ma'am and she says, Oh, that old Howard, he's such a blabber-mouth, there's no tellin' what in the world he might tell you. I don't really wanta talk to her, but I must 'cause she's here in our car.

He said you were like a wildcat, do you know what it means?
Did he really say that 'bout me, young man? I don't know why in the world he would get that opinion of me. I just try to live a happy and full life and now I'm even saved.
Howard Gary's gone home to his wife and kids, ma'am.
What do you mean, young man, I didn't have the slightest idea Howard was married.
Yep, he sure is, Miss Ruby, and he's got four kids. His own mom said he looked like skin and bones and some of his best friends call him, Skinny.
Well, it's all Howard's own fault, 'cause he always took things far too serious.

We're heading for Evansville and Ruby says, Preacher, is it O.K. if I call you, Spare? Dad says, Sure it is, Ruby, when I'm close with somebody, I understand how it is and what it means. I laugh and ask Dad, Where we going; it looks like we're headed towards Evansville and Ruby's still with us? He acts like he can't hear me, so I'll ask him again and he says, She, sure is, Son, I'm taking you home to Maw and then I can give some personal counseling to Ruby. I tell him, O.K., Dad, I'm kind of glad to go home with Maw and Uncle Joe anyhow. Maw said I was to remind you to pay your board before I get outta the car. She said you owe her two weeks already and if you get any money, I need to bring it to her. Dad's not looking happy again 'cause he doesn't like to talk 'bout money in front of people and I know it. He says, Son, sometimes you kinda get your old Dad embarrassed when you say such things in front of people. He pulls out a handful of bills, counts out thirty dollars, hands it to me, and says, Take this and give it to Maw and be sure and tell all your uncles and aunts I paid my board. I tell him, they're gonna believe it, Dad, 'cause I've got the money to prove it. I know he's not happy, but I've got Maw's money, and she needs it more than Ruby.

Dad's seated between me and Ruby as we speed down the highway. A half moon lights up the sky. There's little light, but I can tell something's going on between Dad and Ruby. She's cuddles up to him with his arm around her and several times he kisses her on the neck and she's letting out giggling sounds. I'm getting angry and it's time to stop all their pleasure, 'cause Maw warned me these kind of actions can get out of control and most time it's caused by the devil.

I've gotta let Miss Ruby understand how I feel, so I tell her, I hope you know you're never gonna be a member of the Pilgrim Holiness Church till you stop talking in tongues, wiggling around on the floor, and keeping your dress down. I know she'd probably like to join our church and that's our rules. Suddenly the petting and kissing stops, and Dad and Ruby straighten up in the seat. Ruby seems a little angry and says, Listen, Sonny Boy, I ain't got no idea of joining your Pilgrim Holiness Church anyhow, ain't that right honey? Dad says, I guess you should join the Pentecost honey, 'cause Brother Mills will let you talk in tongues and you can run up and down the aisle all as much as you like. Ruby says, Thank you, darlin', I'm glad you took my side. I know, Dad, will say anything to get close to Ruby.

I can tell Dad's getting a little upset and wanting to get me home as soon as possible. He yells, Driver, can you speed up a little, the boy needs to get home and get to bed. He yells back, Dammit, preacher, I've got this baby down to the floorboard now. Hell, we're goin' almost forty-five miles an hour. I still wanta let Ruby know I don't like what I'm seeing and say, Miss Ruby, I'm not your Sonny Boy, and I'm gonna ask Maw to put you on her Ladies Group prayer list. That always works at home real good. Dads' squirming all over the back seat and says, Oh Lord, oh Lord, not that, Son. Ruby's temper is running high, and she says, I don't have the slightest idea what you're talkin' 'bout, and the last thing in the world I want is to get on any list of a bunch of Bible-toting Pilgrim Holiness grand maws. Dads trying to console Ruby, and says, I guess I'm gonna have to put my foot down someday on my son and let him know who's the boss. Ruby smiles and looks pleased. She says, I sure hope you do honey, and I wanta be there when you do. I'm looking out the window into the night and laugh. I don't care what they do, I just wanta get home.

I'm home and glad. I open the car door and slam it shut, and ask, When are you coming home, Dad? He says, Son you're in good hands with Maw, so don't worry 'bout your old dad. I tell him, I never do, I'm getting like Maw, I'm thinking 'bout turning you over to the Lord. I head for the house and the car takes off for Mt. Vernon. Ruby keeps yelling over and over, Good bye Sonny Boy, good bye Sonny Boy! I never look back, and hope I never meet Ruby the wildcat woman again.

The following morning everyone wants to hear 'bout the meeting in the Holey Roller church and whether Dad paid his board. I wave the thirty bucks in the air, hand it to Maw, and tell them, Dad sure paid his board this time; now he's counseling a lady called Ruby and she's like a wildcat. I explain how Ruby got saved; everyone talked in tongues saying the word **kaseeniki** over and over and how Dad got lots of money selling my pictures. Maw says, One thing for sure, he'll be riding high for 'bout a week and when the money's gone, he'll be home. Joe says, I sure feel sorry for that poor girl, Ruby. Maw wants to know why, and he says, No human being on earth deserves brother Spare with all that money. I tell Maw, Ruby ran down to the altar to get saved, fell on the floor, and began talking in tongues. She was rolling around and wiggling on the floor, her skirt went up almost to her belly, and you could see her silk panties; Howard Gary said they came all the way from China. Maw throws up her arms and says, Goodness gracious child what kinda church service did you get yourself involved in? I try to tell her it wasn't my fault, but she doesn't know what it was like being with a bunch of wild people. She's still upset and tells me, Please, Son, just hush, I don't wanta hear any more 'bout went on with them people, and that woman's silk panties, and they're nothing but a pair of ladies drawers. I don't really care 'bout Ruby's drawers, but I still don't know whether to call them drawers or panties. Maw is leaving the room muttering to her self and Uncle Orie says, Spare can handle any woman if he doesn't kill himself first. Dorie says, She sure sounds like nothing but a hussy to me; we all nod our heads yes, and we're all happy.

Everybody leaves and Maw and me are alone. She puts her arms around me and says, Son, there's something I have to tell you that breaks my heart. There was an accident in the street yesterday and your best pal and friend was killed when he took off running after our iceman's truck. I don't know if she's talking 'bout Bob or Bull till she says, Several people saw it and agreed it was all the fault of your dog, Bull. I still don't know. She's starting to cry and continues on saying, After it happened our iceman, Sam Gander, came in the house almost crying, and said Bull was running after his truck and got under the wheels. Now I know it was Bull; Maw talks slow sometime and if she cries, it's worse. She continues, Bob and some of your friends said they saw it happen, and Sam couldn't help it. Bob cared for him, but he died right away and didn't suffer. I sure didn't wanta see him in pain, and I'll miss him a lot; he was such a good dog. Maw says, I'll say one thing good for old Bull, we never had any scraps go to waste as long as he was around.

It's hard to hold back the tears and were both crying and finally, I'm able to speak. I ask, What did Bob do with him? She says, They took him to an empty field, dug a big deep hole, and covered him over so no animals can get to him. They placed a cross and covered the grave with dirt and large rock. Bob knew you would want some words said 'bout Bull, so he told everyone you and him believe dogs are gonna be in heaven just like lions and lambs, though animals don't have souls like humans. Cotton was there to say some good words 'bout Bull along with your cousins Sissy, Pat and Evelyn. They were crying, 'long with Bob. I ask, Was cousin Titties there, Maw? She says, Yes, he was there, but I understand he had some doubts 'bout Bull goin' to heaven. I tell her, I guess Titties never did forgive Bull for almost p-i-s-s-i-n-g on him in the barn and he probably wouldn't wanta be in heaven with him, either. I always hafta spell vulgar words for Maw.

I'm satisfied Bull is resting in peace, but I still need to see for myself and pay my respects. The field where he lies in his little grave looks barren 'cept for the rocks and a nice cross to show he would have been Christian if he had a soul. I know if he had a soul he would be a Pilgrim Holiness, just like the rest of us. I need to say some good words 'bout Bull myself and I can only think of him bringing me the big toad frog. I look around and there stands my buddy, Bob. I tell him, Thanks for taking care of Bull. Bob is still sad, and soon we head for home. Bob says, Do, you think you'll get another dog, Bid? I'm sure there's never gonna be another dog in my life and say, No I sure don't, Bob, and I'll never love another dog like Bull. We walk a little farther, and Bob says, I know a girl over on the next street whose dog just had six puppies and they're real cute German Shepherd dogs. She wanted to give me one, but Mom wouldn't let me bring it home. I think 'bout Bob's wishes and say, Bob, it might not hurt to just go take a look at some cute German Shepherd pups, even though I know we won't want any.

We're on our way home with a new dog and we name her, Lady, 'cause she looks real good and better than most dogs. I can already tell she's not exactly like Bull, 'cause she squats when she pisses. Maw agrees she's a very pretty and cute puppy, but wonders if she can eat scraps like, Bull. We're happy again, and soon everyone loves Lady, even Cousin Titties.

Uncle Orie plays baseball for Fendrich Cigar Company. They're the best in town and everyone knows it. Sunday afternoon we all go watch Uncle Orie play baseball at the Bucyrus Erie baseball field and Pat says he is the best second baseman in Evansville 'cause nobody can field, hit, run and fight as good as his dad. He's got one problem everybody knows 'bout; when he gets mad his neck starts swelling and Dad and Uncle Joe always walk away from him when that happens. Uncle Joe tells me Orie is one swell brother till he gets mad; Dad says the same.

Heiney Schneider owns the land we go thru to get to the park and charges a dime to pass. He carrys a bucket of drinks around the park all afternoon yelling "SOFT DRINKS, SOFT DRINKS' LAST TIME AROUND' and makes us think he's gonna run outta drinks; but he never does. Everybody says he is the grouchiest guy in the whole park and he shouldn't have the right to charge to hear him moan and groan 'bout everything.

The hot sun beats down and we're all rooting for, Orie. It's the bottom of the ninth inning with the score tied. Orie is at bat with one man on and we are yelling, "Put it in the cat-tails, Orie, put it in the cat-tails." He swings, and BAM! There it goes just to the edge of the cat-tails and Orie is speeding 'round the bases with the crowd cheering and Pat and me are running to greet him at home plate. He slides and dust flies everywhere and the umpire hollers, You're out, You're out, and the park is silent while Orie is dusting himself off and heading for the umpire. I see his neck beginning to swell; this ain't good and everyone knows it. People are booing the umpire and Uncle Orie is up in his face cussing him while Pat and me agree with what he's saying. It's finally over and we lose, but Orie is still mad and Dad and Uncle Joe are afraid to talk to him 'cause his neck is still swollen.

When we get home Maw asks how the game went and Pat says, Maw if Dad only hit it a little further all the way to the cat-tails we would have won for sure, but the umpire was pullin' for their side and we lost. I agree and now we're gonna wait till we play 'em again and it's gonna be a different game with a different umpire.

Ora McCaffry
Top left (sitting)

14

WORLD'S FAIR

It's the summer of 1933. The Great Depression is going on and everyone's read 'bout the Chicago Worlds Fair. Uncle Orie and his family are here at Maw's house and want me to go with them. Pat's hollering, Let Bid go, Maw, let him go, Lady is barking and to me it's like a dream come true. Uncle Orie says, Maw, let the boy go and have a good time, Spare sure as hell can get by preaching for five days, if he ever shows back up from Mt. Vernon. You don't need to worry 'bout the money, 'cause we've been saving some money and my boss just gave me a raise and made me a foreman at Fendrich Cigar Company.

I tell Maw, I'd sure like to ride the big roller coaster I've been reading 'bout in the newspaper, and I've got money of my own. She says, Son, it's 'bout time to get away from your dad for a while, go have yourself a good time and yuh better do just exactly like your Aunt Dorie and Uncle Orie tell you. I'm a little worried what Dad might say and ask Maw how she's gonna tell him. She says, Don't you worry one bit. Anyone deserves a vacation after putting up with your dad and Holy Rollers. Joe says, Hell, he won't even know you're gone unless he needs you to preach somewhere. A couple of kids giggle and Maw says, Start gettin' your things together and stay with your uncle and his family till you leave. Everyone is smiling and nobody more than me. We leave, and Maw is yelling out the door at me to watch my manners, wash behind my ears, and above all, obey my aunt and uncle.

Uncle Orie is far better off in life than Dad and Uncle Joe. He's a boss at Fendrich Cigar Company in Evansville, and during the height of the

Depression, it's a job many people desire. He's prosperous enough to afford a new Ford and our trip to Chicago three hundred miles away. We're gonna stay with Aunt Dorie's brother and sister in law, Mr. and Mrs. Harvey Schumacher for the entire week.

We're up early the following morning, and Orie, Dorie, Pat, Evelyn, Kathryn and me jump in the new Ford with Pat in the front with parents and the rest of us in the back. We don't have a worry in the world and we're gonna have one big time vacation. Life can be no better for the McCaffry family; though the entire country is in big trouble.

The early morning air is nice and refreshing as it blows through the girls' hair. The new Ford is whizzing down the highway 'bout forty miles an hour. The conversation is mostly 'bout what we're all gonna do in Chicago till Evelyn says, Mom, I don't think I can hold it any longer, I've gotta pee bad. Aunt Dorie's not pleased and says, Honey, I told everyone to go before we left and we're no more than ten miles down the road, don't you think you can make it to the next gas station? Evelyn says, I cain't, Mom, I need to go bad. Pat says, We better let her go, 'cause I know how she is. Dorie says, Orie, stop up the road when you see some woods, and we'll let her out. I think I'll go with her, says Kathryn and now, Pat and me might as well go too. The car comes to a halt and we're running down the road heading for the nearest trees. It's not long till we're back in the car and sailing down the highway.

The trip to Chicago is not without further complaints. Kathryn says, Mom, Pat's spitting between the gap in his two front teeth, and it's hitting me in the face. Make him quit it, or I'm coming in the front, and he can sit in the back. I can tell she's disgusted with Pat, and Pat says, I cain't help it, Mom, honest I cain't. I've got to spit when the wind and dust hits me in the face; I know Pat don't like to ride in the back. Dorie says, You kids are just gonna to have to make out and furthermore, I don't hear no complaints from Evelyn or Bid, unless she has to pee again. Pat says, Evelyn won't have to go no more 'cause three times is usually her limit, and we've already stopped three times just for her.

We're halfway to Chicago, and everyone has settled down 'cept for Pat's spitting and Kathryn's complaining. Aunt Dorie wants to sing some good old gospel songs, but Orie says he don't like gospel 'cause Maw made him sit in church and sing Christian songs if he wanted to or not. He wants to sing "Yankee Doodle Dandy", so we sing "Yankee Doodle Dandy". We sing more songs and Dorie says she better quit 'cause she might be losing her voice and we are stopping to eat soon. We pull over in a wooded park area and eat lunch. It's quiet and we're tired, and finally we settle down in the back seat and it's nap time. Kathryn has quit complaining 'bout Pat's spitting for some time and everybody is happy. Late in the afternoon, we finally arrive at Harvey and Mabel's house in Chicago. I'm introduced as their favorite cousin, they hug me and I feel welcome. Harvey is tall and slim with a slight balding head of dark hair, and my new Aunt Mabel is slightly shorter with dark hair, and kinda fast to speak her mind telling what she thinks. She's almost as fast as Aunt Dorie.

Mabel asks, Dorie, is he the boy who answers all the Bible questions and preaches with his Dad?
Yes, he's a fine boy, and we felt he needed some time off from his home life.
I've heard a lot 'bout his father, where's he at?
Preaching, and chasing every split tail he can find.
What 'bout his Uncle Joe? Is he still bootleggin'?
Still bootleggin' and chasing skirts.
That bad, huh, Dorie, it must really be bad for his mother.
Maw is a saint if there ever was one; she just turns 'em over to the Lord when they get acting wild.
Do you think they'll ever change, Dorie?
It's up to the Lord. I just give thanks to the Lord every day that I've got my Orie; and not something like his brothers, the wild ones.

I've noticed the boy seems to speak well and pronounces his words well; far better than other kids.

Yes, he does Mabel, and I think his teacher at school talked to him 'bout it, and now Pat is complaining to me he cain't understand him sometimes.

Well, I guess we could all use some help at times.

His father and uncle could use a lot of help, dearie.

I guess we're just blessed with men like Harvey and Orie, Dorie.

You're right, dear, the Lord has blessed us; I know it for sure when I look at those two wild brothers of Orie's.

Pat and me are listening and I wonder if this is what vacation time is like, 'cause this is what we hear at home. We came here to go on the roller coaster, ride the Ferris wheel, watch Sally Rand do her famous fan dance, and see the skimpy bathing suits at the beach.

The following day, our families take off for a nearby park and enjoy a picnic and games. Everything's going as planned, but the big day at the fair is talked 'bout constantly. Wednesday is Lake Michigan Day at the beach and everyone but Dorie joins in the fun. She sees the skimpy bathing suits everyone is wearing, and says, If someone in church would ever see me cavorting around in a crowd like this, my name would be taken off the books. Cousin Evelyn likes the bathing suits the same as Pat and me, and says she wouldn't mind at all, and Uncle Orie isn't saying anything, but we see him staring at the girls just like us.

Thursday is Fair Day and it's what everyone is waiting for. Pat and me are waiting to hear Aunt Dorie lecture us on being good boys and girls. She says, Children, I want everyone to know we're in a big town and there's no tellin' what goes on at a fair with all the sideshows, and so forth. I want everyone to behave as good Christians, 'cept you Orie, I know you're gonna let your eyes stray everywhere, as most men do.

We stand outside the fair gate looking in awe at its bigness. Pat says, This, is gonna be the best day of our lives, Bid, so let's do everything we read 'bout in the paper or we may never get another chance. Aunt Dorie wants us to ask Orie if there's something we don't understand, 'cause he's supposed to know everything there is to know on earth, but not in heaven.

Yelling and music is blaring so loud it's hard to hear in front of the tents and games outside. Guys wave long sticks and point to signs on the front of the shows showing half naked women, and Aunt Dorie won't look, but we do. They're barking out what to expect inside the shows if you buy a ticket, and Pat and me got our money ready if they let us go. Young ladies stand outside tents dressed scantilly, moving their bodies back and forth to the tune of island music. Evelyn begins moving her hips as they do. Aunt Dorie sees her twisting her butt, and yells, Stop it this minute young girl, don't you ever let me see you act like them, hussies. Orie starts to move closer, but Dorie pulls him back. Pat and me agree; if we don't go inside one of the tents today, someday we'll go and see it all.

Dorie says, Let's quit wandering around everywhere and get goin' on the roller coaster. Everyone is ready and we begin our walk through the fairgrounds looking for the roller coaster and Ferris wheel, and it's not long till we stand looking up directly in front of the coaster. It's everything we imagined, only bigger. We watch people go roaring by screaming and yelling as the coaster keeps diving up and down in front of us. I don't think Aunt Dorie is liking this, but we're here and everyone is gonna go on the coaster as planned. It finally stops in front of us and people get off looking kinda sick, and Evelyn says she's not so sure 'bout getting aboard.

Pat and me are first to load. Dorie says, Children, if you get scared just think of something nice you like and it'll go away. An attendant comes, and we hand him our ticket as he checks the bar in front of us and says, Good luck and hang on. That doesn't sound so good. The rest of the family sits in front of us, while Evelyn is almost in tears. Uncle Orie says, There's nothin' in the world to worry 'bout 'cause people are doing the same thing here every day; don't let it be said that the McCaffry family is chicken.

Suddenly, the roller coaster begins to move slowly and gradually increases speed till we're zooming up and down and around at break-neck speed. The down hills and up hills movement of the huge ride is fast and breath-taking and it's hard to hold onto the bar. Everyone is shouting and screaming as the coaster hits the curves and heads straight down time and time again. Me and Pat begin to wonder if it's ever gonna stop. Evelyn and Kathryn's hair is flying straight back as we move to the top of the coaster and go plunging straight down in a wild frenzy. Pat and me are holding on to the bar in front of us for dear life, and suddenly the coaster slows and comes to a halt. My knees feel weak and I'd like to puke, but I cain't. Pat's sick too, but he cain't talk. I look at the others and they're the same as us. Uncle Orie walks away from us and says, Nothing, to it, kids, just like riding in a boat. Pat and me don't believe him, 'cause he's looking sick like the rest of us. Aunt Dorie looks better than any of us and says, Kids, just get yourself together and we'll go ride the Ferris wheel.

Kathryn and Evelyn take care of their business in the restroom and we gather outside the coaster entrance. Orie says, Gang, where do we go from here? Pat and me are ready to go see Sally Rand do her famous fan dance that Uncle Joe told us all 'bout, and Uncle Orie thinks it's a swell idea. Dorie says, Nobody in this bunch is gonna pay good money to go see some hussy shake her fanny just to get men excited. The only hussy I know is Ruby, the wildcat woman, and she showed herself a lot like some of the ladies here. Pat shakes his head, spits between his teeth, and says, Bid, if Mom doesn't like the idea there's no way in the world we're gonna see her 'cause she makes the rules. I know that's true, cause it's exactly what Uncle Joe told Cotton at Hart Lines.

Dorie says, I'm sorry, boys, but I know all 'bout that hussy, Sally Rand, and her famous dance. We talk 'bout it at our prayer group and it's a sign this world is coming to nothing but sin and temptation. Pat says, Uncle

Joe says the same thing, only he likes it. Dorie is getting like Maw gets sometime, kinda aggravated, and Pat and me won't get involved. Dorie says, Joe's like all men, they think of nothing but one thing and this is no place to lecture you and that's, that. I think Aunt Dorie is getting a little more upset, and she says, We're gonna discuss this at home where all these people around us aren't listening, and by the way, I know who put you boys up to this. It's none other than your Uncle Joe.

We move to the Ferris wheel, and it's just as exciting. Aunt Dorie says, Children, this is the kind of entertainment that's not sinful, so get on and enjoy yourselves and I'm just gonna watch this time. We load up and it begins moving high in the air and it feels like were standing on our heads. It spins 'round and 'round while music plays. It's fun beyond compare, but the girls are yelling to get off and Evelyn yells in front of us, I've gotta pee bad, and I cain't wait. Pat says, I had a feelin' this was comin'. She'll do it every time, Bid, I know just how she is. I think she did, but we're still going 'round and 'round.

Finally it stops, and Pat and me sit atop the huge Ferris wheel and no way to get off till everyone gets off ahead of us. It makes us a little dizzy looking down, but we ain't saying, nothing. Pat's starting to spit between his two front teeth again, and I see someone looking up at us acting kinda mad. We both wanta get down bad, and they're getting off slow.

We finally unload and the rest of the day is wonderful looking at all the side shows. We listen to barkers outside the tents trying to entice us inside to see some people called freaks; or someone who can tell our fortune or foresee our future. We try every kind of food and drink we can hold in our stomach and agree this is the place to find it. Pat says, Bid, when we get home and tell our friends 'bout the roller coaster and Ferris wheel do you think they'll believe us? I tell him, It doesn't matter, Pat, 'cause we have seen the wonders of the world. The only thing is that we didn't see Sally Rand do her famous fan dance.

We bid farewell to Uncle Harvey and Aunt Mabel the following morning after lots of hugs, kisses, and they promise to come to Evansville. I want 'em to meet my family like Maw, Uncle Joe, my dog Lady, and maybe Dad. We take off in the new Ford and they're still waving us goodbye as we round the corner. Everyone has quit complaining 'bout coaster sickness, Evelyn says she's not gonna say anything 'bout peeing, and Pats gonna stop spitting out the window. Things look pretty good for the ride home, and now we can all take a snooze. Pat says, Mom if we ever take another trip we need to bring a can for Evelyn. We agree and Orie says, Amen, and halleluja.

We arrive home 'bout sundown and I give Aunt Dorie and Uncle Orie a hug and head home. Maw's at the door and says, I was gettin' a little worried 'bout you, Son, but I knew the Lord was watching out for yuh. I tell her all 'bout my trip to the fair, the trip to the beach, and how the barkers stand outside the tents and wanted us to come in while the island girls dance and sway their hips. Uncle Joe is listening and says, How 'bout Sally Rand? I tell him all 'bout how Aunt Dorie wouldn't let us go 'cause it's a sin and she called her a hussy. He says, Hell's fire, that woman spoils everything. Maw says, Praise the Lord for Dorie, she's the only one with good sense and morals; if they left it up to Orie, you'd probably still be up there watching hussies shaking and twisting their rear ends.

Maws not done yet, and says, One thing I can say for Dorie, is that she stands up for God and knows sin when she sees it. I'm sure she's gonna tell us 'bout it at the next prayer group meeting. Uncle Joe shakes his head and says, Amen, Maw, that's for sure and we'll hear 'bout it again and again. I ask 'bout, Dad, and Maw says, Son, I haven't heard from that father of yours since he took off for Mt. Vernon with that wildcat you told me 'bout. I ask, Maw, Dad said he was gonna counsel her, what does it mean? Uncle Joe is laughing real loud and Maw turns away from me, and won't answer. Joe says, Spare's counseling her, but not the way most people do. I still don't understand what Uncle Joe means, but maybe Uncle Orie will tell me later. Now it's time for me to check on Lady. When she sees me her tail starts wagging a mile a minute. Bull, could never do that for sure 'cause he didn't have a tail.

The next morning Maw leaves early for the prayer group meeting and Uncle Joe and me are left alone. He seems upset. I can always tell 'cause he's not talking or joking 'bout something. I ask, Is there something bothering you, Uncle Joe? He says, Yes there is, Bid, it's your dad. I wonder what in the world could Dad do that makes Uncle Joe this way. He says, Son, you're dad is goin' 'round bragging to everyone that he's not number one on Maw's list anymore, and I'm number one. If he ever gets back from Mt. Vernon and I find him, I'm gonna whip his ass for sure. I can tell Uncle Joe is real mad and he says, he doesn't mind being on the list, but there's no way in hell he should be ahead of Dad. I ask him if he has any idea how we can find him. Joe says, Hell no, I've looked everyplace he usually hangs out, but he's got to be outta town. He's probably with that crazy woman in Mt. Vernon, but nobody can find her either. I don't know what to say. I tell him, I see Maw's list all the time when we kneel down by her bed and pray before going to bed, and Dad is always number one unless he's preaching. Uncle Joe is smiling, and says, That's the way I see it too, he should be there forever, not me. I tell him, Dad, is usually first, you second, Cotton third, Slim fourth, and Titties fifth, and there lots of others that I don't even know. Uncle Joe seems a lot happier now.

Now he wants to talk 'bout something else. Joe says, Son, you're just gonna have to do something 'bout that old hound dog you and Bob brought home and put in the shed. I ask, You, mean Old Brownie? Joe says, Yeh, I guess, Old Brownie, but he's laying in the shed dying with the mange, and nobody in the world is gonna save that dog. If you don't do something fast he's gonna give it to Lady, and that'll be the end of her. I tell him, Uncle Joe, I could never just walk off and leave Old Brownie to die all by himself in the old barn we found him. People just ran off and left him to die all alone. Uncle Joe don't wanta hear 'bout that, and tells me to get the shot gun outta the closet, take him out someplace, and shoot him.

I'm thinking 'bout what he said. I've never before did something like this; it could be a sin that will send me to hell. Uncle Joe doesn't care; he just wants me to do it, and quick. He's never told me wrong, so I'll do it. I go to the closet, pick up the single barrel sixteen gague, two shells, and head for the shed. When I look at Brownie, I almost wanta cry, 'cause he almost looks dead, and I feel sorry for him. I'm beginning to wonder if I'm 'bout to commit a sin or doing him a favor by shooting him.

This is something I've got to do, no matter what happens, 'cause Brownie is suffering and I'm in trouble 'cause Maw don't know 'bout it. I pick him up gently and try not to hurt him while loading him in the wagon. I know a field Uncle Shave takes me to hunt rabbits, and that's gonna be his buriel place. It's not a good trip to the field and I think 'bout how poor Old Brownie probably never had a good day in his life, 'cept the times he probably was chasing rabbits. It makes me think 'bout how important it is to always take good care of our best friends like dogs and sometimes cats. I'm thinking all the way 'bout the sin I might be committing, and poor Old Brownie doesn't even move or open his eyes.

We arrive at the spot under a big Oak tree and I put Brownie on the ground; he doesn't make a sound. I think maybe he's already dead. I dig his grave deep, step back a few steps, and look at Old Brownie for the last time with tears in my eyes; I pull the trigger. Brownie doesn't move and I see the blood, but don't wanta look at it. I have to do what Uncle Joe said, but it's the hardest thing I've ever done and Maw doesn't even know 'bout it. When I get home, Uncle Joe is still at the kitchen table.

He asks, Did you do your job, Son?
Yes, but don't ever tell me to do it again.
Is there something wrong, Bid?
I don't know how to tell him it's wrong, and say nothing, I'll check on my dog, Lady.

Maw comes home a little later and says, Son, What's happened to that old hound dog in the shed? I'm in trouble for sure now, but I hafta tell her the truth. Well, Maw, I had to take Old Brownie out and shoot him 'cause he had the mange real bad, and I was afraid he might give it to, Lady. Was that a sin, Maw? She says, No, darling, that was no sin 'cause he didn't have a soul, and you put him out of his misery. You did put the shotgun away, didn't you darling? I tell her I sure did and even cleaned it. Maw says, That's fine, Son, always clean up things when you're done.

15

VISITING KENTUCKY RELATIVES

Dad gives me the poke and nod signal after dinner on Sunday. We go outside the house to talk and he says, We're goin' to visit my Uncle Jack and Aunt Becky at their farm in Spottsville, Kentucky, 'bout twenty miles away. He says they're my momma's relatives, he knows 'em well. We'll have one good time going to church, preaching and eating watermelon grown on the farm. It sounds good to me. He warns me not to mention Maw or my home life when get there and I promise him I'll never mention them one time, but he don't believe it 'cause I can tell by the way he looks. I ask him when we're leaving and he says, Monday morning, Son, and when we get to downtown Henderson, they'll be waiting for us. I know where Henderson is 'cause that's where Dad had me preaching and answering questions in the city park. Now, I need to tell Maw and she can get my things ready to visit my Kentucky relatives for the first time.

Monday morning early, we leave from the Evansville Bus Station. Thirty minutes later, we arrive in Henderson where I meet another uncle for the first time. They are Uncle Jack, Aunt Becky, cousins, George, Ray, Francis and Louise. This is the family I've never been told much 'bout 'cept what Maw mentioned. We all hug and kiss and they begin telling me things 'bout my mother I've never heard and I love it. They keep telling me stories 'bout my mother during the trip home to the farm and Dad says nothing.

The young girls are both dressed in long print dresses, short sleeves, and wear no shoes. Both boys wear bib overalls, and no shirts or shoes. The boys are kinda tall and skinny looking and both have a few freckles splattered on their faces. The girls are kinda skinny, long dark hair, beautiful white teeth and have better manners than their brothers. They call Dad, Uncle Spare, and laugh for some reason. I throw my shirt and shoes in the corner of the truck and we talk 'bout what we're gonna be doing next week. It's not long till I can see that Ray is by far the most fun loving cousin of the four. He's got a little glint of mischief in his eyes, and I know I'm gonna like Ray, 'cause he's like my cousins at home. I'm looking forward to being with my Kentucky relatives for the first time in my entire life.

We travel in an old Ford truck from Henderson to the family farm 'bout twenty miles from Henderson. We turn off the main road and down a dusty narrow lane and there's a small frame house in need of paint and lots of repairs. I can see this house has a lot of love and welcome. There are two bedrooms upstairs and a bedroom/living room combination with an adjoining kitchen downstairs. The living room looks comfortable, and you can tell this is where the family spends a lot of time.

Aunt Becky says, Bid, you just make yourself at home and you can sleep upstairs with the boys; Arthur you can sleep in the back room that we call our guest room. Arthur, do you want us to call you Spare? I tell 'em, Call him Spare, 'cause that's all they ever call him at home. Jack says, O.K., it's Spare then. Dad is looking at me and I know he's praying I don't say anything more 'bout home. He's muttering something to himself and it might be 'bout me.

After supper, we go outside and sit on the front porch, and talk 'bout my mother and all the good times they all had together as children. It excites me and I let them know how much I like to hear 'em talk 'bout her. I tell 'em when I'm here on the farm it's almost like being around my mother, even if I cain't remember her. Aunt Becky says, Your mother was a pleasure to be around, and I know she is here in spirit. Her spirit comes from heaven. I try to picture her in my mind and think how she might have run through the house and out onto the porch where I sit, but it's only imagination.

The hot summer air is beginning to cool off from the blistering sun, and a nice breeze is blowing across the front porch. Ray and George appear with a tub and it has the biggest watermelon I've ever seen covered with ice. Jack says, This is how we grow 'em in Kentucky, Bid, and they're sweet as watermelons come. It's not long till we're all eating watermelon, and laughing at some of the jokes Dad is telling. We might even sing some country or gospel songs before the evening is over. I've already decided I like Kentucky living.

Aunt Becky asks, Are you happy living with your dad's folks in Evansville, Bid? I tell her, Maw is just like a momma to me and my uncles and aunts are that way, too. Dad gives me the big poke real good on my side. I'm getting good at knowing 'bout the big poke. I know he's hoping to God I won't bring up anything else 'bout Maw. He always does that to me when he wants me to shut up. I take the signal and say no more 'bout Maw till Becky says, Your maw must be some kind of saint. I tell her, Aunt Dorie called her a saint when I was at the Chicago Worlds fair and Aunt Mabel thought the same thing. Now Dad is really getting nervous. He says, Son, would you like to go take a walk with me for a while? I tell him, No, Dad, I think I'd rather stay here, and talk to my Kentucky folks, and I don't think he likes it. He says, Well, I don't think your aunt and uncle wanta sit and listen to you talk 'bout what goes on at our house. Jack says, Yes, we do, Spare, we sure do. It's kind of interesting. I guess I better stop talking 'cause Dad's giving me the funny look.

It's getting dark and one of the girls brings a coal oil lamp from inside the house and places it near the center of our group. All my cousins are listening to the conversation with interest, especially now that Dad's gonna tell 'bout his military career on the Mexican Border in the U.S. Cavalry.

We're still chomping down on the cold watermelon, but nobody wants to miss this story.

Dad says, Well, folks, I'm not one to brag 'bout some things in my life, but you're the judge. I wanta hear this 'cause it may not be like what Uncle Joe and Uncle Orie told me 'bout at home. Dad says, I was seventeen years old when I decided a military life was for me. I liked the outdoor tough life and I knew it would make my family proud, especially Maw. I left Evansville and after some training at Fort Benjamin Harrison in Indianapolis, I was sent to Brownsville, Texas on the Mexican border. I trained with every kind of weapon in the U.S. Army, and learned how to ride the best horses in the cavalry. I later performed duty near the Rio Grande River, and that's when things began to get rough. One of the boys yells, Uncle Spare, what was your favorite weapon, gun or sword? Dad says, It didn't matter, they all came easy for me. I could handle either, but it seemed like a sword came natural.

Jack and Becky are all ears and enjoy listening to Dad's exploits on the Mexican border. Jack says, Spare, Did you ever get into any battles? Dad says, The, only real battle I ever saw was more like a skirmish, but there was some heavy fighting for a short time. That's expected in the cavalry. Dad's enjoying this, and so am I. He says, I remember one particular skirmish where 'bout fifty of us cavalry men ran into a group of Chiricahua Apache Indians who were raiding back and forth with some Mexican bandits. They usually come over into Texas, steal some horses and cattle, then they run back across the border into Mexico where we weren't supposed to go. George asks, What did you guys do, Uncle Spare, what did you do, did you kill 'em all? Dad says, No, Son, that's not the way it works. You don't do anything till the commanding officer gives the order; you don't disobey orders no matter what. When the captain said, 'Prepare to engage' and finally 'Charge,' every man went for his sword and we took off after the raiders. I guess I can truly say that all of a sudden all hell broke loose. Francis says, Where were you, Uncle Spare, when the charge started? Dad says, I was in my usual place right next to the captain, 'cause he always wanted me by his side or just behind him. He knew I was young, but he could depend on me, and that means a lot. I'm taking a short walk, 'cause it ain't talked 'bout at home that way. Dad goes on, and says, When the captain said, 'charge, men, and don't take pity,' it seemed to set us on fire. The Mexicans and Indians were at the Rio Grande edge of the river when we caught up with 'em and the blood began to flow in the river turning it red. The river was only 'bout a foot deep with water and not very wide, and when the captain didn't stop us, we kept on goin'. Everyone is getting closer to Uncle Spare and I'm moving farther away.

George says, How many of 'em were there, Uncle? Dad says, Probably 'bout a hundred, but when it was over there wasn't one left. We simply cut 'em to pieces with our swords. Jack loves Dad's story and lets loose some cuss words and says, You sure give 'em one damned good whipping didn't you, Spare, what 'bout you, did you kill any of 'em? Dad says, I'd rather not say how many, but it still bears on my mind yet today. Becky says, Did any of your guys get hurt or killed? Dad takes a deep breath and says, Some got wounded including me, but that's to be expected. One of my best buddies was killed and that's how I got my finger shot off. Ray says, Keep on talkin', Uncle Spare, keep tellin' us 'bout the fightin'. Dad says, They had my buddy down and 'bout to scalp him, but I wasn't 'bout to let it happen whether they killed me or not. I charged into 'em, as they shot at me with everything they had, but only hit my trigger finger. I didn't know my finger was gone till the fighting was over. Jack says, I'm glad you told us 'bout your finger, Spare, we kinda wondered if that's how you lost it, but we didn't wanta ask. Dad smiles and says, Life in the cavalry was tough, and it meant a lot to me.

Dad likes talking 'bout his cavalry time. He says, Now you all know 'bout my career in the cavalry, but I never really wanta talk 'bout it just the same as the guys who served in World War I. That's the way with most guys who see action feel 'bout it, and don't wanta ever go through it again. Becky says, We, kinda figured that's what might have happened, but didn't dream you saw all that terrible fighting, and Dad says, It was only a skirmish, but it can live with you forever. I never expected to tell 'bout it, but it's over and I'll just have to live with it probably till I die. Did you get a medal? One of the girls asks. he pauses a while, wipes his forehead, and says, Honey, when my best buddy got killed after I tried to save him, it just wouldn't be right to accept a medal, so I turned it down. Dad won't want me to mention this at home I know for sure, but somehow I've got to tell Uncle Joe.

Every day on the farm begins at six a.m. and Sunday is no different. Aunt Becky says, Bid, Everyone knows you're goin' to be answering Bible questions at our church, so be sure and read up on anything you need to know before goin'. Maw don't even tell me that anymore, so I tell her, I don't need to read anything, Aunt Becky, 'cause it comes easy for me, and she says, Be sure you comb your hair and wash behind your ears, 'cause know how your cousins George and Ray are. She's telling me the same thing Maw tells me every time I go someplace.

We arrive at the small Baptist country church and Dad and me are introduced by an older gray haired minister. He says, We have visitors from across the river with us today. We have with us a young man, seven years old, and his father from Evansville, Indiana. Many of you may have read 'bout him in the paper concerning his knowledge of scripture. Is there anything, Mr. McCaffry, you or your son wish to say to the congregation before I turn it over to you and your son? Dad says, Well, I'd just like to say, I know the Lord has led us to your church this morning, and I don't need to preach 'cause the preacher here has done a good job, or this place wouldn't be packed.

I move forward and face the congregation just like Dad always tells me how to do. They begin their questioning. What must one do to be saved is always the first question and this is no different. Someone says, Name the twelve disciples. A young lady dressed in a long blue print dress with long sleeves asks a couple of questions 'bout women's adornment. Question after question is thrown at me and these people know the Bible well. It finally comes to an end and they stand and clap their hands. I've given them the answers they expected. The service ends around noon and people are outside the church door and we talk. They laugh when I tell some of 'em 'bout my dog, Lady, but they really like to hear 'bout Maw and Uncle Joe. Dad hears me talking and he don't like what I'm saying, and says, I think it's time to go. An elderly lady says, Brother Spare, That boy of yours sure knows the Bible and Dad says, I've did my best to bring him up that way, Sister, but it's been a hard cross to bear without a mother.

We arrive home and it's time to prepare for the picnic at a fishin' spot. A team of mules are hitched to a wagon filled with food and drink. We're on our way. We travel down several dusty dirt roads till we arrive at a large pond where water lilies cover most of the entire pond. Water snakes swim freely everywhere seeming to disregard our presence. George runs to the water's edge and yells, Come on, gang, this is one good lookin' place, and we're gonna catch us some damned good catfish! Aunt Becky hears his remark, grabs him by his ear and says, Young man if I ever hear you using that word again, you'll get your mouth washed out with soap real good. She sounds just like Maw, and Ray quits talking for a while.

Aunt Becky yells, Come and get-it soup's in the kettle. Ray yells back, I'm hungry as a damned bear. He did it again, and Aunt Becky is really mad this time. She grabs him by the ear and heads towards a couple trees. Ray is screaming and yelling saying he won't ever do it again, I feel sorry for my cousin, Ray, and say, Please Aunt Becky don't wash his mouth out 'cause I hear cuss words a lot worse than that at home. She stops, turns Ray loose, and says, What in the world you talkin' 'bout, Bid? I tell her, You should hear some of the things my cousin Titties says, and that ain't nothing compared to what my Uncle Joe can say. You should have been with me when he was running the witch up the alley. I heard words you ain't ever gonna believe. Maw said she didn't want me saying them either 'cause they weren't Christian; if I do hafta say 'em she makes me spell 'em.

Dad's really frowning at me like he doesn't like what I said, and says, Son, you know we don't appreciate what the family says at home, so please don't bring it up again. I tell him, O.K., Dad, I won't, I just thought Aunt Becky ought to know. Becky says, You know, Son, I sure don't know why, but I thought you said your cousin's name was Titties, but I'm sure I must have been mistaken. I tell her, No you're not Aunt Becky, that's his name, Titties, and he's my cousin who lives next door. He's good at cussing, but not near as good as my cousin, Cotton, and my Uncle Joe. They call him Titties 'cause he has tits as big as yours, and he's a boy 'bout fifteen. Dad grabs me again and says, Son, please, for God's sake, say no more, you're ruining our preaching life forever. These Christian people don't wanta hear 'bout your relatives in Evansville. Ray says, I do, Uncle Spare, I'd like to hear 'bout 'em. Dad says, There's one thing for sure, it's not gonna happen, and enough has been said already. They're just a little different, that's all, and sometimes they even embarrass me around Christian people.

Becky calls for everyone to gather near a large wooden camp table filled with food and the huge kettle of burgoo. Louise says, It's time for us to thank the Lord for food and now who is goin' to offer the prayer? Jack says, Well, I think, Bid, should 'cause he sure knows the Bible. When the Lord hears his thanks, He's gonna take it serious and he sure tells it like it is and that's what the Lord likes. After the prayer of thanks, we all run for the table and begin eating and enjoying the food and laughter and fun is in the air.

Arriving home Uncle Jack informs us of the coming day's schedule and says, We're gonna be gettin' up at six a.m. so everyone will be in the field tending tobacco stalks. You know, that's our bread and butter. I need to let it sink in a little farther and ask George, Just what does tending tobacco mean? George acts a little surprised at my question and says, Well cousin Bid, it means you're gonna be out in the field pulling tobacco worms from plants and killing 'em before they kill the plant. I've handled lots of worms going fishin', so that sure won't bother me. I tell Ray, Don't worry 'bout me, Ray, I know all 'bout worms and I'm used to work. George says,

Don't be so sure, cousin, just don't be so sure. You ain't seen tobacco worms this size and walks away laughing. I don't understand why he's laughing.

Monday morning has come fast and I feel as if I've just fallen to sleep. Aunt Becky yells, Come and get-it, come and get-it, you hungry people, breakfast is on the table. We all hit the floor 'bout the same time and there's a mad scramble down the stairs. Dad, Uncle Jack and Aunt Becky are seated and Becky says, Go outside the back door with your cousins and wash yourself at the table where you'll find soap, water and a towel. You better go to the outhouse, too. We return and I notice a big jar of sorghum molasses is on the table and George tells me that's what we call sugar and I'm gonna be eating it from now on. Ray says, Cousin Bid, Sorghum is good, I eat it with a spoon, unless Mom catches me then I hafta put it on bread. I doubt if I ever will.

I soon find out what my cousins mean when they talk 'bout tobacco worms. I'm in the field dressed in bib overalls, a large straw hat, and no shirt or shoes. George begins to show me large green tobacco worms hanging on tobacco stalks. He grabs one and crushes it on the ground. I ask George if they are good catfish bait and he says, I just kill 'em, Bid, I never have fun with 'em. These big worms can kill the plants easy and that's our bread and butter. When our crop comes in 'bout fall, it's the only money we got till the next year. Dad tells me 'bout how important tobacco is, and if we don't have a good crop, we may not eat so good.

The girls are here bringing us cold drinking water and Aunt Becky sent us some food for the noon meal. Before anyone can settle down, it's time to get back to work. I like to work at home, but this is a little different. I tell George, This sure is hot and hard work, cousin, and he says, Oh, this is the same all summer long, we've nothing but work during the day, but when we're done we'll all go down to the pond behind the house, strip off, and jump in. That's how we cool off, and you're gonna like it, cousin Bid.

What 'bout the girls?

Oh, they do the same thing.

Well, I ain't taking no bath with girls, cousin, no matter what.

Don't worry, Bid, them girls are on the other side of the pond, so don't get upset.

The work is done for the day, and we head for the pond. Ray grabs a bar of soap from the outside table, and soon we're splashing around in water naked. This is great, and I tell George, It sure gets worm juice off my hands when I'm scrubbing with lye soap. He says, Yeah, Bid, Mom makes good soap, she can make 'bout anything. They sure like to brag 'bout Aunt Thelma and I'm glad she's my aunt, but Maw can do it just as good, but I'm not telling my cousins.

It's the middle of the week and Dad seems to be getting tired of the hard work, long hours and no place to go. This is something he hasn't planned on. Jack has already told us were not going to town till Saturday morning. I'm having a great time with my cousins, but the work is hard and we spend 'bout eight or ten hours a day in the field. I always look forward to jumping in the pond and having fun with everyone. Thursday morning, Uncle Jack says, I've been over to our neighbor's farm and several of 'em will be coming over here Friday evening to enjoy some homemade ice cream and watermelon. Everyone knows 'bout Spare and they're all bitin' their nails till they meet him and hear his stories. Spare, maybe you can tell us some more 'bout your experiences in the cavalry. Dad's not liking this I'm sure, 'cause I think he might get something mixed up if he tells it again. Dad, says, I really hate to be reminded of what went on down on the border and I don't wanta look like some kind of hero. I've never heard him say that before.

It's Friday afternoon and the day's work is over 'bout four thirty, and we begin getting ready for the visitors. The two neighboring families arrive and after our introductions, Jack says, I've already told you folks 'bout my brother-in-law, Spare, and his son, Bid; if any of you wish to ask him anything 'bout his cavalry career, please go ahead. I walk away and listen at a distance. This is gonna be good, 'cause I know Dad can't remember how many Mexicans were in the battle on the Rio Grand. One of the ladies from the group says, Mr. McCaffry, or should I say, Spare, I wanta know just one thing due to the fact Jack said you don't like to talk 'bout it. I would like to know just how proud your family must be of you while you were serving in the cavalry. Dad says, I can truthfully say my family has always been behind me one hundred percent, but they kinda live a different life than I do as a preacher. One of my brothers has been through a lot himself and only has one lung after losing it in World War I. I always feel sorry for him 'cause I just can't get him to live the Christian life, like I do; Oh, by the way, just call me, Spare. After a few more questions 'bout his preaching, it's time for some fun.

Jack and Becky have arranged for some fun playing softball in the cow pasture behind the old barn. Everybody's in the mood for a game we can all enjoy, and softball is a swell idea. We all take off for the cow pasture. Ray and me lead the way. It's decided that the family of Jack and Becky, including Dad and me, will compete with the two neighboring families in a good slow pitch game of five innings. Jack asks, Spare, did you ever play softball? I don't remember ever seeing Dad play, but he says, Sure, Jack, I'm real fast, fast as they come, and I can go get a ball anywhere; when I'm playing the outfield I'm known to be one of the best. Jack says, O.K. Spare, get out in center field, you kids play on the infield, and Becky you do the catching. The neighbors are allowed to bat first and the game begins. I ask, Ray, Where's my glove? He says, What's a glove? I'm not gonna ask again 'cause I doubt if he ever saw one.

Lots of hitting, lots of errors, lots of laughing and good times are in the air. In the second inning one of the neighbors hits a high fly to center and Dad takes off. He's running with his back to the field, and I know he's only got one thing on his mind and that's to make the catch and show how great a fielder he is. All you can see is, Dad, sliding across the pasture and the ball is rolling out further. Dad is sprawling, and he's not getting up. I cain't see him 'cause of the big tree he slid under, and I'm running towards him with Ray just behind me. He's on the ground and groaning in pain. I ask Dad, What's wrong, are you hurt bad? Now we smell an odor that's familiar to any farm boy. Ray says, Cousin Bid, he's fell in cow-shit for sure, and he's covered from top to bottom. Dad still isn't able to speak and sits on the ground helpless. This is bad, and I tell him, Dad, you're gonna have to get yourself together, clean yourself off and get outta this cow-shit. Ray says, Cousin Bid, it's cow-shit for sure, I've smelled a lot of it here on the farm and I've stepped in some big piles of it myself. One thing you learn 'bout cow-shit, cousin Bid, is that it's real hard to see till you're right on it. Jack and Becky are yelling at us wanting to know if Dad is hurt. Ray yells back, Uncle Spare fell in some cow-shit and hurt himself and he sure is a mess.

The baseball game comes to a halt due to Dad's accident. From across the pasture Becky yells, Son, please don't use vulgar language 'round company. It's not nice to use vulgar words. Use the word manure. Ray seems to be unsure of what his mother is saying. He says, Cousin Bid, is that right; is cow-shit manure? I tell my cousin, I'm not sure either, Ray, but around our house it's always been called cow-shit. My Uncle Shave's wife, Tillie, came into the house one day after being in the barn milking the cow. I said, Aunt Tillie, where's your shoes? She said, Bid, I stepped in some cow-shit, so I left them at the back door. Ray wants to know what I said, so I tell him the truth as Maw always tells me. I didn't say nothing, Cousin Ray; I left her house and went home and told Maw I heard Tillie cussing. Maw didn't answer me, so I guess it's cow-shit.

The game comes to a halt and Jack yells, Spare, go over and jump in the pond and wash off, then come on back to the game. Dad is getting up and is running for the pond. Ray says, Uncle Spare is stark assed naked, but he's gonna have a hard time gettin' the cow-shit off. I had to take two baths in the pond one time and used lots of Mom's lye soap and the family said I smelled a week later. When I cleaned the pasture last week, I should have told Uncle Spare where I put it. I don't want Cousin Ray to feel bad 'bout not telling him. I tell him, Dad wouldn't have paid any attention to the pile of cow-shit, 'cause he had his eye on the ball all the way. I don't think we should call it manure, 'cause it's cow-shit to me, and I think Uncle Joe will feel the same way.

Dad's in the pond and everyone's tired from all the yelling and we decide to call the game. Ray says, Nobody wants to be near Uncle Spare, anyhow. It's almost dark and the visitors decide to go home. Nobody has seen Dad the rest of the evening till bedtime, and he says he ain't gonna talk to anyone 'bout what happened. Ray and me sit on the front porch later after the guests leave, and Ray says, I guess I should have warned Uncle Spare 'bout that pile of cow-shit, but I didn't think he'd run that far out. I sure hope he gets that smell off. Cousin Ray just cain't forgive himself for not telling Dad and I'm tired of hearing 'bout it. I tell him, Ray you're just gonna hafta forget 'bout it. Let's go to bed. The next day not one word is said 'bout the accident.

Saturday morning and the old truck ain't running, so Uncle Jack hooks up his team of mules and we head for Henderson to buy supplies. He has to meet with the bank to get some money on his tobacco crop. Jack says, Spare, it's really been tough these past couple of years trying to put food on the table, and now that the bank has been opened by our new President Roosevelt, it may get better. Dad says, Son, listen to what your uncle is tellin' you and talkin' 'bout 'cause farmers have had it tough. I tell my Uncle Jack, I know all 'bout it, 'cause some of Maw's friends even lost their farms for not paying the bank, but she said things are gonna get better and when they do, we're gonna have electricity put in the house.

After a two-hour trip by horse and wagon to Henderson we arrive downtown and it's' time for me to say goodbye to my Kentucky family. I grab my suitcase from the wagon, walk over and hug and kiss my uncle and aunt, and tell 'em, If anything ever happens to Maw I'd like to live with you, Aunt Becky. She says, That's just fine, Son, just pack your bag and come on over 'cross the river. We love you just like your mother loved you. You're one of us now.

Arriving at the bus station, we board a bus and head for Evansville. It's not long till Dad says, Now, Son, whatever you do, don't mention anything I might have said or done this week 'cause your uncles would only try to make me look bad. I tell him, I won't, Dad, you know I wouldn't tell 'em 'bout you falling in the manure. You can count on me.

Maw greets us at the door and asks how we enjoyed our week with my Kentucky relatives. I tell her we had a great time, and I learned lots of things 'bout farm life and I really like my relatives. Maw asks, How 'bout you, Arthur, did you have a good time the same as your son? Dad says, Well, I had a good time, but you know, Mom, it was my duty to preach and I never got to, but my son did his part in church. Does that mean you're still living for the Lord, Son? She asks, and Dad says, Sure, it does, Mom, I never thought 'bout sinning one time.

When Uncle Joe comes home for supper, I tell him, 'bout our trip and all the fun we had and he asks if Dad behaved all the time. I tell him he sure did, 'cept the time he fell in the manure which we call cow-shit. Uncle Joe starts laughing and wants to know, so I guess I gotta tell him. When I finish telling him and Maw, they are both laughing and Uncle Joe cain't stop. He says, That Spare, that Spare, he's just gotta be the center of attention. When he didn't get to preach, he sure as hell had to do something to get attention. I think it was an accident and so does, Maw. I ask Uncle Joe not mention this to anyone and he promises he won't, but I'm a little worried he will. Maw says, I feel enough is enough; that poor boy can just stand so much. I don't wanta hear no more 'bout this incident. Joe says, Mom, you know I won't say anything to nobody.

Uncle Orie and his family are here for Sunday dinner. Maw says, Listen, children, your brother, Arthur, is doing real good, so he is goin' to offer our prayer of thanks. Dad gives a long prayer of thanks and everyone begins eating and enjoying the chicken and dumplings. Dinner is over and Maw says, It's so nice to have some of my children here on Sunday and it makes me happy. Did all of you enjoy the food? Joe says, Maw, this has been a truly great meal, 'cept there's been an odor and I just can't say for sure what it is, but I'd swear it was cow-shit. Everyone turns and looks towards Dad, as if they suspect he might be carrying the odor. Nobody speaks, but they sure do glare at him. Suddenly, Dad, throws his fork on the table and begins ranting. I knew I just cain't trust my own son anymore, 'cause you've turned him against me and now you're persecuting me. I asked Uncle Joe not to tell, but I guess he did, and now Dad is mad and runs outta the house. He slams the kitchen door and nothing is ever said 'bout the ball game again.

16

THE INHERITANCE

We live in poverty during The Great Depression, but we don't seem to know it and always find a way to have a good time. Nothing in God's world ever makes any of us dream of untold riches till we receive a letter from a New York law firm. We could possibly be the McCaffry heirs to a fortune in Ireland. The letter says the heir to the property in Ireland is from County Cork. Grandpaw McCaffry was from Count Cork and none of us can imagine anyone else is entitled to the money but us, the true heirs. The Martins' are just as enthused as us, 'cause we've always been a close-knit family with a strong bond, and now we're all gonna be rich.

Plans are talked 'bout daily what to do with the money. Rumors are flying 'bout the amount of wealth, and we're sure there must be a large castle with servants and horses are sure to be a part of it. We're no longer referred to as 'Those Crazy Irish.' Now we're rich people to all the neighbors, and suddenly we got friends we never knew 'bout. I hear some people at the grocery store talking 'bout us, and one 'em said, Mary had trouble with the two wild ones before, just think whut it's gonna be like now when they get all that money. I guess they mean Dad and Uncle Joe.

Maw says, We're gonna have a meeting, so we all meet at our house and she starts laying down the law, as she calls it. She says, Hush, I need to talk to you 'bout what money does to people, and the first thing I want you to understand is, the love of money is the root of all evil. Pat says, Says so in the Bible, don't it, Maw? She likes Pat's answer and says, Yes, it does, Son, I guess you're not sleepin' all the time in church. Maw says, I'm afraid if we get lots of money it may be the ruination of our family and no amount of money is worth that. Some people just don't know how to take care of it and end up goin' to hell. Bob says, You mean Uncle Joe and Uncle Spare don't you, Maw? Dad hangs his head down and Joe laughs. Maw says, No, I don't. It's not just them, but they'll probably be the most likely to go wild. Cotton is sitting in the corner listening to Maw's laying down the law, and says, Maw, I heard Aunt Dorie say Uncle Spare and Uncle Joe are already ruined. Aunt Dorie doesn't like what Cotton said, and says, Maw, I really didn't mean it that way, I just meant sometimes it seems like they have more problems than all of us together. Uncle Joe just laughs and says he doesn't care what they say 'bout him, but Dads got his head hanging down and I can tell he's not enjoying it. Dad told me he's a lot like Uncle Joe when it comes to money, and he's not caring what the hell they say 'bout him as long as he gets the long green. Maw says, I've decided one thing for sure, and here's how it's gonna be. I'm just gonna let the Lord handle the whole bunch of you. Everyone is satisfied, and we all begin smiling and laughing and the meeting's over.

Joe works for a small woodworking shop close to home. The hot summer day is half over on Friday. When he comes home for lunch, he says, Bid, get all your buddies together, get some bait, and we'll all go fishin' tonight at Lily Creek. I've been hoping to hear those words for a long time. Fishin' and Uncle Joe seem to go together and we enjoy it. Bob says, I'm tired of listening to stories 'bout all the money, it's time to have some fun. We're off to get bait for the night's trip to Lily Creek, and Lady leads the way.

Joe is home from work and everything is ready to go fishin'. The truck is filled with food, drinks, fishin' supplies, kids and one dog, Lady. Joe gives a quick head check and says,

Cotton, where's Snotty Nose Lindel?
He can't go, Uncle Joe, he's not feeling good.
What's wrong with him, Cotton? If he ain't dead, he should go.

He was in the outhouse last night and a spider musta bit him on his balls.

His mom said both of 'ems big as baseballs. I tried to get a look at 'em, but she shoved me away. Mrs. Sierdorf went over to his house to get a look at 'em, and she told mom, the poor youngun may never be able to have kids. Her husband, Fritz, had mumps once and no matter how much they try, there's no way to get kids. They're Catholic, too.

Pat says, It wasn't poisonous or he'd be dead for sure.

Bob wants to know if we can all go take a look at his balls.

Uncle Joe says, I never could depend on that damned boy anyhow, now the rest of you get your ass to moving or it's gonna be dark before we start fishin'.

Everyone is in high spirits as we arrive at Lily Creek 'bout an hour later. We grab our supplies and head for the creek through a wild area with thick brush and trees. Laughing and shouting is going on and Lady is right in the middle. She's now part of the family. We find the most desirable spot to spend the night and everyone is preparing for the night of fun.

At the water's edge is a large clear area. We take off looking for firewood. A big bonfire will help light up the area. Dad is taking care of the beer and soft drinks, and Uncle Joe is preparing the fishin' lines for baiting. Cotton is smart 'bout fishin' and huntin', so he's helping everyone. This is gonna be one big night and we're gonna catch lots of fish. Lily Creek is only 'bout thirty yards wide and five or six feet deep with lily pads everywhere. The water snakes move 'bout paying no attention to us and everything is perfect for a wonderful night. Off in the distance I hear some big bullfrogs beginning to croak and they sound as if they're saying, belly deep, belly deep, over and over. Bob says, Huckleberry Finn never had it any better than us and would probably love to be here.

Uncle Joe is well known for his story telling ability, and we love to hear it over and over. We like the stories 'bout his hobo-in' and serving in the

Navy during the World War. We never have any doubt 'bout it's truth. We know he wouldn't lie, but Pat says he exaggerates sometimes. We spread a large blanket on the bare ground near the fire and wood is piled high nearby. The fish are beginning to bite and Cotton is pulling 'em in and getting excited. Some of us grab a sandwich and drink, and now its story time. Uncle Joe is the best ever. It's not that he's exactly the best, but we all know he's been there and done that, 'cause Maw told us. Uncle Joe has had been in prison twice and he's an escaped convict, so there is no way in the world we can keep from admiring him. Being in World War I was enough for us to be proud of him 'cause he helped whip the Germans good.

I hand him a cold beer to get him started and he begins now that we're all settled down around the fire waiting for this moment. He begins saying, This, is the true story, lads, to the best of my recollection. I was hoboin' on a freight train in Georgia and things were tough. When I was young, I didn't realize how mean some people can be if they catch you riding on a train without paying. Lots of other guys were doing it, so why not me? There was one thing I didn't know and that is how mean some of those conductors and dicks on the railroad could really be. Well, needless to say, they caught me hobo-in'. I got worked over good by a railroad dick, thrown in jail for not having any money and put on a chain gang working in a turpentine forest for six months.

Pat says, Uncle Joe, Uncle Joe, what's a dick?
It's a railroad cop. I thought I told you before. Now don't interrupt me.
Bob says, Pat will ask him again, don't you think so, Bid?
I know he will, 'cause Pat never gives up till he fully understands. I saw him spit between his two front teeth all the way to the Chicago Worlds Fair. Everyone yelled at him to stop, but he just kept on spitting. Pat's one stubborn cousin.
Uncle Joe says, Pat, stop asking all your damned questions, so I can tell my story.

I whisper to Bob, Uncle Joe told me they're called bulls, but I sure ain't telling Pat or we'd never hear the end of this story.

After 'bout a month on a chain gang, I knew I was gonna do anything to get away. It was hell and the guards were the meanest bastards you could imagine. The work in the swamp was really bad. When one of those big gators or moccasins was swimmin' around in the water nearby, we weren't allowed to stop workin'. I'd made friends with a guy from Ohio who was caught hobo-in'. We had a plan to run. Early one morning when we were having a water break, I saw an opening in a field next to me and decided this is the time to run for freedom. I yelled at my buddy next to me, but for some reason he froze. I cain't stop now 'cause I'm on my way to freedom and I'm goin' no matter what happens, even if they kill me. I wasn't born to be a slave.

Uncle Joe wants another beer; I get him one and he continues his story.

I ran and ran till I thought my lungs were goin' to pop out of my chest, but there was freedom ahead. I thought I've gotta reach a nearby woods and I did. I looked back a couple of times and heard a rifle shot 'bout six or seven times and believe you me that made me run a hell of a lot faster!

Pat says, I'll bet it really did, Uncle Joe, I'd run with all my might, too.
Bob says, See, I told you so, Bid, he did it again.
Joe says, Shut up, Pat.

Uncle Joe continues. I could hear the bloodhounds bellowing 'bout a quarter mile behind me till dark. I waded through swamp water almost up to my neck and at times, my feet and arms were bleeding from scratches, and I was scared as hell. That's when I saw a huge tree with part of its trunk hollowed out and that's where I decided to spend the night. The mosquitoes were eatin' at me all night and there was no way to sleep, and I knew I couldn't start a fire even if I had dry matches. Uncle Joes' looking for another beer, but he's gotta finish the story first. I'm not getting it till he does.

He continues. Hiding inside the base of the big tree was almost unbearable. I kept thinkin' of all the things Maw said to me time after time and I knew I had done just the opposite, but this is no time to cry. I'm gonna fight harder. Now remember this, lads, when you think you can go no farther, just think of your Uncle Joe and what I did. The next morning, I knew it might mean either freedom or my death 'cause I'm never gonna let 'em take me alive. You know how Irish people are, don't you?

Pat says, Yeah, we sure do. Now go on and tell us the rest.
Bob says, He did it again, Bid.
Joe continues.

Well the next morning some daylight and sun began shining into the tree hole where I was hiding and I could no longer hear the dogs. I needed to get the hell away from there as fast as my legs would travel. I knew there was a railroad close by 'cause a couple of times during the night I could hear a train whistle blowing, so I headed in that direction.

Uncle Joe never seems to tire and I know he wants a beer, but I'm not getting any beer till he finishes the story.

I was walking down a dusty lane out in the middle of nowhere when all of a sudden a horse drawn wagon comes along from another direction. To my surprise, I look around my back and there stands a big black man, his wife, horse and wagon loaded with furniture. I don't know whether to run or try and explain what I'm doing here dressed in a prison uniform. From the start, he sensed I was in trouble 'cause of what I'm wearing. I started to run, but it would be no use. I'm worn out and we look each other in the eyes, he says, White boy, you sure got yourself in trouble. I'll do whatever I can to help you, but if we get caught you'll have to say you forced me with a gun or somethin'. That's no problem for me at all 'cause chances are they're gonna wanta kill both of us. I thank him repeatedly and climb into the back of his wagon and cover myself with some old ragged clothes. He hauls me in his wagon down the road 'bout a mile to the railroad and gives me some of the other rags to cover myself. I used them to wear the rest of the way on my trip home. Before I said goodbye, I told my friends, I hope you don't get in trouble. He looked at me, smiled and says, White boy, I've been in trouble all my life. I walked down the railroad track for 'bout a half mile till I heard a train whistle. The train stopped at a rail siding to take water and I crawled into an empty boxcar and headed north.

Uncle Joe is still looking 'round for the beer, but I need to hear the rest of the story and so do the rest of my cousins. We know if he has another couple beers, he won't finish the stories, 'cause it happened before.

He continues. There were times I had to drink water from a ditch and a couple times I ate vegetables from gardens in the neighborhoods. There was one time a farmer gave me some soup his wife had made and it was the best I ever ate. After 'bout a week, I got home and so far nobody has called or asked 'bout what went on in Georgia. I hope they believe I'm dead. When I told Maw part of the story, she says, Son, I quit worrying 'bout you and your brother, Arthur, a long time ago. I just turned it over to the Lord. It's all gonna work out in the end; I know it will because of my prayers and the Bible says so.

Pat says, Sounds like Maw, don't it guys; everyone agrees.
Bob says, See, Bid, Pat did it again.

Joe finishes his amazing story. We check our fishin' lines, eat, drink and put more wood on the fire, and again settle down to hear another story. It's 'bout ten p.m. and dark as it can be 'cept for the firelight. Out in the far off trees, a hoot owl lets out a loud 'whoo, whoo.' This is how we like it. Bob wants Uncle Joe to tell us another story 'bout his time in the Navy. Joe complains 'bout it getting late, but if I get him another beer he's willing to begin the next story. Bob says, Where, is Uncle Spare? I haven't seen him since we got here. Cotton says, Don't worry 'bout Uncle Spare, me and him been talkin' 'bout all the money we're gonna get and he's writing down some of the things we're gonna be buying. Pat hands Uncle Joe a beer and now he's ready to go. Joe begins his story 'bout one of his greatest experiences while serving as an aviation rigger in the Navy at the Great Lakes Naval Training Center in Chicago, Illinois in 1918.

Well, boys, it all began during a period at the Naval Training Center when things weren't the best. Sailors are coming down with the flu in 1918 and there is a lot of sickness and dying around the base. Everyone is on the alert for anyone or anything suspicious 'cause of the high death rate. We know the Germans will do anything to kill Americans in any manner and we are especially on the lookout for spies. We are blessed with a big Irish captain by the name of Mitchell and he's a man whose father comes from Ireland; probably from around Dublin. He was 'bout six feet two inches tall with blue eyes and blond hair and it's well-known that all the ladies love him. He was greatly admired by all his men 'cause he showed no favoritism and knew his job.

Pat says, He was just like us, wasn't he, Uncle?
You can bet your ass he was, and stop asking all those damned questions and let me get done with this.
Bob says, See, Bid, I told you so, Pat's never gonna stop.

Well, boys, Captain Mitchell was officer of the day on this occasion and it was his duty to see that everything around the base is goin' as he instructed. He knew what was goin' on and who could possibly be involved in any kind of suspicious movements around the base. He always carries his pistol strapped around his waist and wouldn't hesitate to use it if he needs to. Captain Mitchell was walking near the mess hall this particular evening when he noticed a light flashing in the mess hall. He knew there wasn't supposed to be anyone in the place at that time of the evening. He ran to the door of the mess hall, unlocked it, and slowly opened the door, and switched on the lights inside and saw someone in the kitchen area.

Uncle Joe is drinking his beer pretty fast and we're all hoping he finishes before he goes to sleep. I'm not getting him anymore and neither are my cousins till this story is over.

Captain Mitchell was surprised when he saw a figure darting around where the food was stored. He yells, Stop, stop, in a loud voice. Instead of stopping, the person heads for the nearest window in a run and that was his big mistake. Just as he reached the window, Captain Mitchell fired two shots and that was all for the man. They later found two bullet holes in the man's heart bout six inches apart. Captain Mitchell received one of the highest medals in the Navy. Nobody ever heard him make any bragging comments 'bout his action 'cept to say, I've always considered it my duty to protect my men and country.

A couple of us thank Uncle Joe for the story. He lies down on the blanket and is going to sleep, and Dad is having a beer with Cotton. Lady is curled up on the blanket between Bob and me and it's time to get some rest.

Pat and me get up during the night and go behind the bushes to relieve ourselves and have a drink. The sun is beginning to show through the trees early in the morning and everyone is up and we begin moving around the camp. Off in the distance we hear a couple of hoot owls, and 'cross the creek a couple of red headed woodpeckers are pecking on a big old hickory tree. Some of us are starting breakfast and Cotton is fooling around with a huge box of fish at the water's edge.

From away off comes a loud yelling. It keeps getting closer to the campsite. Cotton says, I think it's Uncle Shave and Aunt Mary, wonder what in the hell they're yellin' 'bout? Within a few minutes, they stand before us all excited like and begin telling us the law firm in New York called and said the heirs to the money in Ireland has been found and it belongs to the McCaffry's in Evansville. Everyone is yelling at the top of their voice, and things are getting wild. We're all yelling, We're rich, we're rich, and excitement is getting out of control. Fishin' and camping is forgotten and we're in hysteria. Lady squats and pisses a couple times near the fire, barks a couple of times, and seems to enjoy the excitement, but I don't think she even knows why.

Dad is the first to take off for the truck leaving everything he brought to the camp and Joe can't stop him. Joe's whooping it up and hollers for everyone to follow him and Cotton yells, What 'bout the fish and supplies? Joe says, To hell, with that crap, a week from now we'll be eatin' mountain trout. Out of nowhere a big black cat jumps from outta the bushes and Lady takes off after him and I'm running and yelling for her to stop and I'm thinking, oh no, not again. After, a short chase she has him high in an elm tree, and I'm finally able to pull her away. We're the last ones in the truck before it takes off for home and Lady is still barking and pulling on her leash wanting the cat. I'm sure glad it wasn't Midnight.

Everyone is talking 'bout how great life is gonna be. Shave and Mary are in a car ahead of us, and they're the only ones not excited. We're finally home and everyone heads for the kitchen to find out more 'bout our inheritance. Seated at the table is Aunt Mary and Uncle Shave with Maw standing across the room against the wall and not looking happy. We wanta hear all 'bout the money and when we're gonna get it. The kitchen is full and Uncle Shave is the center of attention. Dad says, Brother Shave, Tell us all 'bout the lawyers and what they said. Did they say when I can get my money, 'cause I need it bad and right now? Everyone looks at Shave and Mary and the room fills with excitement. Shave says, Well, it's like this, boys; joke, joke, joke we're joking you, McCaffrys, it's just the opposite; you didn't get the money. The kitchen becomes completely still, nobody says nothing till the shock takes hold, and Orie says, Stop kidding us, Shave, and you better be kidding, now what 'bout the damned money? Shave is beginning to look pale and nobody thinks it's funny, and it's no joke to anyone in the room. Uncle Shave is in trouble. It sounds like we've gone from rags to riches and now we're back to rags in seconds.

Dad doesn't believe it. Joe is left with his mouth standing wide open and everyone else is speechless. I look at Maw and ask, Maw, can they do this to us? She says, Son, I don't want any part of this. Suddenly, Shave realizes he's in dangerous territory and it is no longer a joke to anyone. He jumps up and heads for the back door and all the McCaffry's and Martin's are after him, cussing him with every word ever heard. It's almost as bad as when Uncle Joe cussed the witch. Shave is running up the alley with Dad, Joe, and Orie after him. It's no use trying to catch Uncle Shave. He's the fastest runner in the family 'cause he doesn't smoke. Uncle Shave won't come around for a couple days and he gets a lot more cussing, but now everyone knows we won't ever be rich and he's welcomed back.

We have no more dreams of wealth and Uncle Shave and the rest of the family are back at peace. All is forgiven. Maw keeps shaking her head saying, What in the world are these boys gonna think of next, and Dad is back to normal going back to church. Nobody mentions anything 'bout it till Cotton says, Uncle Joe, we shouldn't have left all our fishin' supplies at the creek. Uncle Joe, says, Well, Cotton, we had a hell of a time for 'bout two weeks, and it was nice to be rich without bootlegging. Cotton says, I guess that means we're just poor again, and Joe says, You can say that again, hell's fire, we might go back to Lily Creek some time and do it again. For some unknown reason everyone is happy and poor as usual.

It's Saturday afternoon after returning from Lily Creek. Bob and me head to downtown Evansville for a movie with Tom Mix, our cowboy hero. We pass through our usual route, the Red Light District, and at the end is a large garage. Its doors suddenly open in front of us. Two guys stand outside and one says, Hey boys, do you vant to make some money? That sounds good to us, 'cause we only got twenty cents a piece in our pockets. We look at each other 'cause nobody offers money unless it's something crooked and Maw warns us 'bout such people. These two guys don't look too good either. They sure don't look like Irish or German and not the usual type we see. Both are dressed in black, wear small black caps, and have more whiskers than Uncle Aden.

Bob says, Where's the money and what we gotta do?
One answers, Come inside and move rolls of linoleum and you get fifty cents.
I ask, Why, don't you do it?
He says, We're Jewish and this is the Sabbath; we don't work on the Sabbath.

Bob and me look at each other and walk outside to talk.

Bob says, These guys are nuts, Bid. This is Saturday 'cause I saw Maw gettin' ready to cook dinner for tomorrow; the Sabbath. I know it's tomorrow, 'cause it's chicken and dumpling day.
Yeah, I know, Bob, but these guys are Jews, and they don't know better yet 'cause Jesus tried to tell 'em once and they wouldn't listen. He's gonna tell 'em again when He comes back and they'll hafta listen then. Jesus loves the Jews, Bob, don't ever forget it.

Are you sure 'bout that, Bid? They look like a couple of nuts to me.
I'm right, Bob. I heard Reverend Johnson preach on it. He said the Jews won't understand 'bout Jesus until the last days, and this ain't the last days. Sometime Dad thinks it is, but me and Maw know better.
Bob says, O.K., let's do it. They gotta be pretty dumb though. We'd do it for a dime.
Sure, Bob, but don't tell 'em.

We begin the job, sweat a lot, they pay us fifty cents each and we take off for Joe Dean's Restaurant. We eat all the hamburgers, ice cream and drink all the pop our bellies can hold, and still have money to see Tom Mix.

Maws just finished cooking. She says, Where you boys been all afternoon? I had to do all the cooking for the Sabbath.

We look at each other, give a sigh of relief and Bob says, We went for a long walk, Maw, and got us some ice cream at a restaurant.

That's good, boys, now go take a bath and get your clothes ready for church tomorrow. You know on the Sabbath I'm not gonna be doing anything but worshipping the Lord and being with my family.

Bob says, Yeah, Maw, we know that but they're some guys that just don't understand what day is Sunday, the Sabbath.

I'm hoping Bob doesn't say no more, 'cause I wanta forget it.

We go outside and Bob says, Bid, do you think we could make another fifty cents next Saturday?

Naw, Bob, we were just lucky. Wait till they hear it from Jesus.

What 'bout the Catholics, Bid? Do you think we should tell 'em 'bout Sunday being the Sabbath, too? They might need to go to the altar like Uncle Spare to get rid of their sins?

Nope, wouldn't do any good. Mrs. Sierdorf says only the priest can help her get forgiven for her sins.

Does she know 'bout the Sabbath, Bid?

Oh yeh, she knows Sundays the Sabbath and she goes to church before us, but she never tells nobody, but the priest everything she does, bad.

Bob and me feel real good tonight 'cause we helped some Jews, made some money, we still got a full belly and we sure know what day is the Sabbath.

17

ELECTION DAY

When I'm in school Mrs. Bethel talks to me 'bout my big improvement in my language and I feel proud, 'cause she says it right in front of Mr. Cottrell, our Principal. She tells me to keep up the good work and she still has her eyes on me. That kinda worries me a little 'cause I'm starting to think 'bout some things that aren't school or preaching.

We have some good arguments at our house when it gets close to Election Day, I like to listen. We're a close knit family till then, and sometimes my folks get kinda mad at each other till it's over. I guess it's like having different views 'bout who is the best guy for president or mayor, but sometimes my uncles and Dad take it a little more serious. The biggest thing Uncle Joe and Uncle Orie argue 'bout though is usually who is gonna be the next committeeman or the trustee, and who's got the money. Usually, Maw, don't get involved unless it comes to sin and religious matters. She wants me to learn by listening, but sometimes Uncle Joe tells me a lot more.

It's one week before the fall election, and tension in the family seems to be growing between my two favorite uncles, Joe and Orie. I don't know why till I sit at the breakfast table on Saturday morning just three days before Election Day. Maw's fixing breakfast when Uncle Orie arrives with Aunt Dorie, Pat, and daughters Evelyn, and Jo Kathryn. Lady slips in the kitchen when the back screen door opens and runs under the kitchen table and lies next to her best friends, Bob, Pat and me.

Everyone is filling their plates and gulping down food, but I'm gonna eat slow 'cause I wanta hear what's going on 'bout Election Day. Bob slips Lady some of his food, Pat slips her some more of his food and she's swallowing the biscuits whole while her big tongue licks all round her mouth. She's enjoying it a lot, and Pat and me glance at each other and smile 'cause we both love her 'cause she's kinda like a family dog.

Aunt Dorie helps Maw get food on the table and some finish and leave the kitchen with Lady. I'm staying 'cause I wanta find out just what's going on 'bout the election and I kinda feel something is wrong between Dad and my uncles. Uncle Orie sits across the kitchen table from Joe and Dad and Maw is acting like something needs to be talked 'bout. She and Dorie seat themselves at the table and Maw says, Boys, we need to thank God for this food, so hush up while I offer thanks. She offers prayer and ends it saying, Lord, have mercy on these boys of mine, amen. Now I know my uncles and Dad are in trouble. She says, Now, boys, I know there have been times when you, Orie, and you, Joe, don't see eye to eye 'bout politics. I also know Orie is the Republican Committee-man and Joe is the Democratic Committee-man. I also know that you, Arthur, don't know who you're for or against from one day to another. Dad hangs his head down and everyone laughs 'cept me 'cause I know what they're talking 'bout.

Maw says, Boys, I know there've been times when election time has brought on ill feelings toward one another and that shouldn't be. This time let us try and be a little more understanding of the other person's views on politics. Dad can't stand it any longer and blurts out, Maw, I've been trying to get these two committee-men together for a long time, but they just won't listen to me. Aunt Dorie, begins laughing and says, Help me Lord, please help me, I can't believe what I'm hearin' from Spare.

I scoot my chair back towards the other side of the room where I can listen and they won't see me laughing. Dorie sits across from Dad, and says, Spare, if you don't stop lying and cheatin' you may end up in hell.

Dad hangs his head a little lower and a couple of tears begin to roll down from his eyes. He says, Maw, I'm only trying to help as I always do during elections. Orie says, Spare, that's why I'm here this morning. I can't figure out which side you're on. I know I'm paying, you, and Joe tells me he's paying you, and I heard Mr. Hunter is paying you. I wanta know just which damned side are you on and what in the hell you're tellin' people at church? I'm having a hard time trying to keep from laughing again, 'cause, Dad takes money from all of them. I hear him tell church people at a prayer meeting they need to vote for Democrats when times are bad, but if they wanta stay in touch with the Lord, vote Republican.

Maw is unable to hold back. She says, Boys, there's one thing I have to say to you, though I don't get involved in politics. I don't wanta see any member of our family voting for a Communist or so-called Reds 'cause they don't believe in God. You know the Communists are having meetings here on the west-side of our town, and I better never, hear of any of you goin' to one of those Atheist meetings. I tell her, Maw, the Bible says if anyone denies God it's the most terrible sin you can commit and it's in the book of Psalms where King David calls 'em fools. I heard Reverend Jefferson say that during the revival. Maw says, You're absolutely right, I didn't raise any fools; I hope not. Aunt Dorie hollers, Amen, tell 'em, good, tell 'em good, Maw.

There's a brief pause and Orie says, Spare, I came here today to fire you from my poll workers list and that's what I'm doin' till you make up your mind whose side you're working for, don't expect any more money from me. Maw, you know I don't believe in unions working against the company who is paying them, but I want no part of Commies. Uncle Joe says, Maw, you don't have to worry 'bout me goin' to any of them meetings, but I'm for labor unions and that's not gonna change. I'm tired of seeing men and women working long hours, six and seven days a week, for eight or ten dollars. By the way, Spare, I'm firing you too, so don't ask me for any more money either. I'm feeling kinda sad for, Dad, 'cause now both my uncles fired him. Tears are running down his face and he puts his arms around my uncles one at a time and begins pleading, Please forgive me, brothers, I only wanta make you both happy and I feel like I'm being persecuted 'cause of my devotion to all of you! I know my uncles won't forgive him till after Election Day no matter how much he begs; they never do forgive anyone till Election Day is over. I've seen Dad's tears many times at revivals and know how easy he can turn 'em on. My uncles' shake hands, hug each other making Maw happy, but I wonder how long the truce will last.

Dad's having a hard time understanding why neither of his brothers will hire him back to work the polls. He keeps asking Maw for her help, but she says, Son, you made your bed, now lie in it. He storms away from the house cussing everyone in the family saying, My family is persecuting me and I don't know what I did to deserve this punishment.

Uncle Joes' got a problem. He planned to use Dad to pay off voters to vote straight Democratic, but now he needs someone else for the job and it's gotta be someone he can trust. He decides it's time to get me into politics. The night before Election Day, a gentleman knocks on our back door and Joe greets him with a good handshake and a hug, and I know they must be pals I don't know 'bout. They sit at the kitchen table and talk 'bout the election coming up tomorrow and how much it's gonna cost the Central Committee. I'm listening, but not understanding, and Maw always says to just listen and learn. Finally the man reaches in his coat pocket and pulls out an envelope and hands it to Joe. He says, I think this should take care of it, don't you think so, Irish? Uncle Joe counts the bills and says, It's gonna do just fine and we'll carry the precinct easy; you can rest assured. They hug each other, shake hands again and the guy leaves. I'm kinda wondering what money has to do with voting.

The man is gone and Uncle Joe spreads two hundred one dollar bills 'cross the kitchen table. I've never saw so much money in my life, 'cept maybe the time Dad sold my pictures in Mt. Vernon. Dads' always told me 'bout this long-green stuff and he says theirs nothing like it in the world. This must be it. Joe pulls his black-jack from his back pocket and says, I'd like to see any son-of-a-bitch try and take it. Bid, don't you say one word to your Dad 'bout this money. Uncle Joe knows he can trust me and I tell him, Don't worry about me, Uncle Joe, I'm not telling him or anyone. I know Dad would ask you to borrow some or if you could spare a little. Uncle Joe says, You're smart, kid, a helluva lot smarter than your Dad. Now listen to what I'm tellin' you.

He says, Come over here and sit down; it's time you learned the business of politicking. This is strictly between you and me and Maw or nobody needs to know 'bout this. I can tell Uncle Joe is real serious and he says, Here's what I want yuh to do. Your dad used to do this, but I never could trust him, but I know I can trust you. Tomorrow at seven a.m., I want you to go to the back room of the barbershop and I'll send people over to see you during the day to get paid for voting the Democratic ticket right down the line. This just doesn't sound right, so I ask,

Uncle Joe, Are we allowed to pay people to vote?
Well, it's this way, Son, both parties do it and it might as well be us.
Uncle Orie, does he pay, too?
Sure, he does, only he keeps most of for himself and that's why we'll beat 'em.
How come Dad can't get money from the guy you do?
Only committee-men get the money, now don't worry 'bout it and you know damned good and well they couldn't trust him with ten dollars; let alone two hundred.

Uncle Joe is acting real serious now and telling me things I've never heard before in my whole life. He says, I'm giving you fifty dollars in one dollar bills and you'll find fifteen half pints of liquor in the back room of the barbershop. Someone will knock on the back door and hand you a small wooden block with a two marked on it or a W; two is for dollars and W is for liquor. Don't talk to anyone and don't let your dad inside, no matter what he says. Above all, don't tell Maw one word 'bout this 'cause she just doesn't understand men's things. I'll be at Mrs. Mattingly's house where people vote just in case you need me. I'm gonna give you three dollars at the end of the day. We'll go buy you some new clothes later and nobody will ever know. I know Uncle Joe never tells me wrong 'bout anything. I tell him, Uncle Joe, you've taken me to the show with you, you've taken me to visit your girl friends, let me play your slot machines and I never got in trouble, so I guess whatever you say is O.K. I did think it was wrong when you told me to shoot Old Brownie, but Maw didn't say nothing, so, I guess its fine. I'll do it. He says, That's fine, Bid; I knew you were my ace in the hole.

We're up early on Election Day and the polls are open at six a.m. I'm in the back room of the barbershop and by seven o'clock, several people have knocked on the door and I'm paying off. Everything is going according to what Uncle Joe told me and I guess I'm now in politics. Nobody has heard from Dad till someone saw him in a car with Mr. Hunter 'bout noon time. Both of them were smoking big cigars, laughing and pounding each other on the back as if they won the election. That's good news for Joe and Orie 'cause both seem happy he's not working for them.

Uncle Joe stops by the barbershop 'bout noon and says, Everythings goin' great and it looks like a landslide for the Democrats. I hear a loud knock at the door and there stands one of Uncle Joe's Democrats who I just gave a pint. I remember seeing him sitting on the side-walk in front of Folze's tavern on Franklyn Street last week. He says, I've already drunk my pint, now can I have the two dollars? I've never had this happen today, so I tell him he better see Uncle Joe, 'cause I gotta have the block with two dollars on it. He doesn't understand and now he wants to know if he can sign up for his poor old sickly wife who just passed away 'bout a week ago. He says, She, was a dyed in the wool Democrat for all her thirty eight years, and I'm sure she would take the W. I don't think it's legal like everything else we do, and tell him to see Uncle Joe and maybe he can figure it out. Around five p.m. I'm out of money and only one pint of liquor left. I'm locking up the place and the guy with the dead wife stands at the door. He says, The guy you call Uncle Joe and the guy I call, Irish, says it's O. K. for me to have the W 'cause her name is still on the list. He hands me the W block and I hand him my last pint.

When I get home, Maw asks, Did it go well handing out the Democrat literature at the polls? I'm a little confused what she's talking 'bout till I realize Uncle Joe may not have exactly told Maw what I've been doing. I tell her, It, went just like Uncle Joe said it would and he thinks his party will win. Maw seems kinda proud of me and says, Well, Son, a little experience in this type of work is good for you even though you're kind of young for politicking. I'm never gonna mention the liquor or the money or she'll skin me alive. I tell her, Thanks, Maw, as long as you're happy with me and Uncle Joe is going to give me three dollars. I kinda feel a little guilty 'cause Uncle Orie lost the election, but he didn't offer me three dollars.

Uncle Orie and his family return for breakfast. Nothing is said 'bout the election and we're all happy. I'm learning 'bout politics and Uncle Orie wants me to work for him next election day. He might pay me five dollars. There's a report Dad and Mr. Hunter aren't happy with the outcome and Dad hasn't been home.

18

NEVER POOR AGAIN

During the summer of 1934, Dad's got a job spray painting at a local furniture shop. Along with a little preaching now and then, it keeps him busy and out of trouble with family and friends. I'm not with Dad during his meetings, but I attend church regularly with Maw and relatives. Evansville is beginning to recover from The Great Depression, but many are still out of work. Dade Park race track draws large crowds six days a week and Dad loves it. He made a couple of trips to the track, but came home broke.

It's the middle of the week and while eating dinner Dad gives me the poke and nod for one of our secret talks outside where Maw cain't hear what he's telling me. I know he's afraid she might put her foot down on him real good, now that he's gambling over at Dade Park. He says, Son, I've got it all figured out how we're gonna get that long-green stuff I always told you 'bout. He knows I've always wanted that bicycle he keeps talking 'bout so, I'm gonna listen to this, and I ask, What're you talking 'bout, Dad? He says, We're goin' to Dade Park and I've finally got a system I cain't lose with. I've heard that a couple times before and ask if I hafta go and he says, Hell yes, Son, you're my new system.

Dad doesn't seem to care 'bout all the times we preached 'bout gambling and drinking beer. I tell him, Dad, what if you see all the people from Kentucky at the track and you're a preacher. He looks kinda surprised and says, Son, you always say things 'bout the bad side of life, and I look at 'em on the good side, and that's the big difference in you and me. Hell you're gettin' just like the rest of our family. Now don't you worry 'bout seeing them kinda people at the track 'cause they don't belong there.

Dad says he's taking off from work at noon on Friday, get a cab and pick me up. I ask him how he's gonna get off from work at noon and he says, They won't fire the best spray painter in Evansville just 'cause I don't wanta work on Friday afternoons. Dads always got things figured out and I ask, Dad, how you gonna get your check before going to the track? He says, It's not a problem, Son, I'll just tell 'em I need it for some sickness in the family and they'll be glad to give it to me, 'cause I'm their best spray man. If I tell Maw 'bout this he's gonna get in trouble and I'll never get the long-green to get my bike.

Dad comes to the house for me at noon on Friday in a Yellow cab and we're off to the races. I've got a bad feeling 'bout this, but Dad's happy and Maw says he's still got a legal right to tell me what to do, and where and I'm going. He tells me 'bout all the hot dogs and pop I'm gonna get, but I'm thinking 'bout what Maw's gonna say when she finds 'bout me going to the races where they gamble, cuss, drink beer, and Uncle Joe says a lotta loose women hang out at the track.

We arrive at the track and Dad says, Hurry up, Son, we wanta get a bet down on the first race 'cause that's where all the big money is on the daily double. I don't have any idea what he's talking 'bout, but he sure must love the daily double 'cause he's almost dragging me along. It's getting close to post time in the first race. Dad's running to get a program and I'm heading to the hot dog stand. I gulp down a couple ice cold drinks and hot dogs and Dad hands me a racing program. He says, Son, this is serious stuff 'cause were dealing in long-green stuff here. Now, this is what I want you to do. You just take a look at the first race on the program and then the second race. After you look at both of 'em, tell me which of the horses' names you think will win. I'm trying to to finish my second hotdog and all he's thinking 'bout is the next two races. I tell him, I don't know anything 'bout horses, and Dad, you should do it 'cause your the cavalry man. He won't listen and says, It's gotta be you, Son, 'cause you're my new system. I have no idea what he's talking 'bout, but I'll do it. He's acting kinda crazy now that it's getting near post time. He says, You're not gettin' it, Son, you're just not gettin' it. Don't you know by now you're gifted; nobody but you can remember all the Bible questions like you and it's bound to be a gift from the Lord. I don't know what in the world he's talking 'bout, but I'll just go look at a couple numbers and horses and see how it comes out. I'm telling Uncle Joe 'bout this for sure.

We look the horses over and I tell him I like Zelady in the first and Poppinlong in the second race, and he runs to make a bet. This is beginning to get exciting. Dad says, Lets go down on the rail and we'll watch the race closer to the horses. I want yuh to understand that if your picks win, you're gonna get the best bicycle money can buy. Now, I'm really interested in who wins the race after he promised the new bike and it's a different deal. I tell him, Dad, the two horses I picked looked prettier and bigger than all the rest, so now you know how I picked 'em. He acts happy to hear that and says, Well, that's fine, Son, but deep down I know the Lord probably guided you. I know he's wrong again, wrong again.

It's post time in the first race and we're standing at the rail. A loud voice comes over the loudspeaker and yells, They're off and running in the first! The announcer starts calling the race every step of the way and I don't hear Poppinalong called one time. They're coming down the stretch and he starts yelling, And on the outside Poppinalong is moving fast, and now he's third, now he's second and as they come to the finish he yells, Poppinalong wins by two lengths. Dads yelling, My system works, my system works! I'm thinking he's gone nuts like all these other people yelling their heads off. I wanta go get our money, but Dad tells me we still have to win the next race to get the long-green.

Dad's excited, but no more than me. I'm thinking of that red and white balloon tired bicycle in the store front at Montgomery Ward. He's looking at the race program for the second race, when a guy Dad knows sits next to him. I look at him again 'cause this guy doesn't have one hair on his entire head, but he's got big bushy eyebrows.

He says, Hi, Spare, it's been a long time.
Hi, Baldy, it sure has.
Last time I saw you wuz when you got shot by Posey Beckham.
Yep, I was eight years old, and I've been shot again, since that time.
Dad holds up his finger and says, Lost, this in the cavalry.
You sure as hell live a charmed life life, Spare.
Yeh, I'm just lucky, I guess.
Heard you been preachin' Spare? Is this the boy I heard 'bout?
Sure is, Baldy, he's smart as a whip.
Son, this is Baldy, a school mate of mine, and he was with me when I got shot by Posey Beckham.
Pleased to meet you, Mr. Baldy.
The boy has good manners, Spare.
I try to raise him right, Baldy, but it sure has been tough since he ain't got a mother. We got the daily double goin' and we need time to look 'em over in the next race. Try not to bother us, Baldy.
I've got the winner, Spare.
Who?
Water Splash, and it's a sure thing. It came right from the barn.
He's a mudder, Baldy.
Not today, Spare, it's fixed.
How do you know?
I'm in on things 'round the barn.
Baldy, you're wrong this time. I got this from heaven, and it never misses.
Who is it, Spare?
Zelady, and it's a sure thing.

Baldy is running to the betting window and doesn't look back, and now I wanta find out 'bout Baldy.

I ask, Who else was with you, Dad, when Posey Bechham shot you?
Two pals, Archie Wilson and Murel Williams.

How come Posey shot-cha, Dad?

He just got married and we were playin' a joke on him.

Was he mad at you?

I guess he was, Son, 'cause he sure as hell shot me and I almost died. Now, let's don't talk 'bout all that old crap that happened long ago. Let's just get Zelady to win this race.

You're right, Dad, I wanta get the bike at Montgomery Ward.

It's getting near post time for the second race and I can tell Dad's kinda nervous. He's talking low to himself, biting his nails and sometimes I hear him say, Help me, Lord, for the boy's sake. Dad's beginning to worry 'bout Baldy's tip and doesn't like the odds on our horse 'cause it's twenty to one, and now Water Splash drops to three to one and it's not looking good for our daily double. Dad wants to go get another bet on Water Splash even if it's not raining and the track's not muddy. I like the way Zelady looks as she parades by us and takes a shit; Dad says now she's gotta chance 'cause she's carrying less weight, but I just wish the race would get over and Zelady wins.

The announcer is yelling two minutes till post time and everyone is headed towards the rail or betting windows. We head towards the rail and a big guy stands next to me with horse reigns around his neck. He wears a black cowboy hat and puffs on a big cigar and looks more nervous than Dad. The announcer hollers, They're off!' and running in the second, and everyone starts acting nuts with their shouting and yelling as the horses head down the backstretch and we haven't even seen the horses yet. The announcer yells," And they're coming down the stretch" and still no mention of Zelady. Dad's going nuts and the guy next to me is yelling and cussing Zelady just like Uncle Joe cussed the witch, Mrs. White. Now they're halfway down the stretch and the announcer hollers, "On the outside Zelady is moving up." The big guy hollers, Put the battery to that no good son of bitch and I don't know what he's talking 'bout. Suddenly as they pass in front of us Zeladys' tail stands straight out and she runs by everything and wins by three lengths.

Dad says, Son, let's go over to the winner's circle and take a look at the horse that answered my prayers. Standing just outside the enclosure, and I cain't believe what I'm seeing till I get closer. There in front of me stands the big cowboy looking guy getting his picture taken and acting like he really loves, Zelady. I cain't understand anything 'bout horses. I tell Dad, The big guy was cussing Zelady just a few minutes ago and now he's down there kissing her on the forehead. Dad says, Well, Son, that guy has probably got problems and you and me haven't. There are really some nuts out here at Dade Park, but you and me aren't like them 'cause we gotta system. I ask Dad 'bout Baldy's horse, Water Splash, and he says, Son, that's just what I'm trying to teach you, don't pay one bit of attention to guys like, Baldy, hell, he never did learn to write in school till the third grade. I knew all along Water Splash didn't have a chance 'cause he's only a mudder. I'm thinking 'bout what Maw's gonna say 'bout all this money.

We might have trouble at home if Maw finds out 'bout this.
Well, she don't need to know anything and don't you dare tell her.
I still think Maw's gonna really be mad when she hears 'bout that big guy cussing Zelady.
Please, Son, don't bring up what you're gonna tell Maw one more time. I don't care what yuh tell her, but don't let her know how much money I've got. If my brothers find out, they'll want me to pay back some old bills I've already forgot 'bout; hell Orie will probably still remember that five bucks he always bugged me about.

Dad's got me by the arm and we head to the cashier's stand to collect our winnings. Dad says, We're rich, Son, we're rich! There'll never be another poor day from now on. I've got a system nobody can beat and I'm gettin' it directly from heaven to you. I know you're gifted, but I never dreamed it would be this way. Whatever you do, don't tell Maw or Uncle Joe 'bout my system, 'cause this is just between us. Do you understand, Son? Dads really excited and I like winning, but I hafta tell the truth. I tell him, I think it was just luck and I didn't ask for nothing from heaven. I can tell he doesn't believe me by the funny look on his face.

The cashier begins counting out the money and Dad's grabbing it almost faster than the clerk can count. The clerk says, That's one hundred and four dollars, mister, so be careful when you leave the track. Dad says, You are absolutely right, buddy, one thing you can be sure of is, that I know how to take care of money. I tell Dad, It's almost as much money he got selling my pictures in Mt. Vernon. He says, Yeah, you're right, Son, but this is a lot easier and that's the way I like it. Now that I've got a system to beat the ponies, I'll never have to work another day in my life and you can have anything you want. From now on my brothers are gonna be asking to borrow money from me and that's sure gonna be a switch. I just might make it hard for 'em just like they do me when I wanta borrow a little to tide me over till payday. Heck, I'll be richer than Mr. Hunter.

Dad's rambling on 'bout his good luck and fortune and how he never will hafta work like ordinary guys again. It doesn't sound right to me. I tell him, Dad, I don't know what you mean 'bout system, and he says, Well, Son, there's no doubt in my mind that you're gettin' this information from heaven. You've always been blessed. All we have to do is hand you a program and when the horses walk by, you can look at 'em and get your inspiration from heaven. That's how we did it today and as soon as you find out the winners, I'll load down on 'em. Dad's got it wrong, I'll tell him again. You know what, Dad, I think you're off a little. I didn't get an inspiration from heaven to say Zelady was gonna win. I really believe when that guy standing close to us yelled, 'Put the battery to that no good bitch' was the secret. When he yelled it, Zelady's tail went straight out, just like someone hit her in the butt real good. Dad doesn't believe me and he says, Listen, to me, Son, there are lots of things you just don't understand. When you're older and educated like me, you'll understand that using batteries is against the law. It's plain and simple Son, you're gifted like nobody ever was. If heaven wants you to have it, don't turn it down 'cause it might even be a sin to not use your gift. I tell him, Well, I don't think

Maw will agree with your thinking, Dad, and he says, Well, for one thing, you're not gonna tell her for sure. I'm puttin' my foot down on that, and it's a rule. I tell Dad, I still think the guy next to us made Zelady run a lot faster than I did.

We head for the entrance and Dad says, Stand here, Son, and wait for me. I've gotta have something to drink to clear my throat. I think the dust on the track caused me to have a chokin' feeling and I need something wet. He's at the stand gulping down a beer without taking his mouth from the bottle and comes back and says, I'm ready now, Son, let's get outta here. I tell him, I saw you drink the beer, Dad, and you know it makes you crazy. You been preaching that everybody else shouldn't do it and the first time you get money, you fall off the wagon just like Uncle Orie and Uncle Joe say you do. Dad's, not liking what I'm saying and says, Now, there you go, Son, accusing me of drinking beer when it was only Coca Cola; it's just that it was served at a beer stand. You shouldn't judge your own dad and you're always trying to find fault with me.

We head for the outside to catch a cab and here comes, Baldy, and he's yelling for us to stop. He's hollering, I've got another one, Spare, I've gotta another one. I don't know what he means, but Dad does. Dad says, Let's get the hell away from him, Son, he's got nothin' but losers, and I sure don't need tips now that I've got my system.

A string of cabs sit outside the park entrance and we get the first cab in line and head home. Dad says, Drop us off downtown at Montgomery Ward, driver, I wanta buy my boy the best bicycle they have. He asks, Do, yuh, want me to wait, sir? Dad says, Sure, driver, nothing's too good for the rich. We walk into Montgomery Ward and buy the best balloon tired American Flyer bicycle they have and we're off for home.

Maw says, I can't believe my eyes at what I'm seeing, Son. Do you mean to tell me that the boy's got a new bike and you're paying your board on time? Dad acts real proud of himself and says, Sure am, Maw, you finally got one rich son and I'll never be poor again and you can bank on that. Maw acts suspicious and says, You robbed a bank, didn't you, Son, have you finally come to this? Don't you know bank robbing can send you to prison for life? You'll be just like that bank robber, John Dillinger. Now Dad is feeling hurt and says, What in the world you talkin' 'bout, Maw, I didn't rob no bank; I got me a system. Maw don't know what he's talking 'bout and says, Well, I don't know what your system is all 'bout, but it can't be what the Lord would have you do. I tell her, That's what I told him too, Maw, but I think he'll start acting crazy again and I saw him drinking beer that he called Coca Cola. He'll hafta go get saved again, won't he, Maw? Maw don't know what to think, but finally says, Oh Lordy, Son, is it that bad? I'm telling her the truth and say, Maw, he's got some crazy idea the Lord is telling me whose gonna win at the races. I think Uncle Joe and Orie will think he's crazier than a loon, don't you, Maw? She says, I think you're right, Son, I'm just gonna leave it to the Lord like I always do. I guess I will too, 'cause I can see that look in his eyes that Aunt Dorie calls, sheepish. I tell her, Maw, there was a big guy who might be a cowboy, guy standing next to me cussing Zelady real bad, calling her a B-I-T-C-H, but Dad was asking Jesus to help him win. Maw doesn't know 'bout races like we do, and she says, Well, Son, you can hear anything at that sin hole. By the way, Son, I'm glad you can spell all the bad words you hear 'round race tracks.

Dad is dressed and on his way out the door without saying goodbye. Maw and me walk to the door and watch him depart in another Yellow Cab. She says, Well, I don't think we'll see your dad for a few days now that he's got some money, but as usual that won't last long. I tell her, You're right, Maw, but I really don't care now that I've got my new bike. When he gets a dollar in his pocket, he just goes nuts, doesn't he, Maw? He's always been that way, Son, only the Lord will ever change him. That's why he's in the Lord's hands.

I'm in the street with my friends and taking turns riding on my new bike and everyone listens while I tell 'bout how we won the money and I got my new bike. A couple of 'em run and tell their parents about our winning at Dade Park, and now all of 'em wanta go and try their luck. On Saturday I ride the bike till mid-afternoon and Maw calls me in the house and says, Son, we've got to start gettin' prepared for Sunday school and church tomorrow, so you're gonna have to stay here and help me. Bob takes off with the new bike and I ask her if she thinks Dad might be in church tomorrow to get saved for gambling and drinking beer? She shakes her head, and says, Don't, be surprised if he doesn't show up for a couple days with the kind of money he had, but he did pay his board and that I didn't expect. I tell her, He's in the Lord's hands ain't he, Maw, and only he knows what's gonna happen to Dad. Maw says, Only the Lord knows what's gonna happen to that boy next, lets just pray for him tonight 'cause I gotta feelin' he's gonna need it.

19

JAIL TIME FOR SPARE

It's Sunday morning and Dad's not home. Everyone is getting ready for church and Uncle Orie comes to the house and says, I've got some pretty bad news for you, Bid. Let's sit here at the table and talk 'bout it. Maw, me, Joe, Bob and Pat, are seated and my heart starts racing; it's gotta be 'bout, Dad. Orie says, I just got a call 'bout twenty minutes ago from the police department in Henderson saying your dad is locked up and he needs a hundred and eight dollars to pay his fine. I don't know the whole story of what he might have done, but that's a hell of a lot of money. Nobody can talk for a while 'cause hardly anyone ever hears 'bout that much money unless you go to the race track of hold a revival and sell pictures. I glance at Maw for an answer and ask, What are we gonna do? Maw, Dad's sure got himself in something bad this time, hasn't he? Maw says, We, will do what we have to do, and put our trust in the Lord. She's always right about everyting, but this time I don't know what she means and it sure doesn't sound good. For once Uncle Joe cain't say nothing and just sits and shakes his head in disgust, then he finally says, What in the hell could he have done that cost that much money? Hell, I could have got outta jail for bootlegging for that kind of money. Maw says, Now, children, this is no time to criticize your brother till we find out what it could be, and it might be just something he did innocently. She grabs her purse and is off to church. Uncle Orie says, Nothing is gonna keep Maw outta church on Sunday, they could hang poor old Spare, and she wouldn't miss church.

Orie says, Sunday morning is the worst time of the week to raise this much money, but I may be able to get it from my boss, Mr. O'Leary, at

Fendrich Cigar. Spare's my, brother, but he sure as hell can get in more scrapes than the whole damned family; but he's still my brother. I'll tell you one thing, if I get his ass outta jail this time, he's gonna pay it back right away, or I'll make him wish he'd never been born. Come on, Bid, let's go get the crazy preacher outta jail or he'll drive the damned Jailers nuts. Joe asks, Do you want me to go along? Uncle Orie says, Hell no, you'd probably get put in jail yourself if they found out you're still wanted in Georgia.

We arrive at Mr. O'Leary's home near the Ohio River in the most exclusive part of Evansville. Orie says, This sure is one hell of a time to call on my employer and ask for money. I know how he must feel and say, I'd hate to even ask for a dollar, Uncle Orie, let alone a hundred and eight. You must really like my dad a lot to do this for him. He says, I do, Son, you know I do, but sometimes he drives me up a wall with some of the silly shit he does. I always remember though two things 'bout him. One thing is that he may not be responsible for some of the things he does. I guess you know he was shot by a neighbor at the age of eight. There's another thing we all did when your mother died that makes me feel kinda responsible 'bout. I ask, What's that? He says, Me and Joe said we'd kinda look after you 'cause your mom, was worried your dad might have a little trouble raising you. One thing for sure, everybody needs somebody and you do need him no matter what he does. I tell him, I guess sometimes I don't know who I'd go to if it wasn't for you, Uncle Joe, and Maw. I'm luckier than a lot of kids, and some kids don't have anyone. Sometimes Maw says I live better than the other half out at Boehne Camp Hospital. Orie says, You're right there, Son. There's a helluva lot worse cases than yours for sure, and I guess she was talkin' 'bout them; but I sure as hell ain't gonna be one of 'em.

I gaze around the outside the beautiful big brick home and imagine what it's gonna look like inside. It might even be prettier than Mr. and Mrs. McDowell's house. Orie is ringing a doorbell and it's the first one I ever saw. After a couple of minutes a big handsome man in a beautiful robe and pajamas is standing in front of me at the door. Immediately he recognizes Uncle Orie and invites us inside his house. He smiles and says, This sure is a little different, Orie, I'm seeing you this time of the morning and on Sunday. Orie says, Well, Sir, I sure appreciate you letting me into your house this early on Sunday morning, but I want you to know I wouldn't be here unless it was something I just have to do for my brother.

I'm listening and looking around the rooms and I know I've finally found the place Maw always tells me 'bout rich people. They must be the other half above us and I don't need to worry 'bout ever being part of it 'cause we're never gonna be rich. I'm thinking if we got our inheritance in Ireland, I could live like Mr. O'leary. This place is beyond compare. The big room we stand in is as big as our whole house, and the furniture, desk, and rugs look like heaven might be. I'm never gonna forget this place and I'm sure gonna tell Maw 'bout the other half.

Orie explains his predicament to his boss. He walks into another room and in a few minutes comes back and hands him the money. Orie says, Mr. O'Leary, let me have some paper and I'll sign a note for you. Mr. O'Leary smiles again and says, No you won't, Orie, you work for me and your word is better than any piece of paper. They shake hands and I wanta give him the kinda shake Dad taught me. I stick my hand out, Mr. O'Leary shakes it real good, and says, You've got a good handshake young man and its not like some wimp; lots of kids don't have one like that. I tell him, Thank you, sir, my dad taught me that, he's the one in jail; it's not my Uncle Joe this time. He laughs and says, I can see why your uncle Orie has you with him. I'm feeling real proud, and Uncle Orie is ready to leave 'cept I don't like borrowing money from a stranger. I like Mr. O'Leary now that I'm part of the loan. Outside Uncle Orie says, Bid, from now on let me do the most of the talkin', but you did give him one helluva handshake, and I'm kinda proud of you for that.

We head for Henderson and Uncle Orie begins explaining things to me 'bout my heritage. He says, Bid, you're at an age now where you need to start gettin' tough. I think maybe you should know something 'bout our family and how we lived when your dad and me were children. When Joe and me were growing up and Maw got married to Lige; our life changed completely. He used to whip our ass for almost anything, especially if we wasted food. We got so we hated the damned sight of him. There were a lot of times he'd grab us by the arms and sling us across the room, but we never let him know how much it hurt. We laid awake many a night planning how we would someday whip his ass good, but damned if he didn't die on us first. Uncle Orie tells me everything 'bout Dad during his early life. I ask, Did my dad really get his finger shot off in the Cavalry, or did he do it himself? He says, He shot it off, sure as hell, Bid, because he just wanted to get outta the army and come home. This is no surprise, but I sure heard a lot of other different stories and none of 'em the same. I tell him 'bout how Dad and me went to Henderson to preach in the park, and he says, This is gonna be a hell of a lot different than preachin' in the park, Bid. Just get yourself ready for this.

I'm doing a lot of serious thinking and we're not talking much till finally Orie says, I want yuh to be just like your Uncle Joe and me have taught you all your life. Above all no matter what they say or do, don't cry, 'cause I don't have the slightest idea what we're gonna run into, but it won't be good. You know I've got my own kids tough as nails and that's the way life is, and you gotta face life whatever it takes. You understand, don't you, Son? I know he's telling the truth like always and I'm getting wiser and smarter 'bout lotta things now. I tell him, I sure do, Uncle Orie. You won't see tears coming from me no matter what.

We arrive at the police station and go inside to the front desk where a big tough looking policeman looks straight in my eyes and says, What'cha need, young man, you here to tell us how to run the place? He sure doesn't look too friendly, and I tell him, No, sir, we're here to get my dad outta jail and we already got the hundred and eight dollars. The policeman smiles at Orie, and says, I don't think you need to tell me who your here for, it's your dad, the preacher, ain't it? I tell him, Yes sir, that's my dad.

Do you know him? He says, I sure do, Son, even heard you and him down in the park preaching 'bout a couple of years ago. I liked you more than him that day and still do. I can tell Uncle Orie doesn't like what's going on between me and the cop. When he starts getting mad his neck starts swelling and things don't get too happy after that. Uncle Orie says, We just wanta pay the fine and get the hell outta here, Buddy, so please let's just get it over with. He says, Sure can friend, and yells, Bring the preacher to the front there's someone here to pay his fine. I feel kinda embarrassed and Orie can see it.

I already feel kinda sorry for Dad, even though he gets into some bad messes. They bring him in to us and he's looking like he's lost everything in the world. I guess Uncle Orie will try and cheer him up. Orie says, You sure are one helluva a looking mess, brother, 'bout like that time you come home after jumping out the window at Joe's bootleg joint. Dad ain't saying nothing, and I don't feel like smiling at all. The cop takes the money and gives a receipt to Orie and comes around the counter and puts his arms on my shoulders. Now, he smiles and says, I'm sorry, Son, I should have used a little more discretion in how I talked to you 'bout your dad. I guess he had us all so mad, we didn't care what happened to him and we just wanted to get him outta here. People have been calling here all morning asking 'bout the preacher. It's kinda embarrassing. We don't like someone making us look bad, but he sure as hell did when he escaped.

Uncle Orie and me don't know nothing 'bout him escaping, and it sounds almost like Uncle Joe when he was down in Georgia. Orie says, Mister, would you mind tellin' us just what he did? Suddenly the officer's mood is changing from compassion to anger. He says, Well, for one thing, he was driving a brand new Essex Terraplane car without a driver's license and he was drunk as anyone I ever saw. He ran that damned car down the middle of the prettiest flower garden in the city of Henderson, and tried to tell us he was flying an airplane. That's not even the end of it. The cop's getting madder all the time and I'd like to get outta here, and so would Dad. The cop says, The worst part is that after we caught his ass and had him in the car with us on the way to the lockup, he jumped outta the rear seat and escaped. He took off running down Green Street faster than a damned race horse and left us standing on the corner. We finally caught him down in the L&N Railroad Yard all huddled up in the back of an empty boxcar. We drug his ass outta there and damned if he didn't say he forgave us for persecuting him. I knew that's what Dad would say and tell the cop, Sure sounds like my dad, he always did wanta fly an airplane and Elmo said someday he might try. Orie says, That's for damned sure; sometimes he gets some damned crazy ideas.

The cop wants to talk more and says, Do you know what in the hell he meant by persecuting him? Hell, if anyone was being persecuted, it was us. This morning when I woke him up, he looked me damned well straight in the eyes and said, 'Brother, I forgive you.' What in the hell is wrong with this guy? You're his brother, you should know. Is he some kind of idiot that thinks he can do this to the Henderson police and get away with it? He almost had me feeling sorry for him after seeing the tears in his eyes. I can tell the cops really getting mad and now, sweat is running down his face while he pulls out his handkerchief and wipes it off. I tell him, Maw told me ever since he read in the Bible how Christians will be persecuted in the last days, he thinks it means him. The cop shakes his head and says, Well, I'll be damned if that don't take the prize. It sure as hell ain't him that's being persecuted; it's us being persecuted by him, a damned preacher. He looks at me real pitiful like Dad does sometimes and says, Do you think you can understand this, kid? I tell him, I sure do, sir, and so does my Uncle Orie and if my Uncle Joe and Maw were here they would understand, too. Uncle Orie says, I just wanta get the hell outta here, but the cop doesn't listen to him.

The cop is getting what Mrs. Bethel calls frustrated and says, We're damned well off to get him outta here. Hell, he'd have us thinkin' we were guilty of something the way he can bring tears on and then tell us he forgives us. He finally finishes, and wipes his brow with his handkerchief again. Uncle Orie says, Mister, I'm sure sorry 'bout all this and I'm sure you understand 'bout this boy of his, so if it's O.K., we'll just be on our way. The cop puts his arms around me and hugs me, and says, Good luck to you, lad, you're sure as hell gonna need it and I sure hope your momma can take this. I tell him, My momma is dead, sir, but I gotta real good grandma and some good uncles. He turns away, shakes hands with Orie, and I give him my good handshake, he smiles and says, You sure got one helluva handshake for a little kid, now please, just take the preacher and get the hell outta here.

We leave with Dad and Orie says, Bid, we need to go see where your dad damaged the flowers. We arrive at the end of the street and it's hard to believe what we're seeing. Orie says, My God, there's not one flower left standing. Dad won't look at us. Orie says, What in the hell did you think you were doing, Spare? Now Uncle Orie begins to act like the cop. There's a whole city block of beautiful flowers all bent over looking like someone mowed 'em down. Orie says, Spare, they should have socked your ass five hundred dollars instead of a measly one hundred and eight. Uncle Orie is really getting mad now, and I see his neck swelling again. He says, Spare, you better answer me when I talk to you, what in the hell happened here? Dad won't answer and Uncle Orie is still yelling at him. Finally he looks at Orie and says, Brother, you're not gonna believe this, but I thought I finally found a way to fly an airplane. Orie says, You're the craziest asshole in the world, Spare. The car you drove was no airplane; it was a damned Essex Terraplane automobile, not a damned airplane. Do you think you can understand what I'm tellin' you? Dads almost crying now and says, Yes, I do now, brother, but at the time I was driving or flying, I really thought it could fly. Orie says, Well it sure as hell cain't and furthermore, it's gonna take some tall explaining to your brother, Viv, at the cab company when he sees the damage to the car. Dad's crying now and tears are coming down fast. He says, Does Maw and Joe know I've been in jail? Uncle Orie starts laughing for a change and says, Spare, the whole damned city of Henderson and everybody in our neighborhood will know 'bout it before the day is out; you, can bet your ass on that.

We're on the way home and everything is getting quiet.

Dad says, Brother, they sure worked me over when they drug me outta the railroad car.

I can see you got one hell of a black eye and your clothes are torn all to hell, says Orie.

Dad, Uncle Joe's gonna laugh when he sees how bad you look, can you kinda slip in without him seeing you?

Orie says, There's no damned way you can slip in, everybody is gonna be waiting at the door.

Uncle Orie, maybe they went to church.

Not today, Son, this is gonna be a day all our family, Martin's and McCaffrys, will be there when your daddy comes home.

Dad says, Well I guess I will just have to stand the persecution instead of love and forgiveness as preached in the Bible.

Orie says, Please, Spare, don't give us any more of your forgiveness shit; just face the music.

Dad, remember when Uncle Joe came home from prison, now you can be just like him when he was treated like the Prodigal Son, but I doubt if they'll have a picnic.

We're home and in the front yard stand Cotton, Titties, Slim, Bob, Pat, Evelyn, some neighbor kids and Aunt Dorie, but no Maw; she's gone to church. I'll cheer him up a little, and tell him, It almost looks like you're a hero, Dad, just like Uncle Joe. He says, Please, Son, don't add to your father's persecution, this is bad enough for me to bear. Dad is headed for the house and everyone is looking at his appearance. He turns and says, Family, I'm sorry for what I did, but please forgive me. Titties yells, You, better get right with the Lord, Uncle Spare. Dad says, I'm taking care of it tonight, Titties, just you watch. Everyone is looking at each other and Cotton says, I know where I'll be tonight; in Maw's church on the front row. So will all of us, hollers Bob. Pat says, It's gonna be something to see when Uncle Spare prays for his forgiveness at the altar. We're gonna hear some good stuff tonight when he confesses and I wanta hear 'bout how he gotta way from them cops. Cotton says, I hope there's something 'bout women in it. One thing 'bout Uncle Spare, he's not like the rest of them Pilgrim Holiness. He always tells 'bout every sin he's done and he don't care who hears it.

Dad's with Maw during the afternoon and pleading forgiveness 'bout getting locked up in jail. He says, Maw, if you'll just forgive me one more time, I'll straighten up, quit sinning, and it'll never happen again as long as I live. She says, Please listen, and try to understand; it's not me you've gotta worry 'bout, it's the Lord. Right now I wouldn't wanta be in your shoes if He happened to come back. Dads crying now and big tears are coming down his face. He says, I know, Maw, I know. I'm gonna get everything taken care of at the altar tonight. Do you think the preacher knows I'm gonna be in church tonight? Maw pats him on the head and says, Son, the whole neighborhood knows you'll be in church tonight. It's up to you and not me to take care of your word to God. Dad says, I know, Maw, I know, and I'm gonna do it. There is something else I been thinkin' 'bout, do you think my son needs to ask forgiveness, too? He was part of my system. Maw shakes her head in disbelief and says, You know better than that, Arthur, it wasn't him that guided you to the sin hole, it was your own way of trying to get rich while doing nothing. Don't you dare try and lay this onto your son, or you'll go to hell for sure.

It's time for church and the service begins with Reverend Johnson in the pulpit. The church is full as usual. Tonight the two front rows on the right are full of Maw's kids and grandchildren we haven't seen for weeks. We could almost call this a reunion like we had when Uncle Joe came back from prison. Sitting next to Maw is Aunt Dorie, and Dad sits next to her with his head down. He's not looking anywhere. Cotton, Titties and Slim are whispering among themselves 'bout 'when's it gonna be time for Uncle Spare? The preacher ends his sermon and everyone begins singing the old favorite song **Just As I Am,** and Dad is heading for the altar. Titties wants to get closer to the altar and hear Dad's confession and everyone else moves with him. Maw and Aunt Dorie don't move and I'm gonna hear this one more time, even if I have heard it a dozen times with Uncle Orie.

Dad is on his knees and the preacher comes to him and kneels beside him. He says, What is it this time, Spare, 'causing you so much trouble? Dad says, You, mean you haven't heard 'bout me, Reverend Johnson, I just got outta jail just like my brother, Joe did before me. I guess it's just the old devil and I know I have a little problem with temptation. The preacher says, It happens to all of us, brother, so you just stay here at the altar and tell Jesus 'bout it. All the kids are moving closer to Dad, but so are other people in the audience including a couple of church deacons. Dad is confessing everything and going well, till he says something 'bout his system, I turn my head to Maw, and tell her, I wasn't part of it, Maw, I tried to tell him it was wrong, and she tells me not to worry, 'cause he's the father and he's the one who should guide me in the right direction and not to race tracks. My friends come closer and ask 'bout what system Dad and me got and they won't quit asking, especially Cotton. This is no place to be talking 'bout horses near the altar. I tell 'em, Cousins, I ain't got no system 'bout betting horses, but Dad had some crazy idea I was finding out 'bout races through heaven. Cotton says, If you do, Bid, be sure and let me know, 'cause even if Uncle Spare did go to jail, he sure had himself a good time for a while.

Dad is raising his arms toward the ceiling and now he hollers, I'm forgiven, I'm forgiven, it's all over. One of the deacons mutters, I sure hope he means it this time. Dad says, It's for good this time, brother Johnson, never again will I stray. Bob and me hear the conversation. Bob says, I'll bet he does stray, don't you, Bid? He understands things like me and I tell him, Sure he will; we all stray, everyone strays at times. When I got my new bike from winning all the money, I wanted some more of the long-green. I'll tell you one thing though, Bob, I ain't gonna do it no more 'cause Maw had a good talk with me. Bob says, Bid, I've been thinkin' 'bout something I heard Uncle Spare say to the preacher 'bout how he jumped out of the police car and got away. Maybe if they didn't ever catch him, like Uncle Joe did down in Georgia, he could be a hero, too. Bob just don't understand the difference in Dad and Uncle Joe. I tell him, No, you got it wrong there, pal. Dad could never be a hero 'cause he talks and confesses too much and Uncle Joe never tells.

Pat joins us and says, When Brother Salvatori was patting Uncle Spare at the altar tellin' him to 'come through clean, what did he mean? I tell him, Dad wasn't telling everything in his confession and the Lord wants to here it all. Pat says, If he told it all, we'd probably be there all night, wouldn't we Bid? Bob says, If Uncle Joe ever confesses, I'm gonna be here with my lunch. We all laugh, put our arms around each other and leave the church. Dad is back in good grace and we all heard what we came for, right along with lots of other people. On Monday morning Dad goes to work and is home early. The best spray man in the city of Evansville has just got fired and Dad is out of work. He must not have been the best spray man they had, after all.

Dade Park is over for the summer, and my life with Dad is getting worse. There's no more preaching or answering Bible questions in the churches and Dad is having a problem with gambling and drinking. I'm going to church with Maw and without Dad, and lots of people are always asking me if he's doing better. I just smile and tell 'em I don't know and Maw says, That's the way to handle things, Son.

20

THE BARBERSHOP

Rumblings of war are all over the newspapers in 1936 and I'm learning a lot 'bout what's going on in the world and everything interest me a lot. I'm almost ten years old and even girls are starting to enter my mind. I read 'bout a fellow named Hitler whose making big splashes in the paper and his Nazi party is active in the United States. In the Far East, the Japanese are ready for war against the Chinese and the people in our country are just coming out of the worst Depression the world has ever seen. I love to read the newspapers for information and the local barbershop is the best place to find out 'bout everything.

The barbershop is only one block from our house and the barber's name is Victor. Maw tells me to call him Uncle Victor 'cause he's married to another one of my cousins and it shows respect. Victor's, not a big guy, only 'bout five feet six inches tall with long, wavy, black hair and everyone seems to like him. I had my first haircut from Victor and he's considered the best barber on the west-side. Victor always treats me like an equal, and we have some man to man talks. We understand each other 'cause he knows all 'bout Dad and my history preaching and going to church. Maw says Victor will someday be in church 'cause he's now number five on her list.

Uncle Victor says I can come to the shop and shine shoes and then I'd be in business just like him. All I gotta do is get the stand, the polish and get Uncle Joe to build it for me. I can use the money a lot 'cause Dad's not around much and if I'm in business I'll be better off than some of my friends. Victor says, Bid, if you set up your stand in here, remember one thing. I ask, What's that Uncle Victor? He says, There ain't gonna be any monkey business, and you gotta keep your mind on the shop and its reputation. I'm gonna do it.

I tell Maw all 'bout Uncle Victor's offer and she agrees as long as it doesn't interfere with my school work and church. Maw says I'll learn a lot in the barber shop and I might meet some nice Christian people. Uncle Joe is started on the shoeshine stand and I'm telling lots of my friends 'bout my business and they cain't come around unless they wanta get a haircut or a shoeshine 'cause Victor doesn't allow any monkey business.

I like the barbershop. I guess you can call it a place of learning, but it's mostly 'bout the neighborhood. I meet new people. There's lots of church people like Pilgrim Holiness, Methodist, Catholics, sinners, saints, good, the bad and politicians while I'm hearing a lot 'bout people I never knew before. Mommas come in with the little ones and I see Uncle Victor frown, but he pats the little devils on the head and says, Hi sweet thing, fights with 'em while they're screaming bloody murder and when it's over, he hands 'em a sucker. I listen to the Holiness people tell Victor how much they need him and his wife join them in the music program. I know he won't, 'cause when the shop closes, he and Uncle Joe take me with 'em to Folze Tavern on Franklyn Street and they drink the beer and smoke the cigarettes. That's not Pilgrim Holiness belief, and if you do it they'll take your name off the books, unless you get saved, baptized and sanctified again like, Dad.

Some of the church people come in and say, What's Spare, and his brother, Joe, up to now-days? Victor smiles and says, I haven't the slightest idea, ask his son, the shoeshine boy. They don't ask. Brother Hilmon comes in for his monthly clipping and Victor says, How, 'bout a shave, but he don't answer 'cause it cost a dime. He gets real happy sometime at our church, runs up and down the aisle, waves his Bible and hollers hallelujah and it almost sounds like the stuff I saw at the Holy Roller church in Mt. Vernon where Dad got all the long-green for my pictures.

Mr. Robinson from our church comes in. He acts like he doesn't know me, but I know him. He talks to Victor and says, Make it fast Vic, I kinda had a bad night last night. Victor asks why and he says, Well Vic, My next door neighbor was beating his wife at two a. m. in the morning and kept me awake all night. He was chasing her outside with a knife and she was screaming and yelling her head off for someone to call the police. Victor says, I'll, bet they threw his butt in jail, didn't they? Mr. Robinson acts like he's not hearing Victor at first till he asks him again and now he says, I didn't call the police, Vic, I learned a long time ago not to get involved in family fights. I kinda wonder if he sinned 'cause he didn't help her, but I remember what Maw said 'bout everyone is gonna answer for their own sins.

My favorite customer is a friend of Dad's named Johnny Rudd. He's one cool customer who comes every Friday afternoon after he quits work on pay day. He's someone with a great sense of humor, good looking, black wavy hair, dresses like Fred Astaire, and a heckuva good tipper. He always says, Hi Bid, how you doing and how's your dad? I always tell him Dad's doing fine even though I haven't maybe seen him for a couple days. Dad dated his sister a couple times when he was living right and going to church. When he quit living right and started sinning, that was the end of the dates. Maw always said she was too nice for Dad anyhow.

I'm beginning to notice girls more than ever before and I stand in the doorway of the barbershop and watch 'em go by. Nelda comes by every afternoon after school and stands just outside the barbershop door and just looks at me without moving. She's my age and in the sixth grade, and the cutest little red head in the entire school. She's got long curly hair that hangs down to her shoulders, lily white skin with a few nice freckles sprinkled over her face and teeth as white as snow. I can find no fault in Nelda 'cept she flirts with lots of other guys and must know I'm here 'cause everyone knows I'm in business. I watch her chewing her gum, blowing bubbles and popping it all over her pretty white face. Victor sees me watching her and tells me to finish shining my friend Johnny's shoes. I guess Victor knows 'bout me and Nelda. I don't know what's happening to me, but I cain't quit thinking 'bout Nelda and the long pretty red hair. I really like the shoeshine business, the money is coming in and I'm thinking 'bout taking her to the drug store someday and buy her an ice cream cone.

Business is kinda slow at the barbershop this early in the afternoon till in walks Dessie Brown who only lives a couple doors from here. She likes to sunbathe in her backyard in the afternoon and she's one real good looker with a shape to match her looks. Cotton sometimes watches and invites me to watch her sunbathe, but I'm in business now and it would be bad to be caught watching her. Cotton is now in Reitz High School and he doesn't care what Uncle Victor finds out 'bout him. He says she don't come out till her husband leaves for work and sometimes he cain't wait that long with the other guys to watch, 'cause he has to get back to school.

Dessie is a woman the whole neighborhood knows 'cause she's probably the prettiest. She's definitely not a Pilgrim Holiness 'cause Pilgrim Holiness don't lay around in the backyard sunbathing. She's dressed in a thin silky looking skirt and blouse with a low neckline showing off her bulging tits with big round nipples, and rouge and lipstick on her face. She says, Victor, this is the first time I've ever entered a man's shop to get my hair fixed, but I've heard you're the best barber around and I've decided I want you to cut my hair. She moves a little closer to Victor and says, Is it O.K. if I just call you, Vic? I can tell Uncle Vic is really getting nervous and I sure wanta see this when he cuts her hair. Victor says, I'll sure give it a try, Dessie, if that's what you want. I know he's getting nervous 'cause his hand is shaking and he knows it.

Cotton and a couple of his pals come in and take a seat. I know they're not gonna get a haircut, but they wanta watch this and I do, too. Dessie is telling Victor just how she wants her hair cut, and we're not missing a word. She says, Vic, this is what I want. Cut it to half way down my neck, trim it and let me have a look in the mirror. She sits down in the chair, her silk dress slides well up above her knees and Cotton and his friends rise up to get a better look. Victor throws the apron over her and begins.

Dessie says, Aren't you the young man who answers all the Bible questions and preaches with your dad?
Yes ma'am, I sure am.
Well, I've heard a lot 'bout you.
I've heard a lot 'bout you too, ma'am.
Just, what have you heard 'bout me, young man?
Well, I heard you're the prettiest lady in the neighborhood.
Well, I sure didn't know that, but it makes me feel good.

Victor is cutting, the hair's falling on the floor, and I'm hoping he don't cut her with his scissors 'cause his hands are shaking real bad. Cotton wants to save the hair but Dessie tells him not to bother 'cause there's always gonna be more coming. I know he doesn't want it for Dessie, he wants it for himself. He puts it in a paper sack, carries it outside and comes back inside the shop acting like he's not interested in what's going on, but I know he's gonna tell everyone 'bout it and act like our hero again. Dessie says something 'bout when it's so hot like today she sure likes to cool off and Cotton wants to know if that's why she sunbathes every day. Victor doesn't like his remark and tells him to get outta the shop, unless he wants a haircut. He and his friends leave with Cotton carrying his sack of hair and a couple of 'em act like their feelings are hurt. Vic is finished and turns Dessie around to look in the mirror and she tells him, Vic, this is great, just like I wanted. He smiles, looks happy, and he's still shaking. He pulls the apron off and her dress slips well above her knees as she steps from the chair. Victor is getting more nervous and I'm enjoying it a lot 'cause she's got tits like I've never seen before. I've never in my whole life saw tits that stick out firm without dropping straight down. I guess that's 'cause most time I've seen babies hanging on 'em from daylight till dark. She asks him how much for the cut and he tells her the same as a man, twenty five cents.

She hands him fifty cents and says, Vic, My hair looks and feels great and it's well worth it. I'm thinking she's a better tipper than my friend Johnny.

I tell Maw 'bout Dessie coming to the shop and she's upset as never before. She looks at me with fire in her eyes and says, I have no idea what this world's coming to. It wouldn't surprise me one bit if they don't starting sittin' in bars and taverns just like men and there's no tellin' what it's gonna be next. Uncle Joe likes the idea and says, Anytime Vic doesn't wanta cut her hair just call on me and I'll do it for free. Maw's getting aggravated and I wanta get away from the kitchen when she gets this way. Finally she says

That woman is nothing but a Delilah.
You mean the one that made Samson lose his strength when she cut his hair?
She's the one, and let this be a lesson to you in the future 'bout such women.
God forgave Sampson, Maw, and he pulled the pillars of the building down and killed all the sinners, didn't he, Maw?
Yes, He always forgives.
The Bible says, judge not lest you be judged.
You're right, Son, you're right, I guess I better not judge.
Why don't you just put her on your prayer list?
That's good thinkin', Son, she's number five.

The following day things are slow at the barbershop, while Victor sits reading the paper and I'm looking outside. There stands Nelda the little read headed sixth grader looking at me again, blowing bubbles and chewing gum. She's wearing new white patent leather shoes and she doesn't move; she just stares at me. I'm afraid to say something to her cause I'm running my business and Uncle Victor may be watching. Nelda walks down the street and Victor asks if she's my girl. I tell him she's my buddy Tommy's girlfriend, but she may kinda like me some.

When I go to bed I'm thinking 'bout Nelda and I have a dream. It's not a good dream like Christians have 'cause, I dream Nelda stands outside the barbershop as usual, but this time she's got tits as big as Dessies', and this is bad for sure. I think it's all happening 'cause I'm seeing and hearing things at the barbershop like never before and sometimes it even sounds like I'm at Uncle Joe's bootlegging joint. If Maw ever knows my thoughts 'bout Nelda and Dessie, she's gonna make me get saved again for sure. Maybe even baptized and sanctified, and then I'd be just like Dad for sure and people would start talking. I may have to get away from the barbershop pretty soon, but I do like making money and being in business for myself.

I've gotta talk to my friend Tommy at school. It's recess time and we all run for the outside toilets to do number one or number two. Tommy, Big John, and me are leading the way. We stand at the long metal urinal and begin splattering it good with Tommy in the middle. If four guys stand at the urinal you get splattered yourself, 'cause you hafta squeeze together. I tell Tommy and Big John 'bout my dream and they laugh. Tommy's not the smartest guy in class and Big John follows him. Sometimes other people say they're slow learners and it makes them come in last and next to last every time we have exams, but we all like 'em both. All my buddies know Tommy's got the biggest dolly whacker in school, and we kinda respect 'em both, even if they're slow to learn.

We finish our piss, Tommy flips his dolly whacker around a couple times, gives it one last shake, while Big John and me watch before he puts it away. We slip ours back in our pants without all the fancy stuff 'cause maybe we feel a little embarrassed after seeing what Tommy was shaking. Our other buddies stand outside holding their crotches, and hollering for us to hurry and saying they cain't hold it much longer or they're gonna go piss behind the outhouse. We don't want that to happen so we go outside to talk. It's gonna be kinda private.

I tell Tommy and Big John 'bout my dream again, and I ask Tommy if he knows much 'bout Nelda. Tommy talks kinda slow and finally says

Well, Bid, I uh-uh-uh showed her my dolly whacker.
You showed her your dolly whacker.
I sure did.
Where at?
My, uh-uh-house.
What happened, Tommy?
She uh-uh, ran.
I guess it scared her.
Probably, so, uh-uh, Bid.

I guess I don't wanta ever see Nelda again now that she saw Tommy's dolly whacker 'cause my buddies say it's not normal and makes us look bad. I'm hoping Maw never finds out and I know Tommy ain't 'bout to tell Maw 'bout my dream.

The barbershop is only one room out of three as part of a double tenement house. The two back rooms are occupied by another cousin. In the back room, I worked for my uncle on Election Day and now suddenly I'm invited to a Sunday afternoon poker game by an older couple, Doc and Sweetzie. They're not considered lovers, but have a close relationship. Doc's been disbarred from practicing medicine and is around fifty years old and graying. Sweetzie is tall, slender, short blond hair and 'bout twenty years old and I think she's kinda hot looking.

The poker games in the back room started during the heat of The Great Depression playing for matches and now that people have a little money, the limit's up to a dime of real money. Doc, comes to the barbershop, gets his shave, haircut, and shine and says, Bid, if you wanta play a little poker on Sunday afternoon, be in the back-room and we'll letcha play with the grown-ups. I've watched 'em all play a lot and it would be nice to try my luck, but when I think 'bout what, Maw, might do, I don't think it's worth it.

Victor says, What'cha gonna do, Bid? Are you gonna play Sunday?
I'd like to, Uncle Victor, but Maw said she'd skin me alive if I ever did something like that.
She would, and she might even blame me and I don't need problems with Maw.

Sunday afternoon I go to the game but don't play. I watch, learn, wish, and later at night I'm in church with Maw and several friends. Walking home she says, Son, where were you this afternoon? Several times I called you and you didn't answer. I tell her, I just visited some friends, Maw, and watched 'em play games. She says, That's fine, Son, but if you go too far away, keep me informed in case I need you. I assure her I will in the future, and feel a sense of guilt, but not enough to tell her the entire story.

The shop closes Saturday evening and Victor, his brother, friends, and neighbors gather in the backyard to sing, play country music and drink beer with Victor till midnight. Victor plays guitar, his brother plays the banjo and neighbors add to the music. It's a hoe-down Tennessee style. I never worry 'bout Dad cause he's not around. When I get home, Maw reads the Bible to me and asks me to promise to never forget what's in it. When we say our prayer next her bed, I silently mention 'bout Nelda and Dessie and ask forgiveness for my sinful dream. Later, before going to sleep, I lie and worry if she finds out 'bout Nelda and my dream. I'm wondering if the barbershop is making me sinful like Dad and Uncle Joe with all my bad thoughts. I finally go to dreamland and I'm hoping I don't dream 'bout Nelda or Dessie and their wonderful charms.

I meet Uncle Joe the next day and he says, Bid, I've been noticing a change in you lately that just don't seem the way things should be goin' with you. I don't feel like it's doing you any good hearing all the crazy stuff that goes on around such places like the barbershop. Some of the people like strangers, politicians and women just don't have your interest at heart like me and, Orie. Remember this, Son, now that Dessies' been in the shop, it'll go to hell for sure. Every damned guy in the neighborhood is gonna find out 'bout it. Uncle Joe knows 'bout everything and I'm hoping he hasn't found out 'bout my dream. He says, I think maybe you need to give up the barbershop business and come with me to meet my new girlfriend. I'm gonna set you up in the newspaper and popcorn business 'cause it's a lot more educational. I tell him I been wanting to leave the place anyhow and I'm ready to start another business. Maybe now I'll quit thinking of Nelda and Dessie.

21

MAW'S DEATH

I'm now ten years old and feel more adult. The great flood of 1937 is over and things are almost back to normal. Uncle Joe and me arrive home after visiting our favorite movie house watching Tarzan and Jane swing through the trees. Maw sits in the living room and looks tired. She tells Uncle Joe to go on to bed and she needs to have words with me. My heart begins to pound 'cause I have a feeling I'm caught for sure. Maybe Maw knows 'bout my sinful dream and my thoughts 'bout Dessie and her big tits. I've got some other sin like going to see the movies with Uncle Joe and I hope it's that 'cause the other might be hard to explain. I ask her, Are you wanting to talk 'bout going to the movies with Uncle Joe? I explain it was only a Tarzan of the Apes movie and there weren't any naked women in it 'cept maybe Jane, Tarzan's wife. Maw's real calm looking, so I know she ain't aggravated. She says, Oh, no Son, it's not that at all, I've known you been goin' to the movies for over two years, so don't worry. I wonder if she has heard 'bout my dream, it's a lot worse than Tarzan and Jane. I'm not saying anything till I'm sure she knows and I'll never be able to explain it. She directs me to sit on the floor in front of her rocking chair and says, We, haven't had much time to talk 'bout lately and I've had something on my mind for a long time that needs to be said. She's looking more tired and worn out than any time I've ever saw her before and I sense this isn't normal. She's always seems to never run out of energy, but tonight it's different.

She wipes her brow and begins to talk. Son, there's something I need to say to you that you definitely need to take heed to. Remember the times I told you 'bout some things in life I'd tell you later, well, I think we're coming to that point in our lives. You're ten years old now and already in your young life, you've done and seen a way of life that no other boy has of your age. You've seen how I tried to raise you and influence your life and beliefs and you saw another side of life your father has shown you. I hope you don't follow in his path. I'm puzzled at what she's saying and tell her, I know what you mean Maw, 'cause he made me do things I didn't wanta do and I don't mean the preaching 'cause I sure liked the people I met. Dad always seemed to get himself in trouble. I was ashamed of him and some of the things he did were hard to explain to my friends. Maw says, I know what you mean, Son, but he's still your dad and you got more sense than he ever had and you're still very young.

She grabs my hand, places it in hers, and I know this is serious. She says, For the first time in my life it's hard for me to get up in the morning. Lately I've been having some terrible headaches and sometimes they're so bad I have to go lie down and take aspirin. It's hard for me to see myself in such condition I don't feel like cooking anymore. I move closer to her and say, Maw, there's nothing in the world I won't do to help you more; just ask me and I'll do it. Everything is becoming more serious than ever and she says, I know you will, Son, I don't know what I'd do without your help at times, but that's really not what I wanta talk to you 'bout,

I'm trying to understand what she's saying to me. She says, I want you to be prepared to take care of yourself in the event I may not be here long. I ask her what she means saying she won't be here at home? Maw is always here when I need her and now it makes me wonder what she's trying to tell me. She pauses a while and I see tears coming in her eye and she says, Well, sometimes the Lord says it's time to come home and that's what all Christians look forward to, you surely understand, don't you? I know what it means but not, Maw, it only means other people. I tell her, Oh sure I do, Maw, but you're still pretty young. I know some people a lot older than you like that Mrs. White who came to our house who was seventy-four when she died and she was a witch. Maw says, Well, Son, I'm sixty three and who knows when it's my time to go. I've heard that before and tell her, Only the Lord, Maw, that's what you always tell me. She is smiling at me and says, You're right, Son, only the Lord.

She seems to be getting more tired and says, If something should happen to me and your dad's not there for you, I want you to go to your uncle Joe and Uncle Orie for your needs, do you understand? I tell her, Sure, I always do that, Maw, but nothing is ever gonna happen to you. She says, Your Uncle Orie has his own family, but I know he'll do his best to help you. Before your mother died, she asked Joe and Orie to look out for you and they agreed. I cain't imagine her not being here, it just wouldn't be the same without her, and I don't like the way she's talking.

I'm gonna ask Maw a question. I tell her, I've always wondered 'bout something, Maw, how come every time I used to ask something 'bout my mother, everybody just hushed up or walked away from me, was it on account of Dad? Was he mean to my mother, Maw? I can tell she don't wanta answer, but she finally says, Well, not really, Son, I guess you could say he just didn't make a lotta good decisions. I know what she really means; it's when he drinks beer he just acts crazy. I ask, Do, you think he really might be crazy when he drinks beer? She says, No I don't think for one minute he's crazy, but he's very easy to give into sin and then he's very sad and remorseful and for some reason it's really hard for him to fight the old devil. I remember something Aunt Dorie said a long time ago 'bout Dad being full of the devil. Maw said later she really didn't mean it that way and the best thing to do is just pray for him.

We're having a good talk, but I don't like the things we're talking 'bout. I tell her, You turned Dad and Uncle Joe over to the Lord a long time ago, didn't you? She says, Yes, I sure did and the Bible says if you bring 'em up in the way of the Lord, they'll return when they're old, it's in the Book of Proverbs. I already believe your Uncle Joe is gettin' his life straightened out. I tell her, I do too, Maw, he's not even going to see the girls in the Red Light District anymore. I asked Uncle Joe, How come you don't go down there anymore, Uncle Joe, and he said, I don't need to anymore 'cause I got a regular girlfriend. Did you know that, Maw? She's not surprised at all and says, Yes, darling, I know all 'bout his girlfriend, Della, and I understand she's a real nice lady and works for your Uncle Orie at Fendrich Cigar Company. I tell her, Maw, I didn't know you knew 'bout my new Aunt Della and she treats me like her own two kids. I like her a lot and sometimes I go with one of her friends to sell popcorn at Bosse Field baseball park or down on Fourth and Main street and sell newspapers and I yell, *"EXTRA-EXTRA—READ-ALL-'BOUT-IT!"* Uncle Joe said I'm in the newspaper business now and no telling how far I can go making some good money. He said he didn't think I should hang around with some of the characters that come in the barber shop and he's looking out for my own good.

Maw seems a little surprised at what I been doing at Aunt Della's house and making the money but I still need a couple questions answered. Maw, there's another question I need to ask you. You know how Dad always wanted to go around preaching everywhere, how come he just doesn't wanta be one of the congregation and sit and listen? She says, Well, that's true, he always tried to be the center of attention for everything, 'cept when he gets caught doing something he's not supposed to. I know that's true, 'cause Dad always wants to have people look up to him, but that's all over now and I'm never gonna bring it up again. I ask her if she thinks Dad's gonna change like Uncle Joe and she says, I don't know, Son, only the Lord knows, but I do believe some day he'll straighten himself up and get on with life. I tell her, I sure hope so, 'cause Uncle Joe says he almost drives him nuts.

I'm enjoying my talk with Maw, even though she seems more serious than any time before. She pulls me a little closer to her and says, Son, there's another very important thing I need to warn you 'bout in your life. She looks me straight in the eyes, squeezes my arm and says, I want you to never in your life deny Jesus Christ as your Savior. I never dreamed she had any doubt 'bout that, 'cause she always knows I love Jesus above all. I tell her, I'll never deny Jesus Christ, Maw, 'cause He died on the cross for me. They'd have to kill me first. I know Peter denied Him just before the cock crowed three times. Peter was really sorry for what he did, but Jesus forgave him. Maw's getting real serious now and she wipes her forehead again and says, I pray with all my heart, Son, but remember Satan is deceiving. Just remember Peter was strong in his faith and Jesus depended on above all, and he still denied him. That's what Satan can do to you and everyone.

The conversation goes on and I can tell by her eyes, she's getting sleepy. Finally, she says, Son, there is one more thing I need to tell you 'bout that you may already know, but I need to say it to you now. There's gonna be some time in your life when you feel you have a problem and there's no way out of your predicament. That time always comes to all of us and it's when you need help from someone higher. You know the Bible verses 'bout how Satan was cast out of heaven with a third of the angels in heaven who followed him instead of God, don't you? I tell her, Yes, I sure do, Maw. I know all 'bout it and I sure like the part 'bout how God kicked him out when he thought he was bigger than God. She says, Well, Son, just remember that you were given to God as a baby, saved, baptized and nobody can ever take you away from Him, not even Satan unless you deny Jesus Christ as your Savior. Remember those other two-thirds of all the angels in heaven are on God's side and they'll look after you if you call on them in prayer. They're called 'Guardian Angels' and they're sure out there, though you can't see 'em.

Maws telling me things 'bout some stuff I really wasn't sure 'bout and I'm never gonna forget. I want her to know 'bout some stuff Dad had me do that just didn't seem right so I tell her 'bout riding through the backwater going to the revival and almost getting run down by the Delta Queen. Maw says, I guess I just wasn't listening when you mentioned some of these things to me, but I'm more worried 'bout your future than some of the crazy stuff your dad did when he was preaching. Maw says, Well, it's like this, Son, when you think you need help real bad, just pray to Jesus and ask him to send his Holy Angels and He'll do it if you're sincere. Never try to fool Jesus in any way 'cause He knows your heart better than you know your own. I tell her, I sure won't, Maw, He knows everything, even every feather on a sparrow and every hair on my head; you cain't fool Jesus for sure.

Maybe she can give me answers. Maw, I wanta tell you 'bout some things that happened quite often when I was 'bout seven years old. I was afraid to tell you then 'cause it involved some older people. Several times when you weren't around, a couple of my older cousins and even grown-ups would throw me in a closet and tell me I was gonna suffocate from something called black-damp. I was over at a friend's house one day and they did this to me and I thought I was going to die in the closet. They were all out in the room laughing their heads off at me 'cause I was begging and pleading with them to let me out. They kept saying things like, He's just like his daddy, afraid of everything. I cried in the darkness of the closet for a long time and kept begging them to let me out, but they only laughed harder and it became worse. I finally curled up in the corner and shut my eyes. If I'd known 'bout the angels, I would have called for them to help me. Maw says she had no idea anything like that ever took place 'cause she always tried to keep her eye on me at all times. She wants to know why I never told her when it happened and I tell her, I would have, Maw, 'cept I was afraid they'd do something even worse. I ask her, Why do people like my friends enjoy treating someone like they did me? Maw says, Son, there's some people who enjoy being mean and a lot is just plain ignorance, just put it out of your mind and forgive them for their ignorance and maybe someday they'll ask Jesus to forgive them. I tell her, I still wake up sometimes at night thinking 'bout it, and I can't stand to be in a place small or where I'm hemmed in like an elevator. Sometimes I even have bad dreams 'bout it. I know one thing, Maw; if I had known or thought 'bout those angels I sure would have prayed for them to help me inside the closet.

I'm happy she's answering my questions. I tell her, My cousin Bob is my best friend and they would make us wrestle each other in the living room while they stood on the side laughing and enjoying it. Bob or me didn't wanta wrestle or try to out-do each other 'cause we're best friends. Sometimes they held us down and made him or me get on top of each other and we knew sometimes people get mad at each other and we didn't want it to happen. Maw can hardly believe what I'm saying, but she knows it's the truth. She says, Son, I don't know how grown people can be so mean, but when I hear such things I only feel sorry for 'em 'cause someday they'll hafta pay for their sins when they stand before Jesus. Maw's right 'bout that and I tell her, I heard you tell Dad that a lot of times when he was cussing and carrying on around you. She reaches over and pulls me closer to her and says, Don't, worry, Son, it's all gonna be just fine when we stand before the Lord.

This is a good time to get some things taken care that always bothers me, but it's not gonna be anything 'bout Nelda or Dessie. Maw, there's something I need to say to you and it's kinda like a confession, I guess. That old rooster Mrs. Brooks called Mr. Rooster, well, me and Bob are the ones who hung him. It was an accident, but we were afraid to tell you. She says, Son, I knew that right away and saw the guilt in both of your eyes. I also know how you saved the boy you called Snotty Nose Lindel from drowning. His mother came and told me how you rescued him. I wipe sweat from my forehead and I'm glad it's finally over and when I tell Bob he's gonna be as happy as me. Maw says, It's all over and forgotten, Son, just like when Jesus when wipes away all of your sins and they're as far as the east is to the west.

Maw's real tired now and she squeezes my hand again and says, Now I'm gonna tell you something I been meaning to for a long time and it's the same thing the preacher told you many times; then you never understood. I know you always wanted to know 'bout Christ returning to earth and I never could tell you for sure and still today nobody knows when He's coming for sure. You have read the Bible with me all your young life and I can only tell you this. The prophets laid out a road map for us in the Bible which we call prophecy and it's all gonna come true. The main thing to remember in your life is that your sins are covered by the cross where He died for the whole world. Above all remember He will be your judge and you will stand before him like the entire world. The secret is 'The Cross—The Cross' where all sin is forgiven for the asking and believing He is the Son of God.

Maw's never been so sincere in her life and she breathes hard as she talks to me while her long silver hair falls down her back almost to her waist. She says, There are signs as we've been told by the prophets, and the very first thing is the Jews must return to their homeland in Jerusalem and become a nation. It will happen, Son, but I won't see it in my lifetime, but it will happen. Satan will then know his days are numbered and he will do everything he can think of to deceive and tempt people all over the world to commit sin. There will be signs of His coming in the skies and oceans will roar as never before. People will live in immorality the same as the time of the great flood when Noah built the Arc. There will be wars and rumors of wars and some will come pretending to be Him and many will follow. She finishes her words to me and reminds me to always be ready 'cause He will come as a thief in the night and nobody knows the hour.

Uncle Joe wants to know what's going on between Maw and me. I tell him Maw's not been feeling well lately and she needed to straighten me out on some things. He's satisfied and says. Well that sure is funny 'cause she just lectured me yesterday and she even believes I may turn into the kinda Christian like a guy named Paul in the Bible. She said he was a character just like me, but that ain't ever gonna happen. I tell him Paul was person who persecuted Christians and God blinded him till he changed his way of life. He be became an apostle and disciple of Jesus and one of the best Christians ever.

Home seems 'bout the same with Dad coming and going, sometimes working and paying board to Maw, and sometimes not. He's working at a new gas refrigerator place in Evansville doing spray painting. He drinks and gambles with some guys at the plant and a couple times book-makers have come looking for him. When he looses his money and don't pay Maw for the board it makes a problem for Maw. When he 'causes her problems it bothers me a lot 'cause she is the most important part of my life.

I'm having a great dislike for my father who's hardly ever here for me and I hate the way he's living. I would love to grab him and pound him, but no way can I physically do this. The only other solution is to tell my two uncles but they'll half-kill him and that would be worse than ever. I'm getting desperate and don't know how to help her. Many nights I lie in bed thinking of ways to solve my problems, and I'm beginning to think there's no way out. I know one thing for sure; if it comes to the final point; Dad's gotta go. I think 'bout calling on the angels she talked 'bout and ask for help, but not yet; maybe he will change. I hope.

The weather is extremely hot for June 5th, 1937. Maw says, we need to get some wash done this morning, and after breakfast I get things ready. Maw has electricity, gas, and a new Servel refrigerator in the house, but still does the washing by hand with a small metal wash board. I stand in the backyard and wait for her to come. I hear some loud noise coming from inside. Maw is trying to tell Dad he needs to pay his board so she can run the house and pay the grocer and some other things, but he don't wanta hear it and starts cussing and yelling and I'm getting madder at my dad. Now he's calling her names that tear through my heart and I'm gonna stop him one way or another. Suddenly the back screen door opens and Dad's bursting out with cuss words all towards Maw. He points at me and says, It's all 'cause of you and Maw I'm in this trouble. I don't know what he's talking 'bout and he's not drunk, but I hate the sight of him; tonight I'm telling my uncles and if they don't take care of him, I will. He leaves and walks away still cussing and when Maw comes from the house I see tears coming down her cheeks. I cry too, and wonder if this is ever gonna end. Tonight I'll talk to Uncle Joe. For the first time in my life I feel hatred in my heart and soul and it bothers me greatly.

We begin the wash and nothing is being said for a while till finally I tell her, I'm gonna take care of Dad tonight. I can't see him mistreating you this way 'cause sometimes I wanta kill him. She turns from the washboard, sweat is pouring down her face, and a couple tears come from her eyes. She wipes her face and forehead and says, Son, just remember what I always tell you.

He will stand before the throne of Jesus and answer for this.
I know, Maw, that's true, but I don't think I can wait till I can see him beat up.
Remember this, Son, the Lord has ways of handling people, and you and me don't have a right to do his work.
I know you're right again, Maw, but maybe if I tell Uncle Orie and Uncle Joe they will kind of help him out with a good whipping.
I'll tell you again. Leave it to the Lord, how many times do I have to tell you?
O.K. Maw, if that's the way you want it, I won't say nothing to nobody.
Son, I've got one of those terrible headaches. I'm goin' in the house, and take a couple of aspirins.
O.K. Maw, I'll do what I can while you're gone.

She comes from the house and starts back to work washing clothes. I stand close to her and suddenly she turns, grabs her forehead, and falls to the ground near my feet. I kneel down on the ground beside her and pull her to me and cradle her head and shoulders in my lap and I have no idea what to do next. I'm crying and pleading with her to talk to me, but she won't answer and her eyes stare up at the bright sunlight. Lady lies down next to me and begins whining, tries to lick my face, and I shove her away. This cain't be happening to my Maw, but it is, and I have no idea what to do. I'm yelling, What's wrong, Maw, what's wrong, speak to me, speak to me, please, tell me what's wrong with you. She doesn't answer and I know it's serious and I call for Cousin Cotton to come. He rushes to my side while I hold her head in my lap and I'm hugging her, while tears are coming down my face like a fountain, and I'm doing her no good. Cotton runs for help yelling for someone to call the doctor, but I'm not leaving Maw this way till he gets here.

Some neighbors are here before the doctor arrives and carry her inside the house and place her on the bed. Soon people gather at the house and some remark how they just can't believe this would ever happen to, Mary, 'cause she's been here forever. It's not long till the whole family is here 'cept Dad. The doctor arrives and says Maw has had a severe stroke and he sees no reason to send her to the hospital 'cause her time on earth is short. I hear the words, and feel like dying myself. Everybody agrees with the doctor, but I can't believe this is happening. I move away from the crowd of people and stand beside the house. Tears stream down my face and I'm hoping they don't see me crying.

I'm not fully dressed and wear only a pair of denim overalls and gym shoes. It's now been almost four hours since Maw was carried inside and I'm still standing outside in the hot sun and Uncle Joe comes from the house towards me. His head is hanging down and I know the news isn't good. He's crying uncontrollably, and puts his arms around me and finally spurts out, She's gone, Son, she's gone. I hear it, but can't believe it. I cry and sob and it's hard to breathe. I ask to see her and he puts his arm around me and we go inside.

Maw lies on the bed with a sheet over her and eyes closed. I kneel down beside her bed like so many times we've knelt and prayed before. I wipe my tears and tell Uncle Joe, She was just like a momma to me. He says, I know she was, Son, and you should never forget it as long as you live. I think maybe she saw this coming when she talked to you 'bout the angels, keeping your faith and forgiveness. I ask him how he knows 'bout our talk and he says, She talked to me, and she was right. We cry harder now and leave the room. Aunt Dorie comes to me and says, I know how much this hurts, Bid, but Orie and I will be there for you. I tell her, Thanks, Aunt Dorie, Maw said you would. Orie is crying and cain't talk for the tears rolling down his face and walks away and stands by himself. Later Dad comes and cries uncontrollably, but I don't talk or look at him.

The following day, Maw lies in a casket dressed in her favorite dress and remains at home. People come from all over the neighborhood and throughout the day till late in the evening. I clean myself up and now I look good in the suit she bought me. It's hard to look at people coming to see her, especially the prayer group women. I hear Mrs. Branson say, We have lost one of our own and I don't know what we'll do without her. Aunt Dorie says, We're moving on without her just like she'd want us to do. Dad is here at home and is doing a lot of crying and telling people how much he loved her, but he never looks at me. I don't wanta be around him and I keep thinking 'bout the morning. My hatred gets worse. I will never forget and I don't want him near me.

Two days have gone by and her body lies in the casket at the Pilgrim Holiness Church where her entire life seemed to dwell. The church is crowded with mourners, saints, sinners, politicians, grocers and lawyers all who knew Maw. Everyone in the neighborhood is there and show respect. People stand outside unable to get seats inside and they don't leave. Children, grandchildren and other family members gather inside along with the prayer group members and the atmosphere is somber with tears showing before the service starts. I sit in the front row between my uncles and Dad sits behind me and still I don't look his way.

The service begins with the preacher reviewing her life and devotion to the church when the church was organized. He tells of the times coming to our house and how she always had the chicken and dumplings and how proud she always was of her family. He tells of how she always checked her prayer list with his and how two of the boys were always at the top and she would tell him, They're gonna come around for good someday and everyone will be proud of 'em, 'cause it says so in the Book of Proverbs. The preacher says, he never once disagreed with Maw. He talks of her devotions to the prayer group and how the prayer group got together and helped form the church and someday she's gonna be wearing a crown of gold in heaven for sure.

The preacher finishes and points to where the prayer group sits and says, It's only fitting that one of you ladies should come up here and say something 'bout your longtime friend. They all turn their eyes towards Mrs. Branson and Mrs. Brown, two of her good friends. The two ladies look at each other and finally Mrs. Branson comes to the pulpit. She is well-versed in Bible scripture and she and Mrs. Brown knew Maw's inner feelings better than other members in the group. She begins to speak in her strong and loud voice. Saying, It's an honor for me to stand before you today and tell you a little 'bout my friend, Mary. In all the years I knew her, she didn't complain or criticize others and when things weren't goin' well at home, she would say her favorite line, "I'm turning everything over to the Lord." Mary always did just that, she trusted the Lord. I've watched her put her last dime into the offering and be happy. I've seen her reach out to someone else who might need help many times. That was Mary Martin, and I'm proud to be a friend of hers forever. I sit thinking every word she speaks is true.

Her eulogy continues on. She says, I'm goin' to ask you for one thing here today that will deeply honor Mary. I want you to wipe away your tears and show your joy instead of grief as we all have. Mary is exactly where she planned to be all her life. She is with her Lord and Savior Jesus Christ. Mary had a firm belief in guardian angels, and I'm sure she didn't suffer in her death as many people do 'cause the angels were surely holding her hand. Let's sing no sad songs for Mary, let's rejoice in her memory. There's a song she loved above all, and I want you to join in with me and sing **The Old Rugged Cross**. The people suddenly change their tears to smiles. All my cousins, aunts, and uncles stop their sobbing and crying and smiles return to their faces. I remembered what she said to me 'bout angels and how important they are in heaven and on earth. I may need their help someday.

Mrs. Branson is leaving the pulpit and the singing begins. The preacher says, This is a time of rejoicing instead of sorrow for everyone. Mrs. Branson said it a lot better than I ever could have 'cause the ladies of the prayer group serve the Lord and the church and now please come forward to see our friend, Mary, before we leave for the grave sight.

I decide to be last in line. This is gonna be something I'll never forget in my lifetime. The line with relatives is long and they proceed to the casket where Maw lies. I'm dreading this trip to the casket and almost crying again. I remember what Mrs. Branson said and hold back tears. I stand at her casket and look down and for the first time in my life, I see the lines and creases in her face and forehead. Her long silver hair is drawn down from the back of her head and lies covering her shoulders. I suddenly realize Maw is sixty-three years old and I'm now ten and she's been with me since birth. It seems as if she just withered away and I have left nothing but memories, but they're good and the very best. My heart is sad as never before, but I have a feeling she's happy being with angels.

We proceed from the church towards the waiting car in the front of the church and I begin remembering things 'bout Dad I can't forget. I remember the day of her death and her walking out of the house deeply worried. I think of Dad's cursing and insulting remarks to her. I walk and rage and anger seem to overtake my thoughts and I hope I won't be near him or I might explode and it wouldn't please Maw; I know that in my heart. The hurt and feelings in my thoughts will always be there and I wanta remember it forever. Maw preached to Dad time after time how everyone must forgive one another or Jesus won't forgive them when we stand before Him. That's something I never wish upon myself. There is one thing for sure in my mind above all: the closeness I once felt towards Dad is gone forever.

The ride to the graveyard is like going to my death. I feel like I'm in some sort of a trance or maybe I'm having another bad dream and this is not real, but it is. I don't wanta talk to Uncle Joe or Uncle Orie, I just wanta be left alone. I stand in the front row near Maw's grave and look across the grave and there stands Dad with tears in his eyes. Even now in all this sorrow, I don't wanta look at him. One of the ladies in the prayer group remarks, I feel so sorry for that boy. I wonder what's goin' to become of him now. Another says, Well, he can't depend on his father, that's for sure. It don't matter to me what people say 'bout Dad, anymore I figure he's got it coming. I know one thing for sure life will never be the same without, Maw.

The coffin is lowered into the ground and tears run down my face without stopping. Members of her prayer group stand near the grave and are humming an old song I've heard a hundred times in church. The humming stops and they sing softly one of Maw's favorite songs, ***I'll Meet You in the Morning***. Faces in the crowd seem to light up with a sense of understanding what her life was 'bout. I know every lady in the group has a firm belief they'll see her in another life. I hear them talk 'bout how life on the other side, after death, is something they look forward to, and they're not afraid of death. I know Maw wasn't afraid of death and she kinda looked forward to seeing the angels.

I think 'bout what she said to me recently when she said she might be called home to meet her Savior. I know her body's been racked with aches and pains and that's gone forever 'cause she said, there'll be no more pain or suffering in heaven. According to her belief, she's gotta new body and with Jesus in heaven forever and ever. I finally understand what she had talked to me 'bout so many times while picking greens or before bedtime. I can picture her in my mind standing before Jesus to get her reward and him saying, "Well done, my good and faithful servant." My mind wanders, and as the ladies begin singing, I imagine her as a young girl with long, golden hair, running through a field of daisies and daffodils having fun with my dogs, Bull and Lady. To me, that would be the heaven beyond compare and I hope for it in my afterlife. The graveside service ends and I grab hold of Uncle Joe's hand. We begin walking towards the car and it seems as if every tree we pass is filled with birds chirping and singing as never before. I hear them, but feel no rejoicing.

Dad, Joe, and me are the only persons staying at home now that Maw is gone. This isn't home anymore, it's just a place to eat and sleep. Dad and me don't talk; we just nod and stare. A couple of days after the funeral, he says, Son, We need to talk. I follow him outside of the house and he begins crying and says, You don't know how much I miss Maw, Son. She meant so much to me and I loved her dearly. I look at him with bitterness and hatred in my heart and soul. I tell him, Dad, I think you must not remember what happened the morning you called her all those dirty names and she had the stroke and died in my arms. He looks at me like he doesn't know what I'm talking 'bout, but I do, and it's good to tell him. He finally says, I can't believe you're talkin' to me that way; I don't know what you're talkin' 'bout. This is crazy, has he gone nuts, he knows exactly what I'm talking 'bout. I'm only ten years old, but this is too much to listen and try to understand. I tell him, Dad, as far as I'm concerned, you're still my dad as Maw told me, but I'll never forget that day. He looks hurt and cries without stopping, and says, Son, you're probably gonna hold that against me till the day you die, won't you?

When he put the question to me 'bout my feelings, it becomes something I never wished to express openly. I look into his eyes, and tell him, Maw always told me to forgive people no matter what they may do to you and I know it's in the Bible 'cause I remember preaching 'bout it. I do forgive you, Dad, but I'll never forget. He's acting more hurt than ever now that I confront him. He can't look me straight in the eyes, but finally says, Son, you look at me as if you could kill me; what in the world could I have done that makes you feel that way? I can't believe he's still denying what took place; it almost sounds like he believes it himself. I tell him, You know, Dad, as well as I do, but you just don't admit it. He says, Son, please don't talk to your old dad that way; you're breaking my heart. I knew that was coming for sure. I tell him, Now that Maw is dead, I really don't care if I hurt your feelings or not. If you ask forgiveness, you have it with all my heart 'cause that's what Maw taught me.

He cries and keeps asking forgiveness without stopping. He says, Will you please tell me if there's anything else I did that makes you hate me so bad? He won't remember this either I feel sure, but I'll tell him. Well, now that you mention it, I remember down in New Harmony when you had me get on the horse during the night and ride through the back-water. I was scared to death that night and all you told me if I can't swim; try dog paddling. Haven't you got enough sense to realize I could have drowned? He acts as if I've deeply offended him again and says, Son, don't you remember I told you I couldn't swim either? It's hard for me to control my anger, but I can't believe what he's saying. I must tell him 'bout Dade Park and the crazy idea he had 'bout me talking to horses, but I know he still believes it.

Remember, what you did with me at Dade Park telling me the Lord was gonna tell me who would win?

Son, I still believe you can talk to horses only you don't put your heart in it the way you should. You should know by now, the Lord's not goin' to help you if you don't have faith; you know I'm a man of faith.
Dad, sometimes I think you've lost it. I asked Maw once if she felt you were crazy but she said no. When you think I can talk to horses, that's too much and for once and for all, don't ever mention it to me again.
Son, there is no way anyone could pick two twenty-to-one horses to win and not be gifted.
I'm finished talking to him, it's useless.
Uncle Joe stands nearby and I go to him.

Joe says, What's goin' on between you and your dad? Is there something I need to know?
Not really. We just kinda come to an understanding and I'm glad it's over.

You're practically grown now and things are gonna be kinda tough for you without Maw, but we'll make it.

I know we will, everything's gonna be fine.

I sit in the house alone on Saturday morning and the sun shines brightly. There's a screeching of brakes from an automobile passing down the street and I rush to the window and look outside. Kids gather around the car and I rush to see what happened and there on the ground lies Lady covered in blood. Kids sob, I can't, there's no tears left; they all disappeared with Maw.

This can't be happening all in one week, my life is destroyed. I place Lady in the same wagon I carried Old Brownie, and head for the field where Bull lies. I do the ritual, place the cross, and cover her grave with stones. No friends stand by, I don't wanta talk to nobody, I just wanta be alone and try to understand.

I tell Uncle Joe 'bout Lady and he shakes his head and says, I don't understand, I don't understand, and neither do I. When nighttime comes and I'm alone I go to Maw's bed and kneel down beside it in the dark. This is where I spent hours upon hours with her praying for many things I never understood, but she always said, Pray and He'll understand. I can't say much of a prayer this time, but Maw always said, Don't forget to thank Jesus for all your blessings. I begin my prayer with, Thank You Lord Jesus, and I choke up with grief. I don't know what else to say, cept I don't know why all this happened, but you do, but why, oh why, dear Jesus. I stay on my knees for several minutes, say amen and walk away and never return to her bed again.

Things will change a lot as far as my life is concerned. Maw's gone and nobody will replace her, but she taught me well and gave me warnings; now it's up to me and if things get real bad I can always call for the angels.

The house I spent most of my life in is sold. There's little money left after paying expenses for the funeral, and the remaining money is shared by her kids. Selling the house means Dad and me need some place to live and our relationship is not like it was when Maw was here. My life as a child evangelist was only for a few short years. People sometimes ask why I quit preaching, but they don't know and I find it easier to just walk away without answering on most occasions. As the years roll on, it's no longer a problem for me.

The influence Maw had on everyone during her lifetime has lasted for decades and she could have never imagined its outcome. Her firm belief in Bible scripture proved to be her legacy above all things. Proverbs 22-6, "Train up a child in the way he should go and when he is old, he will not depart from it." All of her children, grandchildren and many other lives were changed by her philosophy of life and faith in her religion. All became good citizens with many serving their country in the military and government life. Victor and his wife joined her church and became members of the church orchestra. Shave, her youngest son, became a leader and follower of the church his entire life and accomplished much in bringing in followers. Joe, whom she predicted would be like Paul the prophet changed his life entirely and devoted the rest of his life to the church where she raised him. The influence he had on the next generation of followers is still felt today. Dad didn't change his lifestyle till later in life at the age of sixty; he became a staunch and reputable member in the Church of the Nazarene for the last twenty years of his life. He gave up his desire for the La Fendrich Cigars and booze, and carried his Bible at all times. He helped many others seek Christ before he died at the age of eighty-two. The church she loved so much has grown and been instrumental in helping people in the community and many troubled youth have found help through its' guidance.

Maw would surely be proud of the two wild ones, Spare and Joe. Bob and I became Soft Shell (Southern) Baptists. The biggest hero of all her grandchildren was Titties. He married his grade school teacher and she was the favorite of everyone.

Fifty years after Maw's death, Pat and I talk 'bout our youthful days. He has taught school in Indiana high schools and coached football his entire life and helped guide many young people to better lives. The years have turned our hair to grey, but memories of Maw and our roots remain strong. I ask, Cousin Pat, tell me one thing we can remember from Maw's life that helped guide you in life. He says, There is one lecture I'll never forget. I can almost quote her remarks she made at every Fourth of July church picnic.

"This is the Fourth of July, our day of freedom from England. Be proud of our wonderful country and above all never forget your roots and this great state of Indiana in the Heartland of America. Protect your country with your lives if called upon and always above all serve our God!"

Maw had this life and believed in a better afterlife. I gave her another life in this book due to her influence on me and my wonderful relatives.

The End

Arthur B. McCaffry
Bid, Age 14

978-0-595-41479-6
0-595-41479-6

Printed in the United States
88837LV00004B/25/A